ADHD
NATION

ADHD NATION

The Disorder. The Drugs. The Inside Story.

ALAN SCHWARZ

Little, Brown

LITTLE, BROWN

First published in the United States in 2016 by Scribner
First published in Great Britain in 2016 by Little, Brown

1 3 5 7 9 10 8 6 4 2

Copyright © 2016 by Alan Schwarz

The moral right of the author has been asserted.

A CIP catalogue record for this book
is available from the British Library.

ISBN 978-1-4087-0657-2

Printed and bound in Great Britain by
Clays Ltd, St Ives plc

Papers used by Little, Brown are from well-managed forests
and other responsible sources.

MIX
Paper from
responsible sources
FSC® C104740
www.fsc.org

Little, Brown
An imprint of
Little, Brown Book Group
Carmelite House
50 Victoria Embankment
London EC4Y 0DZ

An Hachette UK Company
www.hachette.co.uk

www.littlebrown.co.uk

TO DAD
For my square roots

CONTENTS

CONTENTS

PART 4

ADHD
NATION

A trial of amphetamine therapy brought about striking behavioral changes, a decisive improvement in school performance, and a consequent uneasy peace among the warring factions. It was difficult to argue with success.

Leon Eisenberg
Minimal Brain Dysfunction in Children
June 1970

INTRODUCTION

Attention deficit hyperactivity disorder is real. Don't let anyone tell you otherwise.

A boy who careens frenziedly around homes and busy streets can endanger himself and others. A girl who cannot, even for two minutes, sit and listen to her teachers will not learn. An adult who lacks the concentration to complete a health-insurance form accurately will fail the demands of modern life. When a person of any age has a combination of these struggles—severely enough to impair his daily functioning—with no other plausible explanation for them, then he could very well have a serious, if still somewhat mysterious, condition that medicine has decided to call ADHD.

No one quite knows what causes it. The most commonly cited theory is that the hyperactivity, lack of focus, and impulsivity of classic ADHD result from some sort of dysfunction among chemicals and synapses in the brain. A person's environment clearly plays a role as well: a chaotic home, an inflexible classroom, or a distracting workplace can all induce or exacerbate symptoms. Unfortunately, as with many psychiatric illnesses, such as depression or anxiety, there is no definitive way to diagnose ADHD, no blood test or CAT scan that lets a doctor declare, "Okay, there it is"—all one can do is thoughtfully assess whether the severity of the behavior warrants a diagnosis. (After all, we all are distractible or impulsive to varying degrees.) One thing is certain, though: There is no cure for ADHD. Someone with the disorder might learn to adapt to it, perhaps with the help of medication, but patients young and old are generally told that they will deal with their abnormal brains for the rest of their lives.

1

As for medications—for a long time Ritalin and now primarily Adderall, Concerta, and Vyvanse—they quite remarkably improve concentration and impulse control. Not unlike the painkiller OxyContin and antianxiety agents like Valium, they are powerful drugs that can be dangerous and addictive, particularly when taken improperly. All told, however, they have done considerably more good than harm; they are not the Devil's work. If a diagnosis of ADHD has been made by a qualified and responsible health professional then the decision to seek treatment through medication, either for yourself or your child, is not unreasonable.

The American Psychiatric Association's official description of ADHD, codified by the field's top experts and used to guide doctors nationwide, says that the condition affects about 5 percent of children, primarily boys. Most experts consider this a sensible benchmark.

But what's happening in real-life America?

Fifteen percent of youngsters in the United States—*three times* the consensus estimate—are getting diagnosed with ADHD. That's millions of extra kids being told they have something wrong with their brains, with most of them then placed on serious medications. The rate among boys nationwide is a stunning 20 percent. In southern states such as Mississippi, South Carolina, and Arkansas, it's 30 percent of all boys, almost one in three. (Boys tend to be more hyperactive and impulsive than girls, whose ADHD can manifest itself more as an inability to concentrate.) ADHD has become, by far, the most misdiagnosed condition in American medicine.

Understandably encouraged, drug companies such as Shire (the maker of Adderall and Vyvanse) and Janssen (Concerta) have targeted the United Kingdom and Europe as the next big growth areas. The U.K. was the first to bite, partly due to advertisements such as one from Concerta, which announced that "Kids Get on with It" and promised "Peace Time" for adults; whereas at most 1 percent of children in 1990 had been diagnosed with ADHD, the rate has quadrupled and keeps climbing, with prescriptions more than keeping pace. Dissatisfied with this robust market, however, drug companies are funding slews of studies and hiring physician groups to spread the gospel of ADHD and the wonders of their medications. One Shire campaign was called "ADHD: Making the Invisible Visible," which gathered worldwide so-called experts and broadcast how all nations should follow the United States' exemplary handling of ADHD.

Few people in the thriving ADHD industrial complex acknowledge these warning signs. Many are well-meaning—they see foundering children, either in their living rooms, classrooms, or waiting rooms, and believe the diagnosis and medication can improve their lives. Others have motives more mixed: sometimes teachers prefer fewer troublesome students, parents want less clamorous homes, and doctors like the steady stream of easy business. In the most nefarious corner stand the high-profile doctors and researchers bought off by pharmaceutical companies that have reaped billions of dollars from the unchecked and heedless march of ADHD, an American phenomenon trying to go global.

Some onlookers blame the new millennium's quick-fix, just-take-a-pill ethos, or simple Internet overload. But the rancor surrounding ADHD stretches back at least half a century, back to when the disorder carried the less marketable name of minimal brain dysfunction. A U.S. government hearing in 1970, not long after Ritalin emerged as a way to calm critically hyperactive children, examined whether too many kids were being put on "behavior drugs." As the percentage of American children diagnosed increased persistently through 2000, media reports staged recurrent tugs of war between parents testifying that Adderall was their family's lifeboat and those decrying the overmedication of children. Many claimed that this hostility only stigmatized kids with ADHD and discouraged parents from seeking help; then again, whatever stigma there was didn't prove very dissuasive. Diagnoses have continued to be handed out so blithely, at the hint of any problem, that today one in seven American kids turns eighteen having been labeled with ADHD—no longer a niche minority but a sprawling swath of the nation's future. Shockingly, it's almost certain that kids *misdiagnosed* with ADHD outnumber those with the legitimate, clinical problem, leaving the disorder so muddied that no one quite knows what to make of it at all.

The ADHD explosion has become, to some, literally laughable. Stephen Colbert dubbed it "Meducation," and profiled a doctor who prescribed Adderall to children *without the disorder* simply to improve their grades. "Shocking!" Colbert said. "There are children in America who haven't been diagnosed with ADHD." *The Onion* sardonically profiled a four-year-old girl stricken with "Youthful Tendency Disorder." These ribbings are routinely decried by ADHD support groups as disrespectful. Perhaps, but advocates also bring satire and skepticism upon themselves with preposterous sales messages, flitting back and forth from asserting the gravity of the condition (which one article says "impair[s] life functioning 24/7") to celebrating its purported positives. Some "Famous People with ADHD" rosters claim that Stephen Hawking, Abraham Lincoln, Isaac Newton—even Socrates—quite possibly suffered from ADHD, too, implying that it contributed to their inner genius and encouraging the hesitant to join their "very good company." (Many such lists sit on websites surrounded by ads for ADHD medications.) The disorder's longtime support and lobbying group, Children and Adults with Attention Deficit Hyperactivity Disorder (CHADD), has published a run-down of "12 Amazing ADHD Superpowers," among them "Multitasking," "Laser-focus," and "A strong moral compass." It's a curious list, given that *inability* to stay on task and *deficient* focus are among the disorder's official core symptoms.

Occupying a uniquely bizarre place in American culture, let alone medicine, ADHD has become the brain disorder some choose to fake. Because Adderall, Concerta, and other drugs can instantly boost any person's motivation and focus, whether for term papers or tax returns, the pills move from medicine to performance-enhancing drugs, steroids for the brain. Thus ADHD gets caught in a tenuous balancing act between treating the ill and tempting the healthy— fostering spurious diagnoses not just among adults, who can take themselves to accommodating doctors, but children, too, because some parents will exaggerate their child's symptoms to get them a prescription. The doctor nods and says, "Let's try Concerta and see if it helps"; when it invariably does, and the child's schoolwork improves, the ADHD diagnosis appears confirmed. Yet the doctor might as well have said, "Try these platform shoes, see if they make him taller."

And so the number of diagnoses only keeps rising, to the point where millions of kids today are labeled with a brain disorder they probably do not have, changing their self-image and personal narrative forever. Yet this doesn't seem to bother a lot of powerful people. A pitch-perfect example came in 2013, when the *New York Times* broke the news that ADHD diagnoses had reached that staggering 15 percent of children nationwide, and 20 percent of boys. A prominent doctor responded in child psychiatry's top scientific journal: "These numbers are actually all good news. . . . It appears that we are getting close—after more than 2 decades of advocacy—to identifying and treating a majority of children and adolescents with ADHD." What he and so many others do not see, or want to see, is that their fervor for finding every kid with even a whiff of ADHD has left an awful lot of dolphins getting caught in their tuna nets.

THIS BOOK TELLS the story of the longtime forces that put us here, told primarily through the experiences of three people.

One is a nationally renowned child psychiatrist, all but the father of ADHD and its medications, who now has serious misgivings about his role in, as he puts it, "a national disaster of dangerous proportions." Then there are two kids: A seven-year-old girl who was misdiagnosed with ADHD, and a fourteen-year-old boy, under tremendous academic pressure, who faked symptoms to his clueless doctor to score steady supplies of Adderall. Both spent ten years suffering through the consequences. While their ordeals were not necessarily common, they also are not nearly as rare as most people realize, and represent the rising collateral damage from the ever-escalating war against ADHD.

Despite this tale's dozens of other characters—kids and doctors and parents and teachers and drug companies and more—this is not a *they* book. It's a *we* book. It's the story of how we, as a society, have allowed what could be a legitimate medical condition to become diluted beyond recognition, and beneficial medication to become a serious drug problem. It is something we all must discuss.

Because whether it's just one child or today's six million, if we're going to tell a kid that he has a permanent, potentially devastating brain disorder, we'd better damn well be right.

PROLOGUE

Rain pelted the white Ford's windshield as it drove up Interstate 684 toward Connecticut. An old man was wedged in the passenger seat, cane crossed over his creaky legs. The wipers whooshed. The trees rushed past. The man didn't know quite what he was in for. He was intrigued, even excited, but also nervous.

Dr. C. Keith Conners had spent more than fifty years as one of the world's most eminent child psychologists, a man renowned for pioneering the recognition and treatment of a once unappreciated childhood malady: attention deficit hyperactivity disorder. As a young researcher in the early 1960s, Dr. Conners had pinpointed just how much a new drug—Ritalin—could calm severely hyperactive and impulsive children. He developed and later marketed a questionnaire to pinpoint a child's symptoms of impulsivity and inattention, helping doctors diagnose millions of youngsters nationwide. He evaluated new and better drugs on behalf of pharmaceutical companies. He led the most important studies and headlined the biggest conferences. If one person put ADHD on the medical map, it was Keith Conners.

Yet now, at eighty-three and barely mobile, Dr. Conners had started to consider his job well done as done a little too well. When he started, and began encouraging doctors to locate and often medicate children with acute issues, he couldn't conceive that in 2015, more than six million children would be labeled with ADHD, many of them misdiagnosed by lazy doctors just checking off boxes on his questionnaire, and then prescribing medication with little regard for side effects and risks for abuse. He didn't foresee drug companies contorting his science into shameless advertisements that exploited parents' fears for their chil-

7

dren's futures, while also promising better grades at school and more chores done at home. Now Big Pharma's latest frontier was adults, a market ripe for indoctrination.

As the car turned toward Hartford, Conners sighed: "I struck a match, and I didn't know how much tinder there was around."

Didn't know until recently. Enjoying a comfortable retirement in Durham, North Carolina, Conners had started reading *New York Times* articles about improperly diagnosed kids feeling inferior, damaged. College students pulling all-nighters to write term papers and cram for exams were popping so much Adderall that some became addicted, delusional, and occasionally suicidal. High school juniors, menaced by scholastic pressure, were taking and even snorting the drug before the SATs. Perhaps most horrifying of all, ten thousand toddlers as young as two—against all published medical guidelines—were being put on Ritalin to treat their supposed ADHD.

Reading about these children rousted not just Conners's curiosity, but also his conscience. So in June of 2015, Conners got himself wheel-chaired to the Raleigh-Durham airport for a flight to New York City. The next morning, he was driven up to Connecticut to sit down with two children—former children, actually—who had become casualties in medicine's longtime crusade against ADHD.

One was Kristin Parber, who as a seven-year-old in the late 1990s got diagnosed with ADHD when she almost certainly did not have it. Distractible, yes. Rambunctious, certainly. But as her parents watched dozens of children in their Philadelphia suburb thrive on Ritalin, they joined the wave. The experiment went fine, until it didn't. Turns out that, more than anything else, Kristin had one of those square-peg personalities that didn't quite fit her world's round—and shrinking—holes. The human brain has evolved over many thousands of years, yet only in the last hundred, a blip on that time line, have we demanded that each and every young one sit still and pay attention for seven hours a day. Kristin couldn't. But was that really her underlying problem?

The other was Jamison Monroe. Down in Houston, around the same time that Kristin was being evaluated for ADHD, the only affliction Jamison had was a whopping case of high school pressure syndrome. When his grades began to slip, Jamison tried some of his friend's Adderall and, literally overnight, began acing his exams again. So he went to his doctor, pretended to have ADHD, and after a careless pseudo-evaluation got himself prescribed steady supplies of Adderall. Jamison's grades kept rising. He loved his Adderall. Until he loved it just a little too much.

Kristin and Jamison crossed paths in 2009—and now, all grown up, were working together in central Connecticut. They wanted to meet Keith Conners as much as he wanted to meet them. Heck, it was Conners's questionnaire that had been used to diagnose them with their purported ADHD in the first place. If Conners's motivation for the three to meet was conscience, theirs was more catharsis.

The car pulled into the driveway in, of all reconciliatory settings, a small town called Bethlehem. Conners took a deep breath and uneasily hoisted himself out of the car and onto his cane. He toddled up the gravel driveway, leaning on the cane so hard that his arm shook.

Kristin and Jamison warmly greeted their visitor at the door. The three made their way to a room, sank down into leather chairs, and told their stories.

Those tales all descended directly from one moment, eighty years and two hours away—when an unknown Rhode Island doctor had some kids who needed help.

PART ONE

Chapter 1

FIDGETY PHIL'S
ARITHMETIC PILLS

The Emma Pendleton Bradley Home sprawled across thirty-five wooded and restful acres on the outskirts of Providence, Rhode Island, beckoning the children nobody else wanted. Opened in 1931, it teemed with dozens of toddlers to teenagers whose uncontrollable behavior drove their desperate parents to this hospital, one of the first to focus on disturbed and difficult kids. Only blame was unwelcome. The children were overseen and educated, to whatever extent possible, by a team of nurses led by a young physician named Charles Bradley.

Dr. Bradley could not bear to witness pain in a child, let alone inflict it. But sometimes he felt he had no choice. To help investigate just what might be wrong with these youngsters' brains, he would perform a pneumoencephalogram—a spinal tap—in which a needle inserted into the child's spine would inject bubbles of air or other gas that would then float up the spinal column into the brain, pushing out fluid and allowing abnormalities to appear more clearly on an X-ray. Beyond the torturous procedure itself, the kids' subsequent searing headaches wrenched children and staff alike. If only something else, anything, could take that pain away.

On a hunch, Dr. Bradley decided to try a new over-the-counter sinus reliever called Benzedrine, which in its short lifetime had also been found to improve mood in adults. He gave the 10-milligram tablets to thirty children for a week to see if they would help. The experiment failed miserably—the headaches remained as bad as before. But something else happened instead, a change so spectacular he could hardly believe it.

The children became less raucous. They listened. They learned. For perhaps the first time, they enjoyed success, praise, and a drive to perform better in school. "I can't seem to do things fast enough today," one child remarked. Another said he had "joy in my stomach." They tore through math problems like never before and practiced their handwriting with a focus previously unthinkable. One said, "I start to make my bed and before I know it, it is done!" Some even called their medicine "arithmetic pills."

Dr. Bradley was shaken. He and the hospital's staff gave these troubled kids the most nurturing environment possible, teaching them new social and behavioral skills so that they could acclimate, someday, to the outside world. Bradley was not looking for a magic pill and didn't necessarily want one. But as a scientist at heart, he knew his finding deserved more study.

By pure happenstance, Bradley had discovered a way to make children slow down and pay attention—a pursuit as old as parenthood itself.

SOMEWHERE IN WHAT we now call France and Spain, on undiscovered Paleolithic walls and ceilings, cave drawings undoubtedly depict boys running wild, oblivious to their mothers' cries, their antics scaring wild boar away from their fathers' cocked and poisoned spears. Irrepressible Dark Ages children surely vexed nobles and serfs alike. And for all his renown, Gutenberg has subjected centuries of kids to books on which they would rather not focus.

As early Western medicine explored treatments for various ills, it also ruminated on short attention spans. In a 1775 medical textbook, the German physician Melchior Adam Weikard posited that an overly distractible person's "fibres"—what we would now call nerves or temperament—"must not be bewildered or affected by any clamour or by any disturbance." A person with such a constitution, Weikard wrote, "studies his matters only superficially; his judgments are erroneous and he misconceives the worth of things because he does not spend enough time and patience to search a matter individually or by the piece with the adequate accuracy. Such people hear only half of everything . . ."

Weikard recommended that "the inattentive person is to be separated from the noise or any other objects; he is to be kept solitary, in the dark, when he is too active."

The earliest careful consideration of inattention as disease appears to belong to Sir Alexander Crichton, a Scottish doctor at the turn of the nineteenth century so prominent that Russian tsars later wooed him away to be their personal physician. At Westminster Hospital in London, Crichton tended to patients afflicted with fevers, coughs, worms, itches, and hysteria, the last of which he found particularly compelling. He spent six years writing a two-volume textbook, *An Inquiry into the Nature and Origin of Mental Derangement*, in which he explored what he called "the cause of insanity and the various diseased affections of the human mind." Considered one of the first English texts to systematically delineate what we now call psychiatry—he investigated such diverse topics as joy, judgment, and genius—*Mental Derangement* launched Crichton to such lasting prominence in Great Britain that King George IV knighted him.

"On Attention, and Its Diseases" receives an entire chapter in Crichton's massive work. It ponders what leads a human mind to concentrate—free will, motivation, education—before describing how, among the overly distractible, "Every impression seems to agitate the person, and gives him or her an unnatural degree of mental restlessness":

> People walking up and down the room, a slight noise in the same, the moving a table, the shutting a door suddenly, a slight excess of heat or of cold, too much light, or too little light, all destroy constant attention in such patients, inasmuch as it is easily excited by every impression. The barking of dogs, an illtumed [*sic*] organ, or the scolding of women, are sufficient to distract patients of this description to such a degree, as almost approaches to the nature of delirium.

Notably, soon after Crichton offers this rather stark description of mental disease in adults, he cautions that distractibility in a child was normal—an inherently youthful trait that deserved not to be quelled, but cultivated. Each child, he wrote, has a different "mental diet" he can digest. (As Crichton put it, with a whiff of autobiography, "Every public teacher must have observed that there are many to whom the dryness and difficulties of the Latin and Greek grammars are so disgusting that neither the terrors of the rod, nor the indulgence of kind entreaty can cause them to give their attention to them.") He lamented that young people unsuited to conventional educational methods certainly had other natural talents and should not be labeled "dunces during the early part of their lives."

Inattention got a little levity in 1845, when the German physician and psychiatrist Heinrich Hoffmann made a Christmas gift for his three-year-old son, Carl Philipp. Dr. Hoffmann liked to doodle pictures to soothe crying children, so he wrote and illustrated a book of fanciful drawings of quirky boys and girls, accompanied by jaunty verse. He called it *Struwwelpeter*, or *Shock-headed Peter*. He later expanded it with "The Story of Little Suck-a-Thumb," "The Story of Augustus, Who Would Not Have Any Soup," and "The Story of Flying Robert."

Among these was a story about Zappelphilipp—as alliterative luck would have it, "Fidgety Philipp"—who was annoying his parents at dinner:

Fidgety Phil driving his parents crazy

Heinrich Hoffmann

Let me see if Philipp can
Be a little gentleman;
Let me see if he is able
To sit still for once at table:
Thus Papa bade Phil behave;
And Mamma looked very grave.
But fidgety Phil,
He won't sit still;
He wriggles,
And giggles,
And then, I declare,
Swings backwards and forwards,
And tilts up his chair,
Just like any rocking horse—
"Philipp! I am getting cross!"

(Sadly, Hoffmann's clearly simple amusement at children's eccentricities—particularly those that drove Mom and Dad nuts—did not survive the ages. Some 150 years later, as debates began to rage over the existence and medical legitimacy of attention deficit hyperactivity disorder, ADHD advocates excavated and held up Fidgety Phil as unassailable proof that the condition had been recognized since way back in the mid-nineteenth century—and medically recognized at that, given Hoffmann's being a psychiatrist. Today, Fidgety Phil no longer entertains children; he all but diagnoses them. The official definition of ADHD, published by the American Psychiatric Association, still honors Heinrich Hoffmann's little boy with Hyperactive Symptom No. 1: "Often fidgets with or taps hands or feet . . .")*

A more formal theory of impulsivity as organic disease arrived in 1902 during a lecture series before the Royal College of Physicians in London called "On Some Abnormal Psychical Conditions in Chil-

---

*In another revisionist twist, Hoffmann's book was later translated into English by none other than Mark Twain—whose Tom Sawyer has also been cited by psychiatrists as a boy with ADHD.

dren." Sir George Frederic Still was a pioneer in the nascent field of pediatrics—to that point, few doctors paid much attention to maladies specific to children, preferring instead to view their bodies as those of undersized adults. Dr. Still studied twenty children who exhibited what he called a "defect in moral control"—characterized by "spitefulness," "shamelessness," "cruelty," and more, appearing almost oblivious "to the good of others or to the larger and more remote good of self." His case illustrations included an eleven-year-old boy who could not resist the urge to grab two other children and slam their heads together; kids who showed "a reckless disregard for command and authority"; and one who tried to immolate a cat. These children, understandably, demonstrated what Still called "quite abnormal incapacity for sustained attention."

But Still took one less banal, and genuinely groundbreaking, step forward. He contended that although such behavior could appear in children who were either "idiots" (of extraordinarily low intelligence) or who had incurred some sort of brain injury or illness (meningitis, for example), some offered no physical explanation for their behavior at all—and appeared of average or better intellect. These kids' hyperactivity and impulsivity, Still suggested, resulted not from their conscious choices, or from bad upbringing, but through some unexplained misfiring within their brains. Now, did those children have what we now call ADHD? Almost certainly not. Although impulsive and inattentive, to be sure, most if not all would be characterized today as having oppositional defiant disorder, antisocial personality disorder, or some other condition defined more by pure aggression. And yet, even more spuriously than Fidgety Phil, Still's twenty children have since been flown as flags of primordial ADHD. None of this, of course, is Still's fault; his work legitimately advanced the study of impulsivity and hyperactivity in children, for claiming that otherwise intelligent youngsters were having problems due to something beyond injury or disease.

Yet ultimately, it was the disease of one little girl that, some thirty years after she died, would change the course of ADHD, and in many ways psychiatry itself. Her name was Emma Pendleton Bradley.

Emma was the only child of George Bradley, a Rhode Island businessman who, in the mid-1870s, had enjoyed the good fortune of meeting an entrepreneur named Alexander Graham Bell while the latter was fiddling with a precursor to his "telephone" so that a disabled girl in Providence might communicate. Bradley befriended Bell and eventually helped organize the National Bell Telephone Company. He became a millionaire—a billionaire in today's dollars. His daughter, Emma, was born into an idyll of privilege and possibilities. But that all changed when Emma turned seven and contracted encephalitis, an insidious virus that inflamed her brain tissues and left her epileptic, palsied, and mentally retarded.

Institutions of the period focused almost exclusively on adults with the severest of mania, so George Bradley could find no treatment for Emma. Brokenhearted the rest of his life, Bradley left his entire fortune upon his death in 1906 to establishing a proper facility for mentally challenged children. ("Out of this misfortune of our only child," his will wept, "has grown the purpose and the hope that from the affliction of this one life may come comfort and blessing to many suffering in like manner.") The effort took twenty-five years, but in 1931, the Emma Pendleton Bradley Home opened for dozens of children with a wide range of maladies, some physical but mostly emotional. The facility was run by Dr. Charles Bradley, George's grandnephew, a young Harvard Medical School graduate devoted to children's mental health.

The hospital aimed not just to house the kids, but to offer special education, Boy Scout–type activities, and sports. Part of their medical care would include experimental treatments. One of them was an intriguing new drug for adults just coming to market.

AROUND THIS TIME, 250 miles south in Philadelphia, Smith, Kline & French Laboratories needed a hit product, and fast. The company's top-selling prescription medicine in the 1930s was Eskay's Neuro Phosphates—an elixir that, its label promised, would ease a person's "defective nerve-cell nutrition" and "nerve fog," while also "restoring nervous energy." (It contained 17 percent alcohol, more than any Cabernet.) This was not pharmacy's future. SKF needed a jolt, and fittingly found one in what we now call amphetamine, or speed.

It came to the company from Gordon Alles, a chemist in California, who a few years before had tinkered with various compounds he thought might relieve asthma or nasal congestion. Some appeared promising, but Alles was most intrigued by one chemical's unexpected psychological effects when he injected it into himself. He immediately noticed a "feeling of well-being" within him—as well as, he added, conversational wit. Further refinements produced a substance that would leave people instantly energized—sometimes too much and for too long, leading to sleepless nights—and with a euphoria unknown even in the Roaring Twenties. Smith, Kline & French saw such potential in Alles's drug that the company licensed it before knowing exactly what medical condition the stuff might actually treat. Finding out was a lot easier then than today: Lax federal regulations did not require any proof of safety, let alone efficacy, before a drug was released for public experimentation. So SKF sent boxes of what it called "benzedrine sulfate" to any doctor willing to try the drug on patients with various ills, from asthma to postpartum depression.

One of the very few physicians willing to experiment with children was Charles Bradley, the Emma Pendleton Bradley Home's new medical director. Bradley was neither cruel nor reckless—he felt such empathy for his young patients' inner misery, and such desperation for anything to help, that he would try anything scientifically promising. He already had designed a new chair in which children receiving spinal taps could feel less tortured. Now, he thought, perhaps this benzedrine sulfate might relieve those kids' subsequent headaches—and if it boosted their spirits for a few hours like it did in adults, so much the better. Dr. Bradley selected thirty children aged five to fourteen, twenty-one boys and nine girls, to receive morning doses of benzedrine sulfate for one week.

The trial floored Dr. Bradley and his staff. The kids' headaches remained awful, unfortunately, but something peculiar occurred instead: They immediately showed more interest in school. They not only focused on their lessons, but wanted more. Their comprehension, speed, and accuracy improved, too. These changes arrived on the first day of treatment and disappeared the moment it ended. Even those children who did not respond quite so well still usually showed some academic improvement.

Moreover, the pills calmed the otherwise uncalmable. Most of the children had either distinctly fewer mood swings or "a sense of well-being, even to the point of mild euphoria," Bradley wrote, echoing Alles's findings. Not all reactions were positive, he cautioned: There were several cases of nausea, insomnia, and heightened anxiety. As he wrote up these results for a paper in the November 1937 edition of the *American Journal of Psychiatry*, Bradley dutifully warned of these effects. He pondered why a drug known to stimulate activity and thought processes in adults would make these children less frenetic. This almost-too-simple result would have demoralized the entire hospital, he noted, "had not the improvement been so gratifying from a practical viewpoint."

While awaiting reaction from the scientific community, Bradley began treating more children with Benzedrine, and for months at a time—if nothing else, the pills made life easier for both the kids and what became less harried nurses. The staff began more carefully measuring the children's behavioral and academic improvement. One eleven-year-old boy, listed as having a 114 IQ, was once so daydreamy that he would complete only three pages of arithmetic problems a month; on the drug he blew through twenty-seven. (He also went through fourteen more pages of spelling work.) Not all children showed such a boost; some even regressed. But words that therapists used to describe them in the final report were striking: "attentive," "serious," "concentration better," and "neater and more careful work."

Bradley concluded that amphetamine lowered the children's distractibility and, perhaps less directly, influenced mental performance "by altering the emotional attitude of the individual toward his task." He later added: "In view of the practical importance of satisfactory school progress to all children, the therapeutic possibilities of amphetamine sulfate in this regard become attractive." One should note Bradley's second use of the word "practical"; he was saying that Benzedrine might not seem the most honorable method for altering children's behavior, but growing educational demands on children might require it.

Bradley knew he had discovered something equal parts important and seductive. Repeating himself again, he cautioned that the medication should not be considered a cure-all, however tempting that may be—its benefits lasted only as long as the pills did. He warned that the children's underlying physical and mental problems still needed careful psychosocial therapy from trained professionals.

Ambivalent about his discovery, Bradley didn't complain when officials at Smith, Kline & French essentially ignored it. The pharmaceutical landscape had changed drastically in just those few years. A major scandal erupted in 1937 when more than a hundred Americans, many of them children, died after taking a new antibacterial syrup for strep throat; it turned out that the manufacturer had used an antifreeze-like toxin during the production process and had never conducted even basic safety tests. (To this point, the drug business had been overseen by the American Medical Association, essentially doctors themselves.) This stunning episode led directly to the passage of the 1938 Food, Drug, and Cosmetic Act, which gave the Federal Drug Administration—a precursor to today's Food and Drug Administration (FDA)—the power to keep a product from the public until it was demonstrated to be safe.

And Benzedrine was not necessarily safe. It cleared sinuses, yes, but users grew quite fond of its boosts in mood and acuity. Smith, Kline & French's first amphetamine product, a lipstick-shaped cylinder inserted into the nose and sniffed—it did not yet require a prescription—was so immediately pleasurable that news reports began describing people who would disassemble the container, remove the amphetamine-soaked gauze, and chew it for the high. The bad publicity continued in 1937 when *Time* magazine, through which America received news en masse to an extent inconceivable today, published an article headlined "Pep Pill Poisoning" that described students at several midwestern universities taking the "new, powerful but poisonous brain stimulant" to stay up nights on end to study. When a Purdue student died soon after taking the pills two years later,* the tragedy was reported widely enough that Benzedrine's dangers became too conspicuous for SKF to sell it as a tool to control children's mental states. Especially when those youngsters' troubles, let alone medical condition, didn't even have a name.

SKF executives ultimately decided to market Benzedrine in pill form to treat something on which it showed at least a defensible, if not drastic, improvement: depression in adults, particularly women. Bradley's insight into amphetamine's even greater influence on children's behavior foundered in the literature for twenty years with little recogni-

---

*Medical records now suggest that the young man also had a heart defect that probably played a significant role in his death.

tion from the scientific community. But anyone who came across the papers could sense something seminal, extending past child psychiatry to parenting and education itself—a quick-and-easy way for children to be turned from difficult to calm, from scattered to studious.

BY THE LATE 1950s, the United States had changed drastically since Bradley's first experiments. World War II soldiers had returned to form a middle class with unprecedented promise and economic clout, raising children with growing expectations that they aim higher. The Soviet Union launched Sputnik, leading to President John F. Kennedy's promise to win the space race through science and education.

Soon, in a professor's office at Johns Hopkins Medical School, science and education collided much as they had on Charles Bradley's hospital grounds a generation before. Dr. Leon Eisenberg was a nationally renowned psychiatrist with a particular interest in children. His young protégé, Keith Conners, came across the Bradley papers and wanted to explore further—but not through Bradley's relatively crude experiments. Eisenberg and Conners decided essentially to reproduce Bradley's work through far more scientific and reliable methods. To validate the drug's before and after, and to remove bias, no one would know which children received the medication and which received only placebos. The project received permission from Johns Hopkins and funding from the National Institute of Mental Health (NIMH), marking one of the first times the federal government would subsidize a trial of psychotropic medication in children.

In 1962, a barrel the size of an oil drum arrived at the doctors' offices in Baltimore. It brimmed with more than a hundred thousand small pink capsules. But not Benzedrine. This was a new and virtually unknown drug. Its scientific name was methylphenidate hydrochloride. Brand name: Ritalin.

Chapter 2

DR. CONNERS

Old Mrs. Howarth was well into her eighties, a sweet, gray-haired widow whose clapboard home smelled of dust and Old West leather. She had been one of the Utah Territory's hearty early settlers, back during the Civil War, but now, in the mid-1930s and nearing a lonely death, she needed help living alone. The highlight of many days came when a four-year-old boy brought her a pot of fresh soup. Sometimes he fed the chickens out back. Rather than scamper away, though, the boy stayed and listened to her stories of cowboys and covered wagons. He enjoyed the tales, but even before kindergarten he could sense that merely letting the old lady share her memories warmed her as much as any soup. He learned that he liked listening. These were Keith Conners's first therapy sessions.

In tiny Ophir, Utah, there wasn't much to do during the depths of the Depression. Named after the Old Testament mine that supplied King Solomon with gold and silver to build the first temple of Israel, Ophir liked to dream that it, too, might house some hidden treasure. But the place was really just a copper mine with some houses dotted about the rim of the canyon. In one of those homes lived Michael and Annie Conners and their three children.

Michael, like most men there, worked in the mine. He ran the hoist that lifted debris from the recent blast up and out of the earth. It was pretty good work for a man with little formal education. Originally born Michael Zezza, the son of Italian immigrants who had worked on railroads from Wisconsin out to Idaho, Michael ran away at sixteen to find whatever work he could, including as an undersized boxer. He decided this required a persona more Irish, so he took the surname of the road on which he had grown up—Conners Street. Pugilism didn't last long, though, and Michael fell in love with Annie Merle, a farmer's daughter from southern Utah. Billie Beth was born in 1926. Then came twins, on March 20, 1933—a girl, Carol, and a boy, Carmen Keith. They weighed less than three pounds and barely survived.

It was just the first of several health scares that shaped Keith's young life. He was a perfectly normal boy who liked to steal apples from a neighbor's orchard and play with toy cars and soldiers, which he stored in an old wooden box that had once held dynamite at his father's mine. He spent first grade in Ophir's one-room schoolhouse. Then, at six, his appendix ruptured. The resulting peritonitis was potentially fatal; the same infection, before antibiotics, had recently killed Rudolph Valentino. By sheer luck Keith survived, only to find himself again near death three years later when he contracted rheumatic fever. The doctor insisted that any bodily movement could further damage his young heart, so Keith had to lie on his stomach and remain as still as possible for eleven months. With nothing else to do he began reading some of his older sister's high school books, including *The Dialogues of Plato*. He devoured the entire *Encyclopedia Americana*, A to Z. He taught himself chess.

Most of all, Keith listened to the family's wood-cabinet Philco radio. To the great envy of the healthy fourth-graders stuck in the schoolhouse, Keith stayed home and lost himself in hour upon hour of *The Shadow*, *The Lone Ranger*, *The Green Hornet*, and other radio serial programs, turning the spoken words into elaborate, imagined scenes. His favorite was *The New Adventures of Sherlock Holmes*. Not only was the title character smart and slightly weird, traits with which young Keith was beginning to identify, but he picked the locks of mysteries just by listening and thinking.

After recovering from his rheumatic fever, Keith became so good at chess that he won Utah's junior championship (and began hustling old duffers down at the local club). He spent just one year in high school. The most austere teacher at West High, Mrs. Henderson, recommended that the clearly gifted young man take some early-entrance exams that were being given by the University of Chicago. He won a full scholarship. At sixteen, leaving home for the first time, Keith

Conners boarded the eastbound California Zephyr train and rumbled across the Rockies and beyond, twenty hours to Chicago.

Adoring the University of Chicago's focus on Great Books and philosophy—Plato's *Dialogues* still spoke to him—Conners graduated in 1953 at age twenty and was nominated for a Rhodes Scholarship. This presented two problems. First, he was no athlete, and the Rhodes

Courtesy of Keith Conners

Keith Conners, age fourteen

emphasis on body as well as mind required all recipients to embrace some sort of physical endeavor. (He barely qualified through some makeshift intramural basketball.) But then, all candidates still had to be in perfect health to participate in Oxford's sports activities, and Conners's rheumatic fever had left him with a heart murmur. The examining physician wouldn't clear him. Conners needled and cajoled and finally persuaded the doctor that the murmur was nothing to worry about. He got the sign-off on his health forms.*

---

*So Keith Conners's career was partly launched by coaxing a reluctant doctor to give him what he wanted—foreshadowing the future problem of patients seeking ADHD medications.

Conners so enjoyed Oxford's psychology courses during his two years overseas that he set his sights on getting a master's in the subject when he returned Stateside in 1955. He was accepted at Harvard and arrived there a bit of an odd man out. Cambridge teemed with New England prep-schoolers; he was the Utah rube. This difference became clearer during one of psychiatry's most infamous investigations: Harvard's study of lysergic acid diethylamide, or LSD.

An experiment to assess this new substance's effects—which at the time were still presumed to be medical, not recreational—required volunteers in two groups to drink a cup of orange juice. Half the cups had LSD dissolved into them, the other half some vodka. Neither group knew which it had gotten (the vodka was made tasteless) and researchers, who also didn't know, sat behind a one-way mirror and watched exactly how loopy the subjects became. After drinking his cup, Conners became so deliriously wasted—friends had to carry him home—that the observers figured he had gotten the LSD. But the log said he had gotten vodka. This befuddled the research staff until they learned that Conners, although not religious, had grown up among so many Mormons that he had never consumed an ounce of alcohol in his life.

Conners sobered up in time to get his psychology doctorate from Harvard in 1960. While considering career paths, he received a letter from a prominent Johns Hopkins psychologist named John Money, a pioneering researcher in gender identity. (Only a few years later, doctors at Johns Hopkins performed the United States' first gender-reassignment surgery.) Dr. Money invited Conners to Baltimore to work with him on the study of hermaphrodites. Conners wrote back: "I'm not sure what a hermaphrodite is, but I know I'm not going to want to spend my life working on them."

Dr. Money, if a tad disappointed, appreciated the cheekiness and showed Conners's letter to another Johns Hopkins iconoclast, Leon Eisenberg. Dr. Eisenberg wanted a smart, young partner to help him investigate overlooked emotional problems of young people.

His first target: an intriguing, yet vexingly nebulous, condition recently dubbed hyperkinetic impulse disorder.

*　　　*　　　*

IT'S HARD TO fathom today just how much psychiatry dismissed children up through the 1950s. The field considered them to be, essentially, little adults—with similar emotional labyrinths to explore, almost always through years of Freudian talk therapy. When the powerful American Psychiatric Association in 1952 published its first catalog of psychiatric conditions, the *Diagnostic and Statistical Manual of Mental Disorders*, almost all considerations of young people were lumped into one small category rather obliquely called "Adjustment Reaction of Childhood." (This phrase raised several questions, including what stage of life these children were adjusting from.) Only a few sentences described children's troublesome behaviors, ranging from nail-biting and thumb-sucking to violence and cruelty.

Leon Eisenberg cared about children as few in his field ever had. He was convinced that their psyches were not just adults' writ small; their problems were distinct, and their treatments should be, too. Eisenberg's outlook built on the work of his Johns Hopkins mentor, Dr. Leo Kanner, who had written the first English-language textbook of child psychiatry and was the psychiatrist who first described autism in the early 1940s. Eisenberg extended Kanner's autism work by assessing how children's language patterns over years could predict their autistic behaviors as adults. He developed theories not merely through talk therapy with individual patients, the strategy used by most of his field, but by conducting formal scientific studies to generate rock-solid evidence. With Eisenberg, one of the first psychiatrists to trade squishy observations for hard-and-fast data, other scientists at Hopkins joked, "Finally, a psychiatrist who can count."

Still, if any area of science could defy categorization and cold calculation, it was the behavior of young children. This was clear among kids whose conditions fell short of schizophrenia or severe depression; when talk turned to hyperactivity and impulsivity, traits shared by all children to some extent, separating unusual from normal was almost impossible. There had to be a physical explanation, most likely an early, even prenatal, brain injury. This view took hold to the point that when a child in the 1950s was particularly uncontrollable, he—it was almost always a boy—was often said to have "minimal brain damage."

The brain-damage theory began to crumble at, somewhat coincidentally, the Emma Pendleton Bradley Home in Rhode Island. Charles Bradley had left as medical director in 1948 and was succeeded by Dr. Maurice Laufer. Dr. Laufer eventually noted that too few of his hyperactive and impulsive patients had any past brain injury to explain their troubles. Something else had to be responsible, even if no one knew what that could be. So he coined a new term for their condition, something more dulcet: hyperkinetic impulse disorder. "In brief summary," he wrote, "hyperactivity is the most striking item. This may be noted from early infancy on or not become prominent until 5 or 6 years of age. There are also a short attention span and poor powers of concentration, which are particularly noticeable under school conditions." This observation foreshadowed the ultimate definition of attention deficit hyperactivity disorder a generation later. Similarly prescient was Laufer's recognition that parents, after being told that their child actually had an identifiable medical condition, felt "a great sense of relief concerning their own and the child's responsibility for the problem."

As for treatment for hyperkinetic impulse disorder, despite Bradley's experiments at the same hospital, amphetamine had developed too mixed a reputation to consider giving it to children. On the one hand, its vast use among soldiers in World War II to increase alertness and mood in combat was viewed as almost patriotic, a means to Allied victory. (Winston Churchill personally authorized the use of 72 million Benzedrine tablets by British troops, although some took so much they began to hallucinate and see tanks drive sideways.) But news articles about Stateside Benzedrine addiction were commonplace, to the point of satire: In 1947, the musician Harry "The Hipster" Gibson released the song "Who Put the Benzedrine in Mrs. Murphy's Ovaltine?," a giddy number about an even more giddily addicted housewife. Smith, Kline & French countered the bad publicity by releasing a slightly tweaked formulation of the drug and rebranding it Dexedrine, but that, too, kept minting addicts. In the rare cases a parent wanted to try medication on a child, nonamphetamine options were preferred. Some hyperactive or emotionally unstable children were given the tranquilizer Nostyn, which was marketed to doctors as "safe for your little patients too." A similar product, Atarax, was advertised as "lengthening the child's attention span for better schoolwork and easing his relations with teachers, classmates, and parents," a strategy used in later ADHD ads. But these drugs typically caused worse side effects in children than adults, so the entire concept of giving them to any beyond the sickest young people remained frowned upon.

Back at Johns Hopkins, Eisenberg still saw too much promise in Dexedrine to renounce it altogether. He was anything but a drug maven—he viewed talk therapy to be vital to the treatment of children. ("It's time to stop pulling drowning kids out of the river," he insisted, "and start heading upstream to see who is pushing them in.") He gave up on no kid and would pursue any aid that formal science could pinpoint. A responsible, well-structured Dexedrine study would have to meet three vital conditions: Some children would receive medicine, others only placebos, and others nothing at all (making the study "controlled"); pure chance would decide which patients fell into each group ("randomized"); and no one, from the kids to the teachers who observed and rated their behavior, could know who had received medicine and who did not ("double-blind"). Shortly before the trial began, Eisenberg recruited Keith Conners, who shared his enthusiasm for formal science and concern for kids.

Their Dexedrine experiment took place over two months in 1961 at the Boys' Village of Maryland, a reformatory facility for delinquent teenaged African American boys,* most of whom would today be diagnosed with behavioral disorders other than ADHD but who were still quite uncontrollable. The Dexedrine did appear to improve the boys' behavior; on the downside, they lost their appetites to the point that many lost five to ten pounds. This effect surprised no one, as amphetamine was already a popular diet pill for adults, and it worried Conners and Eisenberg. Yet they saw enough promise to urge further experiments, which they called "a compelling social necessity."

Eisenberg and Conners knew the public wasn't ready to give amphetamines to children. Perhaps doctors and parents could accept a relatively new drug that was almost identical to amphetamine, a pick-me-up for

---

*Any cynicism regarding Eisenberg's experimenting on African Americans first would be wholly unfair. If anything, he wanted to help them more; Eisenberg took a special interest in providing care to underprivileged, minority children, and became an early proponent of affirmative action.

adults called Ritalin. That pill had much less baggage. In fact, from the start, Ritalin was a love story.

LEANDRO PANIZZON ADORED watching his young wife, Marguerite, play tennis. He was a chemist for the Swiss pharmaceutical company CIBA—short for Chemische Industrie Basel, or Chemical Industries of Basel—who had spent years fiddling with the molecular structure of amphetamine, for little reason other than to maybe stumble on something that would increase Marguerite's energy and focus on the court, but be less addictive. (And, while he was at it, slim her waistline.) In the mid-1940s he wound up with a formulation that did all this and more—turning Marguerite, known as Rita, into a tennis-playing machine. She loved it as much as he did her. So he named it Ritaline.

To distance itself from amphetamine's sketchy history, CIBA termed the chemical formulation of this drug "methylphenidate." The company released it to the American market in 1956 as Ritalin, a treatment for narcolepsy, chronic fatigue, depression, and erratic behavior caused by senility. (Again, only in adults; the medication was untested in children.) Early advertisements for the stuff in medical journals presented galleries of middle-aged and elderly men looking lethargic and depressed, with the message, "All are candidates for Ritalin." CIBA went so far as to develop a liquid version that psychiatrists could inject into their patients right there in the office, something illegal today; this method would "help psychiatric patients talk," one ad said, "in as little as 5 minutes."

Fresh off their promising Dexedrine results, and knowing that methylphenidate and amphetamine were close molecular cousins, Eisenberg and Conners suspected that Ritalin might similarly improve the behavior and schoolwork of particularly difficult children, but with fewer side effects. Conners visited two facilities near the Johns Hopkins campus in Baltimore: a group home for kids whose truculence made them unsuitable for placement with a foster family, and a psychiatric treatment center for what were then called "disturbed children." None had a specific diagnosis; they just clashed with traditional and increasingly distraught family settings. But the kids had some hope. When Conners visited the homes for the first time, he was struck by how much the youngsters craved his attention. He felt like a visitor to Bangladesh who finds children pulling on his clothes plaintively. The sensation stuck with Conners for the rest of his life.

Conners arranged for seventy-eight children to take the little pink capsules for ten days—half getting Ritalin and half placebos—and were examined before and after in about a hundred different physical, behavioral, and emotional categories. The Ritalin kids jumped out immediately. They became less impulsive. Their alertness improved and, along with it, their ability to learn. Side effects were relatively tame: Many children lost their appetites, others struggled to sleep, and a few became more anxious than usual. But the trial was a resounding success. The paper Conners and Eisenberg wrote up for the *American Journal of Psychiatry*—the field's most respected journal—was titled, "The Effects of Methylphenidate on Symptomatology and Learning in Disturbed Children." The headline might as well have been: "Hey Everyone, Ritalin Works."

However, just as with Charles Bradley a generation before, the psychiatric establishment roundly shrugged. Experienced doctors weren't necessarily hostile to the findings; they just didn't care. Psychiatry's stock and trade was Freudian analysis, and any suggestion that some pill could do anything that their intensive (and profitable) talk therapy could not was blasphemous. Upton Sinclair had once put it best: "It is difficult to get a man to understand something, when his salary depends upon his not understanding it."

The Conners/Eisenberg paper did impress some people, though. The National Institute of Mental Health was encouraged enough to consider funding further Ritalin research. Then, weeks later, came a more eye-opening offer.

Conners was sitting in Eisenberg's second-floor Hopkins office discussing their young patients when someone knocked on the open door. He was a salesman-looking fellow, early thirties, in a dark suit, white shirt, and tie. He introduced himself as a representative of a very appreciative CIBA Pharmaceuticals. The man slid a piece of paper out of his pocket and placed it on Eisenberg's desk.

"Here you go," he said. "For further studies."

It was a check for $5,000. As the man left, Eisenberg closed the door behind him and turned to Conners.

"Watch out for these guys," Eisenberg said. He walked back to his desk, put the check in a drawer, and never mentioned it again.

AS CONNERS INVESTIGATED how Ritalin affected children's behavior, others debated just what to call that behavior itself. "Minimal brain damage" was falling out of favor, for two reasons: First, such children were showing no signs of brain damage, minimal or otherwise; second, it was just plain unsavory. More than thirty other terms began making the rounds instead, including "organic drivenness," "character impulse disorder," and "cerebral dys-synchronization syndrome."* One doctor even proposed "Hoffmann's disease," to honor century-old Fidgety Phil.

Two doctors at the Child Guidance Clinic in Little Rock, Arkansas, Samuel D. Clements and John E. Peters, were determined to come up with a better name. *Hyperkinesis?* Too restrictive, they felt, because some children were relatively calm; they just couldn't concentrate. *Attentional deviation syndrome?* Didn't capture hyperactivity. These kids . . . well, there was just something off with their *functioning*. And there it was, staring back at them: minimal brain *dysfunction*.

The term gave mothers more than just a tasteful phrase to use at the bridge table; it reified the syndrome within the medical community by being equally malleable and disprovable. (Any exasperating behavior from a child, almost by definition, could be ascribed to who-knows-what at least minimally askew within the brain.) Rather than explore this overinclusiveness, the most prestigious journals, including the *New England Journal of Medicine*, happily accepted it. One paper said that minimal brain dysfunction was "a mysterious something" that experts were "not able to clarify . . . to any great extent." But its existence was "beyond doubt." In 1966, Clements led a US Department of Health, Education and Welfare (HEW) project that would further define MBD for either the skeptical or understandably confused. His three-part report spanned more than one hundred pages and

---

*The 1968 edition of the *DSM* grudgingly settled on "hyperkinetic reaction of childhood," which it only briefly described as "overactivity, restlessness, distractibility, and short attention span, especially in young children." The term never gained any real currency.

represented a playbook for clinicians to make the diagnosis. Suddenly, minimal brain dysfunction was not just recognized by the medical establishment; it had received the government's seal of approval.

Eisenberg and Conners got the ultimate endorsement, too—being wooed away from Johns Hopkins by the even more prestigious Massachusetts General Hospital and Harvard Medical School. But their interests were beginning to diverge. Eisenberg focused on improving minorities' access to psychiatric services and admitting more women into Harvard's medical programs. Conners was left in charge of seeing young patients, counseling families, and running all research in child psychiatry, including continued tests of Dexedrine and Ritalin in children.

Conners was less concerned with MBD's name than creating a tool to measure its symptoms. Some questionnaires used by doctors asked how often the child would "wrestle and horse around," "play hooky," or, question 13, "get into tricks at Halloween," not exactly the stuff of which science is made. Conners spent years developing a list of thirty-nine more straightforward and objective items such as "inattentive," "quarrelsome," or "excessive demands for teacher's attention," using formal statistical methods to confirm that these really were the most telltale categories to pinpoint MBD. The youngsters were ranked from 0 ("not at all") to 3 ("very much")—but not by doctors, who, Conners explained, could not possibly evaluate youngsters' behavior during short office visits. Teachers, who spent as much time (or more) with children as parents did, were best situated to make the "astute observations" required to judge the truly dysfunctional.

By late 1969, Conners presented what he called his Teacher Rating Scale in a paper in the *American Journal of Psychiatry.* The questionnaire could allow doctors everywhere to assess MBD and make diagnoses in a more accurate and standardized fashion. It would do even more than that, though. Conners's tool would quite precisely measure a kid's behavioral symptoms before and after a trial of Dexedrine or Ritalin— and, in some ways, became an invitation to try.*

---

*Conners needed no questionnaire to assess the effects of Ritalin on himself. Late one afternoon, following an exhausting day in the lab, he had to attend an eight p.m. lecture by Harry Harlow, a behavioral psychologist famous for locking young monkeys away from their mothers and studying their emotional demise. Knowing he'd never stay

"The drug," Conners had written shortly before, "has energized the children, apathetic and discouraged by previous school failure, into making use of abilities available to them." This message was still a little too stuffy for CIBA, which appreciated Conners's conclusions but still needed something punchier for a Ritalin-for-kids advertising campaign—a promise that would speak to doctors and parents alike. It succeeded. One medical-journal ad altered the picture of a young boy,

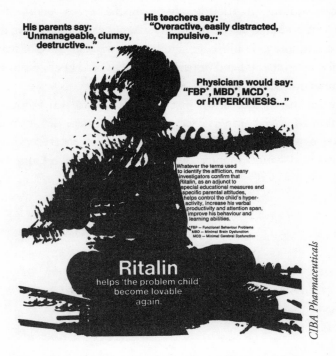

maybe five or six years old, to make him appear to be shaking violently, as if electrocuted. But CIBA's wonder drug would calm him down, and so much more. Ritalin, the ad declared, "helps the problem child become lovable again."

---

conscious for the whole thing, Conners found the tub of Ritalin capsules so generously donated by CIBA and took one. Within thirty minutes he snapped awake and thought to himself, "This is fantastic!" He kept working until eight. He skipped dinner. He zoned in on the lecture, chatted with folks afterward, and stayed up until three in the morning. Just one dose felt so great, so beguiling, that he never tried the stuff again for the rest of his life.

Leon Eisenberg was growing uncomfortable with this enthusiasm. However rooted in science, Conners's symptom questionnaire measured not necessarily a child's behavior, but outsiders' *impression of it*—their *tolerance* for it. The evaluations remained dangerously subjective, allowing a parent or teacher to circle 2's and 3's depending on their own values, even whims. Eisenberg cautioned: "Whereas the adult comes for treatment largely because of his own distress and at his own initiative, the child comes to our attention because of his family's or his community's initiative. Who, then, are we to classify diagnostically: the child, the family, the community, or all three?" He feared now that the Conners Scale, unleashed upon the real and imperfect world, would begin green-lighting widespread overuse of Ritalin.

America would soon learn just what Eisenberg was talking about. Mere months after Conners's scales were published, debates over Ritalin moved way beyond scientific journals. They entered newspapers, television, and—most remarkably—the halls of the US Congress.

Chapter 3

FROM MBD TO ADD

As tips go, this was a doozy. In the spring of 1970, Robert Maynard, a national correspondent for the *Washington Post*, heard that the Omaha, Nebraska, school system was—wait, *what?*—prescribing "behavior modification drugs" to thousands of their difficult students, most of them black. This news resonated deeply with Maynard, himself a black man who had spent years covering the cauldron of civil rights and the nation's inner-city riots. So when he learned that thousands of black kids were being hit with drugs, not just fire hoses, he flew to Nebraska to pursue the story. His exclusive sparked a summer in which Ritalin broke through and into the national debate.

"Omaha Pupils Given 'Behavior' Drugs," the *Post*'s page-one headline blared. Maynard reported that 5 to 10 percent of children in the elementary school system—perhaps six thousand total—were taking Ritalin, Dexedrine, or other drugs to control their hyperactivity and other disruptive antics, all part of a "behavior modification program." Many parents from Omaha's mostly black north side said their schools were coercing them to go to the clinic of one Dr. Byron B. Oberst, a local pediatrician, who would put their children on medication to make them more manageable. Maynard accused school officials and local doctors of staging a campaign to, as he put it, "drug black children into quiet submission." One ten-year-old boy named Mackie said, "I'd be acting crazy fooling around at the board and stuff and the teachers said, 'Mack, do you have one of your pills?' I say, 'Yeah.' So I took one and we went out and played and I came back and I felt more like doing my work." Children as young as eight were carrying pills to school and trading them during recess like candy, telling each other, "Here, you try my yellow one and I'll try your pink one."

The school's head of health services didn't understand the fuss. "It makes them happier," he shrugged. Dr. Oberst explained his prescriptions "made these children become more successful" and steered them away from "vandalism, riots and anarchy against society."

This ardor notwithstanding, making kids happier with amphetamines was not the most popular of concepts by the summer of 1970. Dexedrine had become perhaps the most widely abused drug in the United States—more than hippies' marijuana, more than Timothy Leary's LSD, more than the heroin that would soon kill Jimi Hendrix and Janis Joplin. In the 1960s, doctors prescribed amphetamines so willingly—for weight loss, depression, all but hangnails—that an estimated four billion tablets were dispensed by American pharmacies per year, or enough for every man, woman, and child in the United States to have twenty apiece. The United States military handed out Dexedrine so freely that an estimated 7 percent of its Vietnam forces became abusers and addicts.* About eight hundred thousand Americans were dependent on amphetamines, about three hundred thousand of them flat-out addicted—and many of them average housewives. These addicts weren't the young beatniks and hippies so reviled by the establishment; they were, in many cases, the establishment itself. There was talk about banning amphetamine in the United States altogether, its medical uses be damned. Instead, the federal Controlled Substances Act placed unprecedented restrictions on the handling of addictive pharmaceuticals like Dexedrine and Ritalin. Prescribers were now required to maintain a special government license, fill out much more paperwork, and prescribe no more than a thirty-day supply at a time. Drug companies could not produce such medications in quantities higher than the government deemed clinically necessary.

---

*Then there were athletes, whose teams placed bowls of "greenies"—Dexedrine tablets were green—in locker rooms to combat the exhaustion of the long season. *Ball Four*, the rollicking 1970 baseball exposé by the rabble-rousing pitcher Jim Bouton, described players popping the pills "just to get their heart beating"; after watching Pete Rose run and just miss a diving catch, one player remarked, "Five more milligrams and he'd have had it."

It was the ultimate buzzkill. US production of amphetamine plummeted an astonishing 90 percent in only a few years. Stimulants could no longer be handed out as mere pick-me-ups for tired professionals, but only for narcolepsy or short-term weight loss. And for a children's malady just now hitting America's living rooms: minimal brain dysfunction.

NEWSPAPERS LARGE AND small seized upon the *Post* report on the rampant deployment of Ritalin on youngsters in Omaha. Media outlets went out and appraised the use of Ritalin in their own local areas and usually found similar stories. NBC's prestigious *Huntley-Brinkley Report* broadcast a segment on minimal brain dysfunction and the swelling numbers of children taking drugs for it. The Food and Drug Administration ordered its own investigation into what might be happening in communities around the United States.

The *New York Times* responded with an article that more than tacitly endorsed Omaha's methods. It rather airily (and unjustifiably) claimed that as many as 20 percent of all American children had minimal brain dysfunction, "making it a problem of epidemic proportions"—and that they needed Ritalin just as diabetics did insulin. It discussed a six-year-old boy from Providence, Rhode Island, named Jackie D., who fought with other children, was too clumsy to ride his bike, and had learning problems; after going on Ritalin, the article explained, "Now he is quiet, coordinated and has even done well enough in his lessons to be promoted to second grade."* To illustrate the transformation Ritalin could bring, a different boy was asked to draw a person—before going on medication, and then after. The first scratching was a small, faceless blob; the second, a detailed figure with a big smile.

Reporters, from small newspapers to major television news departments like NBC's, sought out doctors who could comment on where Ritalin came from, and naturally wound up interviewing the men per-

---

*The boy's being from Providence, the site of Charles Bradley's amphetamine experiments, was no coincidence: His pediatrician was Dr. Eric Denhoff, who had worked with Bradley decades before and was now in private practice.

haps most instrumental in the research: Eisenberg and Conners at Massachusetts General Hospital. The doctors told all who would listen to relax, that scientists were on the case. "There's nothing new about it," Conners said, referring to Ritalin's dating back to the 1950s. Regarding the inevitable question of whether Ritalin could steer kids toward drug addiction later in life, Conners explained that there was no evidence of that risk—in government-funded studies, to boot. Dr. Eisenberg got a little impatient with any outside suggestion that stimulants could harm children. "When used properly, they are remarkably safe," he said. "Even safer than penicillin."

Some people didn't buy it—particularly Cornelius E. Gallagher, a New Jersey congressman. A self-styled tough guy from the docks of Bayonne, Gallagher scheduled an official House of Representatives subcommittee hearing for September in which he would examine these issues, essentially putting the use of Ritalin in American children on public trial. If the government was going to support research into minimal brain dysfunction, Gallagher explained, it would darned well find out just what it was supporting.

Mail arrived in Gallagher's office in bundles from parents and doctors nationwide. One man said that his daughter's elementary school teachers and nurse were insisting she be diagnosed with minimal brain dysfunction, joining four others in her class; the school, he wrote, "made me feel as though I was a stupid, neglectful parent who was only doing my child harm by not giving her this Ritalin." The Harvard Center for Law and Education and the American Civil Liberties Union considered suing school systems in order to publicize such tactics. But other letters were less approving of Gallagher's interest. A physician from Columbus, Ohio, lambasted Gallagher for having "the audacity" to question medical professionals: "What do you know about the hyperactive child and about the problems that they have incurred in school? What do you know about the family that is besieged with phone calls from irate teachers that the child is destructive, uncooperative, has a short attention span, won't learn? . . . Problems of taking care of children, their medical needs, should rightfully be left in the hands of pediatricians."

Congressman Gallagher called the hearing to order at ten a.m. on September 29, 1970. Keith Conners was not there, for reasons lost to history, but his name came up within minutes. A top official at the US Department of Health, Education and Welfare, Dr. Thomas C. Points, detailed how most of the government funding for minimal brain dysfunction drug research had to gone to Harvard's Dr. Conners, totaling $450,000—including $120,000 that very month. Points continued that Dr. Conners's studies had found Ritalin and Dexedrine to be "safe and clinically effective." In fact, kids who were denied medication, Dr. Conners had found, were at risk for "psychoses and sociopathic personality." There was no danger of children becoming addicted either now or later in life—according to Dr. Conners.

Every mention of this mysterious Keith Conners frustrated Gallagher more: "Yes. But Dr. Conners has been involved in this for some time. He is obviously a dedicated scientist to this thing. Where do we have some other dedicated scientist who may question this?" A few minutes later, Gallagher spat, "Certainly there must be some other way than merely having a proponent of a program view it 'objectively,' as you tell me Dr. Conners is doing. . . . We have hundreds of thousands of children, millions of dollars of taxpayers' money involved in this, and we are going on the basis of one or two opinions that are being formed now?"

With Conners absent from the hearing room, the doctors left to answer Gallagher's most pointed round of questions were the architects of minimal brain dysfunction—Drs. Clements and Peters from Little Rock. Peters did most of the talking, his assertions sounding plausible but increasingly spurious upon closer inspection. While claiming that between 5 and 20 percent of children had minimal brain dysfunction, he said, "I think those of you who have not seen children of this kind don't know what we are talking about." (*But Doctor Peters,* Gallagher mused, *if so many children are this disordered, how hidden could they be?*) When concerns were raised that teenagers could abuse the drugs like some of their parents undoubtedly had, Peters explained that—as luck would have it—kids outgrew minimal brain dysfunction by the age of twelve, so no worries there. Trying to reassure the panel of his personal credibility, Peters said that he had prescribed Ritalin to his own young son, to great effect. He testified that he had never, not once, seen or heard of any parent being pushed by a school system into medicating their child. So help him God.

Gallagher thanked Dr. Peters for his comments. Then, with impeccable timing, the congressman played his ace in the hole: He called to testify one Margaret Youngs of Indianapolis, Indiana. Mrs. Youngs looked every bit the tractable housewife: dark dress draped over a necktied blouse, her Mary Tyler Moore hairdo framing a fleshy, midwestern face. But she sat straight at the heavy wood table, just down from Drs. Clements and Peters. They didn't remember her. But she sure remembered them.

The Youngs family left Ohio back in 1963 and settled in Little Rock, Arkansas. They enrolled Mickey, their third-grade girl, and Ross, two years younger, in Hardin Bale Public School. Mrs. Youngs testified that teachers there decided within weeks that both children had minimal brain dysfunction and needed Ritalin. The principal recommended she take them to the local MBD clinic run by two prominent doctors—Clements and Peters—and gave her some of their introductory pamphlets while explaining that her own daughter was also on Ritalin for MBD. Mrs. Youngs refused to take the pamphlets. Her children might not be academic superstars, she said, but brain disordered they were not.

Mrs. Youngs described how the school spent three years pushing her to send the children to the Clements-Peters clinic and join what was becoming a concerted experiment on behavior-altering drugs for difficult, class-disturbing children. Other families had faced the same pressure, Mrs. Youngs said. Some gave in, others resisted. But all feared that speaking up would result in retribution to their kids. "Step by step," Mrs. Youngs told the committee, Hardin Bale officials "were plotting a well-laid plan for soliciting children . . . to be used as guinea pigs." When the school had invited Dr. Clements to speak to parents about MBD, she went and directly asked him why medication was necessary. "If you are going to worry about the use of drugs," he replied, "I suggest you don't give your children aspirin." Teachers grew so disgusted with Mr. and Mrs. Youngs's resistance to put their children on Ritalin that they threatened legal action—ultimately demanding that the parents write a letter to the school that stated, for the record, that they refused the school's recommendation.

Other local doctors had hopped on the MBD bandwagon, too, Mrs. Youngs continued. One day, when Ross went to the family pediatrician for a sore throat, the doctor asked him about his grades. Ross replied C's and D's. "Dr. Flack asked my son how he would like it if he could get A's and B's," Mrs. Youngs testified, the physician's name eliciting some chuckles from onlookers. When Ross said yes, she said, "Dr. Flack proceeded to write out a prescription for [Ritalin] and told my son this would help him to do better in school. I was in the room at the time, but the conversation by Dr. Flack was directed completely to my son. I refused the prescription and, needless to say, Dr. Flack was no longer my family physician."

Three years into the ordeal, Mrs. Youngs said, her family fled Little Rock for Indianapolis, where Ross began thriving academically without drugs.* She had kept up with some of her Arkansas friends who said the school was still pestering them to visit Dr. Peters and put their kids on Ritalin.

Gallagher asked Dr. Peters to respond.

"If she was pressured," he said, "I think this is terrible."

THE HEARING AND drama of Mrs. Youngs's testimony were covered in newspapers nationwide. Discussion no doubt took place at countless breakfast tables and watercoolers. But none of these conversations included Keith Conners himself—he didn't even know the hearing had taken place until several weeks later, when someone from NIMH happened to mention it over the phone. Ensconced in Cambridge, focusing only on his patients and ongoing research, he shrugged at missing the first government hearing about the field he had helped forge. He took the entire business as political grandstanding, laymen sticking their noses into science they did not understand.

Like so many doctors before and since, Conners focused on the world inside his own office doors—doors that welcomed real children with real struggles and needing his real, and often successful, intervention. His symptom questionnaires helped isolate the child's core problems. His Ritalin could provide true relief. He saw these results every day. He didn't care what the malady was called, whether it be minimal

---

*Ross Youngs is now fifty-nine and a successful entrepreneur in Ohio.

brain dysfunction, hyperkinesis, or the next *nom du jour*. In Conners's mind, the children he saw at Mass General, mostly unruly and recalcitrant boys, had already been diagnosed by the adults around them with something far worse—a malady he called, if only to himself, "rotten little kid syndrome." If he could spare a child even one more day with that label, one more needless castigation or disapproving stare, he would do so.

Among all of Conners's inspirations—from Eisenberg to Aristotle—perhaps none affected him more than a little eight-year-old named Lenny, one of his earliest Boston patients. However bright and handsome, Lenny showed the hallmark, indiscriminate recklessness of MBD: dashing headlong over a couch or into his younger brother, frantically raiding the kitchen cupboards, or climbing out his second-floor window and dangling his feet over the roof. His teachers complained that Lenny ignored rules and instigated misbehavior from other students. His mother was at her wit's end, left alone while her husband worked long hours and took frequent business trips. He complained that her parenting was to blame—a charge she also heard from neighbors.

"You've felt miserable about this situation for a long time," Conners told her during an early appointment. "Others have given a message that it was your fault. It seems that you have been feeling pretty angry about that, perhaps even angry at the child as well for disrupting your family life."

Tears welled in the mother's eyes. She began to weep openly. "I can't begin to tell you how . . ." she stammered.

Conners finished her thought so she didn't have to say it out loud.

"That you felt like killing him?"

She nodded. More tears.

"He's really a sweet boy," she said. "But no one ever listens to me to understand what it's like. I always feared it was my fault because I can't help yelling at him all the time. It's just nonstop. I try to control myself but he never stops."

Conners knew that the family would need some serious talk therapy to survive. But he also knew that Lenny—and certainly the mother—needed faster relief. He suggested Ritalin.

Lenny was transformed. He not only behaved better but developed awareness of his behavior itself. It wasn't long before he told Dr. Conners: "I had to tell Mom that she didn't have to yell so loud anymore, because I get the message and can do what I am supposed to." The mother felt vindicated—the problems clearly were not her fault—and relieved, ready to provide calmer discipline on her easier child. Conners never forgot how Ritalin had liberated this entire family from the guilt, anger, and frustration caused by one difficult boy, allowing them—and his teachers—to build a more nurturing environment for all.

Tales like these, whether witnessed in real life or recounted in a scientific journal, resonated more with Conners than any distant congressman. Children with minimal brain dysfunction did not necessarily need conventional twice-a-week psychotherapy, but they usually needed these drugs. Hesitation to prescribe them merely prolonged unnecessary agony, as if ignoring the screams of a child with appendicitis. Conners was by no means the only prominent clinician to adopt this mind-set. Consider this passage from the first full book devoted to minimal brain dysfunction, published in 1971 by the psychiatrist and emerging firebrand Paul Wender: "It would not be hard to argue that in many instances psychotherapy of children with this syndrome virtually constitutes malpractice—a harmful withholding of useful treatment from a child."

Conners did have a softer side, of course. One day, he traveled down to New York to meet with a television producer named Joan Ganz Cooney. She was convening about a dozen top names in child education and mental health to discuss her idea for a new public-television show, one that would use music and puppets to introduce preschoolers to letters, numbers, and the like—yet rooted more in science than shtick. She invited Eisenberg and Conners to share some of their research and insight—not regarding Ritalin, needless to say, but their other work on learning processes in young children. (Conners's seat at the round table happened to be beside the *Where the Wild Things Are* cartoonist Maurice Sendak, who doodled one of his shaggy beasts on a napkin that Conners has kept to this day.) The meeting became Conners's only contribution to the show, and he drove back to Cambridge and his patients unsure anything would come of it. He was wrong. You know it as *Sesame Street*.

Most of Conners's freelance work, though, was for companies seeking to capitalize on America's growing interest in MBD. No firm used him more than Abbott Labs, which thought it could please both sides of the debate by releasing a new medication far less potentially addictive than Ritalin and Dexedrine: a drug it called Cylert. Conners conducted Abbott's first clinical study of Cylert's effectiveness in impulsive children, finding that it did provide some short-term moderation of symptoms with fewer side effects.* Abbott then asked him to convene a symposium called "Clinical Use of Stimulant Drugs in Children," in which the field's top names—the loudest being Wender's—gathered in sunny Key Biscayne, Florida, to reconfirm among themselves how countless American children were going untreated for MBD and suffering without medications they might need well into adulthood. Conners not only chaired the symposium but edited a hardcover compendium of the papers delivered there. Abbott paid for the book to be published and made it available to doctors nationwide. Taped inside the front cover, quite neatly and helpfully, was an advertisement for Cylert.

(Not to be outdone, CIBA, the makers of Ritalin, published its own "Physician's Handbook" for diagnosing MBD, which conveniently included form letters for a clinician to explain the syndrome to teachers. The book was written by Drs. Peters and Clements of Little Rock, Arkansas.)

Growing enthusiasm for minimal brain dysfunction did face some push back. In 1975, Peter Schrag and Diane Divoky, husband and wife education writers, published *The Myth of the Hyperactive Child*, a blistering indictment of the entire MBD concept. The book sold briskly among parents and attracted serious reviews in the popular press. Later that year, a Colorado pediatrician named Barton D. Schmitt eviscerated the medical establishment in a journal essay: "Labeling troubled children as having MBD has almost become a national pastime." He continued: "It has become an all-encompassing, wastebasket diagnosis for any child who does not quite conform to society's stereotype of

---

*Conners specifically reported no ill effects on the liver, accurate during his eight-week trial but ultimately flat-out wrong. Cylert was later linked with more than a dozen deaths from liver failure and was removed from the market a decade ago.

normal children. . . . Almost any behavior short of psychosis has been attributed to MBD."

As diagnoses rose, so did skepticism of just what doctors were truly identifying. If the syndrome were *minimal*, why use such serious medications to treat it? If it involved the *brain*, why didn't anything show up on any cerebral scans? And what constituted *dysfunction*, anyway? What was wrong with these kids medically? The critics did have a point.

Claiming to hear and respect these concerns, the coterie of MBD experts gathered to rework and reword the syndrome of childhood hyperactivity. The doctors succeeded—by coming up with yet another new name, the one that would explode into a true cultural phenomenon.

DR. VIRGINIA DOUGLAS, one of the first women to join the otherwise male-dominated club of child psychiatry, stepped to the podium and delivered the 1971 presidential address to members of the Canadian Psychological Association. Her speech described her longtime work with hyperactive children. She theorized that the problem was not insufficient body or impulse control. It was insufficient *attention*: attention to tasks before bolting away; attention to instruction; and attention to the emotional and societal warning cues that normal children heed. This was an entirely new construct—and one that really did capture what doctors were seeing, what parents and teachers were complaining about.

Dr. Douglas's paper single-handedly redirected the study of hyperactive and impulsive children. Naturally, Keith Conners invited her to present her insights at his MBD symposium in Key Biscayne the following year. Young researchers sensed a paradigm shift and pursued a reconsideration of attention among girls, who had generally been underrepresented in investigations of hyperactivity. Research into Douglas's theory popped up everywhere. By the end of the 1970s, more than two thousand studies and papers examined this new concept of "attention deficits."

The American Psychiatric Association's previous *Diagnostic and Statistical Manual of Mental Disorders*, dating from 1968, had described obstreperous and impulsive children as having hyperkinetic reaction of childhood. But Douglas's theory took such hold that this nomen-clature, especially its reference only to hyperactivity, was considered too restrictive to encircle this growing population of troubled children. The less official but more popular term, minimal brain dysfunction, was on its way out, too. ("Minimal" didn't exactly convey anything worthy of respect or governmental funding.) The treatment and recognition of these children's problems—and the future of the field—would stem from the name that the revised *DSM,* scheduled to arrive in 1980, settled upon. Paul Wender, who had thundered some years before that not giving an affected child Ritalin was grounds for a malpractice suit, worried that no term would ever fit: "If we could find this hypothetical seventeenth-century physician who had first described the condition," he wrote during the negotiations, "we would be able to label it after him and rechristen it as, say, 'Krankheit's syndrome.'" (Krankheit is German for "disease.")

In the end, it became essentially "Douglas's disease." On page 41 of the new 1980 *DSM,* the headline rang: ATTENTION DEFICIT DISORDER.

Whereas hyperkinetic reaction of childhood had been described in two fuzzy sentences, attention deficit disorder got four and a half entire pages—detailing the syndrome and instructing precisely how doctors should diagnose it.

A. Inattention. At least three of the following:
  (1) often fails to finish things he or she starts
  (2) often doesn't seem to listen
  (3) easily distracted
  (4) has difficulty concentrating on schoolwork or other tasks requiring sustained attention
  (5) has difficulty sticking to a play activity

B. Impulsivity. At least three of the following:
  (1) often acts before thinking
  (2) shifts excessively from one activity to another
  (3) has difficulty organizing work (this not being due to cognitive impairment)

(4) needs a lot of supervision

(5) frequently calls out in class

(6) has difficulty awaiting turn in games or group situations

C. Hyperactivity. At least two of the following:

(1) runs about or climbs on things excessively

(2) has difficulty sitting still or fidgets excessively

(3) has difficulty staying seated

(4) moves about excessively during sleep

(5) is always "on the go" or acts as if "driven by a motor"

It was a stripped-down Conners Scale. Twenty years after Leon Eisenberg had encouraged Conners to pursue objective measurement of behavior, and a decade after Conners released his first thirty-nine-item checklist of symptoms to assess, a child's diagnosis of attention deficit disorder had been trimmed down to a Chinese restaurant menu of sixteen items—and in some ways only eleven. Bowing to Douglas and Wender, a diagnosis did not require any symptoms from the hyperactive list; a child could receive either disorder code 314.00, "ADD without hyperactivity," or 314.01, "ADD with hyperactivity." Not requiring turbocharged behavior was an overt attempt not to exclude girls, and to ease diagnoses for all.

More disturbing, the symptoms absurdly overlapped. Any child "easily distracted" would have "difficulty concentrating," too. One who "fails to finish things" also "has difficulty sticking" to them, and "shifts excessively from one activity to another." (The most ridiculous was separating "sitting still" and "staying seated.") Having one or two of these tendencies almost by definition meant having six or eight. Researchers led by Conners claimed that statistical and other factor analysis justified these interlocking symptoms, but the construct was clearly tautologous: Any child who even *seemed* to have ADD in any way would qualify. A few people involved in the definition did recognize this. Dr. Judith Rapoport, a no-pushover young researcher at the National Institute of Mental Health, warned the team: "ADD could replace oedipal anxiety as a new universal explanation; I urge restraint."

Rapoport got steamrolled. The symptom list stood. And along with it, the final *DSM* manual stated:

> *The disorder is common. In the United States, it may occur in as many as 3% of prepubertal children.*

THREE PERCENT. BUT that number wouldn't stay so low for long.

Chapter 4

COLLISION COURSE

Conners had just finished yet another talk on attention deficit disorder and was packing up his notebooks when a bubbly, full-bodied fellow named Steve Stein walked up and introduced himself. It was May 1986, the annual meeting of the American Psychiatric Association (APA), at the Washington, DC, Convention Center. Conners was there to talk ADD. Stein had come to talk business.

Since the APA had sculpted "attention deficit disorder" in its 1980 manual, the number of diagnoses had grown briskly, with hundreds of thousands of new children identified each year. Freed from the ugly minimal brain dysfunction moniker, more and more parents were visiting child psychiatrists and pediatricians to assess whether their difficult and distractible kids had this more palatable problem; the diagnosis, and the Ritalin pills that often followed, went down increasingly easily. Little reassured people more than using Conners's questionnaires, which had versions for teachers and parents and left diagnoses blessed by the father of ADD himself. Conners had always made his scales available free for anyone who asked—as he moved from Harvard to the University of Pittsburgh and then to George Washington University through the 1980s, he and his staff photocopied and sent countless tests a year to doctors across America.

Then Steve Stein, a psychologist who marketed psychiatric questionnaires, approached Conners with a proposal.

"I'd like to license your scale," Stein told Conners at the Washington convention. "You'd get ten percent on every one."

"No one's going to *buy* it—they get it for free," replied Conners, who was a little uncomfortable turning his academic instrument into a business venture. Commercialism wasn't exactly becoming of a university professor, after all, and he made a perfectly comfortable $50,000 a year as it was.

Stein pressed on. Doctors loved quick-and-easy score sheets, ADD was on the rise, and the Conners name would make a great selling point.

"We'll more than match your current salary in the first year," Stein promised. "If we don't, I'll *kiss your ass*."

Conners relented. If he earned a few bucks, great. But more important, he sensed that widespread use of his ADD scales might bring some order to the disorder—more and more doctors had started just winging the diagnosis. This carelessness had also caught the eye of the glacial *Journal of the American Medical Association*, which lamented in

CONNERS' RATING SCALES

Child Name:_____ Child Age:_____ Child Sex:_____ Teacher:_____

Instructions: Read each item below carefully, and decide how much you think the child has been bothered by this problem during the past month.

Not at All	Just a Little	Pretty Much	Very Much	CTRS-28
0	1	2	3	1. Restless in the "squirmy" sense
0	1	2	3	2. Makes inappropriate noises when s/he shouldn't
0	1	2	3	3. Demands must be met immediately
0	1	2	3	4. Acts "smart" (impudent or sassy)
0	1	2	3	5. Temper outbursts and unpredictable behavior
0	1	2	3	6. Overly sensitive to criticism
0	1	2	3	7. Distractibility or attention span a problem
0	1	2	3	8. Disturbs other children
0	1	2	3	9. Daydreams
0	1	2	3	10. Pouts and sulks
0	1	2	3	11. Mood changes quickly and drastically
0	1	2	3	12. Quarrelsome
0	1	2	3	13. Submissive attitude toward authority
0	1	2	3	14. Restless, always up and on the go
0	1	2	3	15. Excitable, impulsive
0	1	2	3	16. Excessive demands for teacher's attention
0	1	2	3	17. Appears to be unaccepted by group
0	1	2	3	18. Appears to be easily led by other children
0	1	2	3	19. No sense of fair play
0	1	2	3	20. Appears to lack leadership
0	1	2	3	21. Fails to finish things that s/he starts
0	1	2	3	22. Childish and immature
0	1	2	3	23. Denies mistakes or blames others
0	1	2	3	24. Does not get along well with other children
0	1	2	3	25. Uncooperative with classmates
0	1	2	3	26. Easily frustrated in efforts
0	1	2	3	27. Uncooperative with teacher
0	1	2	3	28. Difficulty in learning
Not at All	Just a Little	Pretty Much	Very Much	

Multi-Health Systems, Inc.

One of the earliest commercially marketed Conners Scales, circa 1989.

1988 that clinicians were prescribing stimulants "for almost any child presenting with a behavioral or learning problem." Unfortunately, such concerns were clearly not shared by the psychiatric community, because as we'll soon see the APA at this time was yet again *loosening* the criteria for a child to be diagnosed in ways that instantly bumped diagnosis rates by 15 percent. Perhaps the Conners Scale could help standardize things, Conners and Stein reasoned. In 1989, they released it to the waiting market.

Hundreds of thousands of the things soon sold every year. Numbers would later double, triple, and more. Conners Scales were delivered by the bundle into eager doctors' offices throughout the United States— and almost overnight became the iconic test for attention deficit disorder. If a child might have ADD, you took him to the doctor, and did a Conners Scale.

ONLY THE CRUELEST of critics would deny that many children were benefiting from their diagnosis of ADD, and a subsequent prescription for Ritalin. No one knew quite how or why the medication worked. But work it did, at least in the minds of desperate parents and teachers. However the psychiatric establishment chose to define the problem, and through whatever metabolic magic Ritalin provided relief, it could allow the long unteachable an education, and the otherwise intolerable more nurturing relationships at home. Clearly, when an ADD diagnosis was handled judiciously, real lives could be reshaped.

Newspapers everywhere hailed these triumphs in compelling stories that introduced parents to all things ADD. Everyone recognized the behavior at issue—almost every article invoked the cartoon strip *Dennis the Menace*. (*Time* magazine illustrated its story with a drawing of a manic Dennis with his neighbor saying, "He's really fast. He can go from zero to driving me bonkers in less than ten seconds.") Parents learned that doctors had a name for their own Dennis's antics, and an emerging, almost simple, solution.

For example, there was seven-year-old Matthew of Simpsonville, South Carolina, whom *USA Today* described as a former terror in the classroom who would ignore teachers' instructions. But he improved greatly on Ritalin, which Matthew appreciatively called his "thinking pill." There was eleven-year-old Jeremy, whose mother wept while discussing Ritalin's effectiveness in an Associated Press article syndicated to newspapers coast-to-coast: "There has been such a remarkable change in this child. From the time he was seven he talked about suicide. Now he's on the student council and is so thrilled with life." Another mother wrote to the *Chicago Tribune*: "My son has been on Ritalin for 2½ years. It has made a difference between day and night. Before everything was a battle. . . . Now he's so much more responsive. He's just a bright, sweet little boy." A local woman who counseled parents of ADD children told the *Miami Herald*: "Why do we have to let kids fail before we help them?"

When Ritalin worked, one Harvard-affiliated doctor raved to the Associated Press, "the parents want to kiss you on both cheeks." Doctors began hanging ADD shingles and creating all but diagnosis assembly lines. One Detroit clinic built a practice servicing hundreds of kids and soon developed a three-month waiting list; its doctors said they had diagnosed about three-quarters of their young patients with ADD, with almost all of them going on medication. When schools faced criticism for perhaps growing a little too enthusiastic about Ritalin's effects, they questioned what the big deal was. The superintendent of the Baltimore County school district remarked: "All we do is refer children to medical help, the same as we would if a child had problems seeing a blackboard. We would tell the parents and they would have the child's eyes examined."

While some parents took their educators' nudge to heart, others sued school officials for coercion and other misuses of power. Families unable to pay for their own attorneys, which was most of them, were sought out and then represented by lawyers for a group that had been itching for years to take on the Ritalin machine: the Church of Scientology, the controversial religious group founded by L. Ron Hubbard that, among other divisive stances, decried the use of all psychiatric medications as "chemical straitjackets." In 1987, through its wing known as the Citizens Commission on Human Rights, the church arranged protests outside psychiatry conferences, where objectors wore shirts emblazoned with "Psychiatry Kills" and "Psychbusters." Children were given posters that said "Love Me, Don't Drug Me." Some supporters took their message to the skies by commissioning a plane to fly with the banner "PSYCHS, STOP DRUGGING OUR KIDS" trailing behind it.

Dozens of lawsuits—many filed, others threatened—claimed that doctors were putting their children on Ritalin without disclosing its possible side effects. These downsides went beyond the insomnia and loss of appetite for which amphetamines and Ritalin were well known. (And, in the most extreme cases of ADD, perhaps worth enduring.) Some children developed tics. Pharmaceutical companies' clinical trials of methylphenidate showed that some kids hallucinated on the product, either seeing and hearing things that weren't there or feeling as if insects were crawling under their skin—harkening the side effects of Benzedrine abuse among World War II soldiers. And evidence was mounting that the drug, when used for years, appeared to be correlated with some children's growth being suppressed by an inch or more.

School systems roundly denied having strong-armed parents, although one New Hampshire district did admit that it had told the family of one troubled boy that he could not attend school without Ritalin, and defended its stance in open court. As newspapers large and small began writing articles in which anti-ADD parents and doctors faced off against their pro-ADD counterparts, the conflict naturally spilled into the top showcases for such drama: national daytime television talk shows hosted by Oprah Winfrey, Geraldo Rivera, Phil Donahue, and more. Mrs. Jones would rejoice in how Ritalin had turned around her Billy's life; Billy, sitting cherubically next to her, would agree and say he's a much better boy in school now, to audience applause. Mrs. Smith would then counter with how her school had forced Ritalin on her rambunctious but altogether adorable Katie, who would then recount for the gasping audience how Ritalin made her stay up all night and hear voices. This theater was pumped into the homes of millions of parents, many of them dealing with these issues themselves.

Most lawsuits fell apart before they reached trial. Even when pushed or merely encouraged to get their kids evaluated, schools asserted that parents got the ultimate diagnosis and medication from doctors, not them. As for those doctors, they claimed they were merely following what the psychiatric establishment had blessed as scientific and safe. Then, even when a lawsuit might have had some merit, the fact that the Church of

Scientology was behind much of the hostility didn't help. The group's antipathy for all psychiatry went so deep that officials claimed that psychiatrists deserved "the blame for all drug abuse and related crime" in the United States; Hubbard himself called mental health professionals "psychotic criminals" who, if they "had the power to torture and kill everyone, they would do so." In comparison, pro-Ritalin forces were understandably seen as far more credible, especially when there were so many success stories with the drug—a number that, any reasonable person would admit, outnumbered nightmare scenarios by many times.

Yet this rancor over Ritalin still spooked vast numbers of parents who were weighing the drug's pros and cons. For the first time since Keith Conners's first Ritalin trials, prescriptions for the drug *decreased*, and drastically. In Baltimore, the site of one lawsuit, Ritalin prescriptions had doubled every six years since the early 1970s; from 1987 to 1991, they dropped by almost half. Nationwide, prescriptions decreased at least 20 percent. After Ritalin's three-decade rise, a substantial portion of parents were now reassessing the drug and even the legitimacy of the ADD diagnosis itself.

Parents of ADD children found their judgment and even morality had become part of a nasty national debate. They felt threatened. They craved support and understanding. They found it in a new group called Children and Adults with Attention Deficit/Hyperactivity Disorder, or CHADD.

ON THE FIRST Wednesday of every month, at 7:30 p.m., the doors to the auditorium of the Florida Medical Center in Fort Lauderdale opened to area parents yearning to talk about attention deficit disorder. One mother discussed how teachers were punishing her son for behavior that wasn't his fault. Another mom said her son had ten televisions going on in his head, and that Ritalin had blissfully turned nine of them off. Get-togethers like these were starting to sprout all over Florida, thanks to a small group of parents with ADD children who had formed CHADD in 1987. Their goal: to provide support for families feeling frustrated and isolated from not just their children's ADD, but its societal perception.

Few knew that their disorder's name was, once again, being changed by the American Psychiatric Association, which continued to flail for the perfect moniker. Coined in 1980 in part to accommodate girls, the term "attention deficit disorder" now didn't evoke the kids (particularly boys) in whom hyperactivity was the dominant symptom. Although a few behaviors to look for were "difficulty remaining seated" and "butts into other children's games," pure overactivity got a little lost. So for the revised *DSM* published in 1987, the APA rejiggered the disorder's official symptoms and, just to be clear, changed the name itself, to attention deficit *hyperactivity* disorder. This switch seemed fine—everyone knew hyperactivity was part of this soup anyway—until, right on cue, it developed its own problems. Just as before, some girls weren't hyperactive enough for doctors to diagnose them. So the APA monkeyed with the name yet again. After ever more sound and fury, the fourth edition of the *DSM*, in 1994, kept the term "ADHD" but then carved out a sub-diagnosis called "attention deficit hyperactivity disorder without hyperactivity"—the rough equivalent of spaghetti and meatballs without meatballs. The resulting confusion persists to this day, when most people skip the hassle, just say "ADD," and leave it at that.*

By any name, CHADD served them all. One of the founders, a psychologist named Harvey Parker, explained to a Florida newspaper: "We try to make parents understand they're not alone. They didn't cause the problem. Once they understand, it takes a lot of the guilt off them." Of course one of the meetings' main topics was Ritalin, of which many undecided parents remained wary. To this Parker and other CHADD parents would always trot out the same analogy: "If your child had trouble seeing in the classroom, you'd get him glasses, right? This is the same thing—it helps you focus." Parents nodded and spread the word. The Fort Lauderdale meetings quickly grew so crowded that a West Palm Beach chapter opened one hour north. Organizers hoped that about seventy parents would come to the first meeting; it drew three times that. "It's great to sit in a room and know you're not alone," one mother said. Chapters began appearing nationwide, serving parents of an ADHD population then approaching 4 percent of school-aged children, or about two million.

---

*"ADHD" will be used for the remainder of this book because it does remain the disorder's correct name, except in direct quotations that use other terms.

Headquartered in south Florida, CHADD grew so fast, with hundreds and sometimes thousands of parents signing up each month, that it developed some serious political muscle. It persuaded Congress to classify ADHD as an official learning disability to be covered under all educational and government-assistance programs. It lobbied for Ritalin to be moved from a Schedule II controlled substance, where the most dangerously abusable medications resided, to Schedule III, which would help ease its reputation, loosen caps on production, and allow parents to receive renewable prescriptions rather than have to visit a doctor every thirty days. (It lost that argument.) The US Department of Education collaborated with the group on two educational videos, one for parents ("Facing the Challenges of ADD") and one for teachers ("One Child in Every Classroom").* CHADD produced a public-service announcement called "A Child's Call for Help," which was seen by nineteen million television viewers and prompted almost 100,000 calls to CHADD's toll-free number for more information. By mid-1995 the organization was thriving, with 34,000 members in 640 chapters nationwide. To many people, including some high-level government officials, its mission had been as virtuous and misunderstood as the children it was representing.

That image was swiftly shattered, though, when a PBS documentary uncovered more than disquieting ties between CHADD and Ciba-Geigy, the manufacturer of Ritalin. Ciba had given CHADD close to $1 million since 1989 to attract parents and fuel its growth. And worse, the organization did not disclose this funding—neither parents, doctors, nor government officials had any idea that CHADD was advocating for expanded use of Ritalin while also being supported by the company that sold it. That public-service announcement, which concluded with a formerly out-of-control gap-toothed boy telling viewers "Thank you for helping me," had CHADD's logo but no indication that it had been paid for by Ciba. A spectacularly dopey Ciba representative responded to PBS on camera: "CHADD is essentially a conduit" for company messaging regarding Ritalin.

When John Merrow, the documentary's investigative reporter, deftly

---

*"One Child in Every Classroom" was catchy but dangerously wrong. If 4 percent of children randomly had ADHD, then about one-third of classrooms would have none at all.

sprung CHADD's relationship with Ciba on parents and others, people who moments before had praised the organization for its efforts—usually repeating the "Ritalin is just like eyeglasses" mantra—grew either flabbergasted or furious at the organization's coziness with Big Pharma. One mother, a proud CHADD member, furrowed her brow and said, "Who is working for whom?" A Drug Enforcement Administration (DEA) official quivered in rage when he heard that CHADD had lobbied his office to loosen controls on Ritalin production while concealing its funding by Ciba. The Department of Education, upon learning that it had spent $750,000 on ADHD educational videos that were essentially advertisements for Ritalin, declined comment but later stopped distributing the films and distanced itself from CHADD. The organization's response to its relationship with Ciba, meanwhile, was delivered by Parker, who appeared befuddled by all the commotion. "We see it as a *responsibility* of the drug company to give us that money," the group's cofounder said. "They owe it to the parents who are spending their money on medication. They owe it to these families to give them something back." *

However brilliant, the 1995 PBS documentary aired only a few times—this was before television could be replayed on demand on digital video recorders or iTunes—so it briefly stung CHADD but couldn't do much to slow the ADHD train. The small minority of parents who saw the show and appreciated the conflict-of-interest issues were vastly outnumbered by those who welcomed the ADHD diagnosis as an explanation for their child's behavior, and Ritalin the antidote for it. Hundreds of thousands of children each year continued to get diagnosed. This enthusiasm led Ritalin production not just to recover from its 1990, postlawsuits low, but to increase a stupefying 400 percent in just five years. ADHD was zooming along faster than ever.

Then something fascinating happened. As if breaking a sound barrier—or in this case a dissonance barrier—ADHD diagnoses reached a point where the disorder was no longer particularly rare. It was almost common, especially among boys. Finding another fam-

---

*The film was so controversial that some PBS executives, many of them with recently diagnosed children themselves, wanted to spike the documentary before it aired. Merrow had to purchase additional liability insurance and show the certificate to higher-ups before it was broadcast.

ily who understood the challenges of an ADHD child was as easy as attending a Little League game. Parents could look around at their growing company and say to themselves, "Wait, why are we feeling bad about this?" This expanding ADHD community was ready to be emotionally mobilized—inspired not just to tolerate its situation but to embrace it, celebrate it. No one stepped up and led them through the seas of stigma more than Dr. Edward Hallowell.

A child psychiatrist at Harvard University Medical School, Dr. Hallowell told anyone who would listen how realizing he had attention deficit disorder was the single most cathartic and empowering moment of his life. Hallowell had been distractible and impulsive as a child on Cape Cod in the 1950s. His home life certainly didn't help. His father was so emotionally volatile after serving in World War II that he received shock treatment at a psychiatric hospital. During a visit home he grew so enraged that he threatened to kill his wife; she convinced him to have sex instead. Nine months later, Edward was born. The boy was a handful and his mind wandered some, but he was clearly intelligent and could focus on subjects he found interesting. He attended prestigious boarding schools, then Harvard, then Tulane Medical School.

In 1981, as a child psychiatry fellow at the Massachusetts Mental Health Center in Boston, Hallowell attended a lecture about children with ADHD. Right there in the audience, he felt like he'd been hooked up to a car battery. "That's me!" Hallowell told himself. He determined that day to devote his career to helping others with his disability.*

Hallowell treated ten years of young patients with ADHD (using the gold standard Conners Scale for diagnoses) before deciding with his colleague, Dr. John Ratey, to write a book on the subject. But the result, *Driven to Distraction*, would stand out from the other ADHD books on the market. It would explain the disorder to the lay reader, yes, but it would also attempt to convince parents, children, and others that this surprisingly widespread condition, when treated properly, can be "powerfully positive." (Ratey joined Hallowell in claiming he had ADHD himself.) They provided case studies of people whose lives had

---

*Although having ADHD himself is one of his primary selling points, Dr. Hallowell has never been formally evaluated for the disorder. He is self-diagnosed.

been ruined by either not recognizing they had the condition or having parents who didn't care enough to intervene. But fear not:

Mozart would be a good example of a person with ADD: impatient, impulsive, distractible, energetic, emotionally needy, creative, innovative, irreverent, and a maverick. . . . You might describe many with ADD as having a "special something," a hard-to-pin-down yet undeniable potential. If that potential can be tapped, the results can be spectacular. Albert Einstein, Edgar Allan Poe, George Bernard Shaw, and Salvador Dalí were all expelled from school, and Thomas Edison was at the bottom of his class. Abraham Lincoln and Henry Ford were pronounced by their teachers to show no promise. The novelist John Irving nearly flunked out of high school because of an undiagnosed learning disability. There is a long, long list of people who achieved greatness in adult life after performing abysmally in school due to undiagnosed learning disabilities. Unfortunately, there is a longer list of those people whose spirits were broken in school, who therefore never got the chance to realize their potential.

While such passages undoubtedly inspired parents of severely ADHD children to replace stigma with hope—a laudable service long overdue—it turned the diagnosis completely around, from scary to alluring. Parents who thought their child had a "special something" or "undeniable potential," which is to say all of them, were told that behavioral difficulties could very well lie rooted in something that wasn't just an impediment to the likes of Mozart and Einstein, but *what made them special in the first place*. Of course, these claims were pure bunk. The fact that Einstein got booted from grade school (which was true) could not be attributed to ADHD; most people would agree that Lincoln and Edison were not underachievers; and no science had even remotely indicated that kids who do get diagnosed wind up novelists or transcendent composers as a result. But at its core, *Driven to Distraction* was not science. It was marketing. It told current ADHD families what they wanted to hear, aroused the undecided, and left skeptics in their dust.

Driven to Distraction flew off bookstore shelves so fast in the mid-1990s that Random House scrambled to keep up with demand. The book ultimately sold more than a million copies and was translated into a dozen languages, making Hallowell and Ratey millionaires. Hallowell in particular enjoyed his overnight celebrity; his enthusiasm for ADHD became validated with nods during every media interview and applause at every speech. Doctors began approaching Hallowell at psychiatry conferences and saying—in these exact words—"Thank you for filling my waiting room."

Hallowell almost single-handedly recast ADHD and Ritalin as things not to be feared, but embraced. In 1996, he told *Parade* magazine, "This is a good-news diagnosis." (Later, he told a television interviewer that ADHD is "very much in the American gene pool—we're a country that was really founded and created by people with ADHD. We're a nation full of ADHD, which is why we're so exciting and interesting.") Within months several picture books appeared for young children to learn about their ADHD, including *Eukee the Jumpy Jumpy Elephant.* "No matter how hard Eukee tried, he just couldn't sit still," the narrative goes. "So his teacher suggested Eukee and his parents go see Dr. Tusk."* Eukee explains to Dr. Tusk that he gets in trouble at school for not paying attention. The doctor reassures Eukee that lots of kids are like him, and tells Eukee's parents, "It's not his fault. Just like it's not someone's fault if he or she has trouble seeing and needs to wear glasses." The doctor turns to Eukee: "We can give you some medicine. It will help you pay attention better and feel less jumpy inside." Immediately, Eukee receives hugs and smiles from his parents. He gets happy-face stickers and other prizes. His teacher writes on his paper, "You're the best!"

"Soon, everyone began to feel better," the story concludes. It fades out with a song:

> *I can do the Elephant March, and listen to what I am taught*
> *I keep my trunk and tail to myself, and I like myself a lot*
> *Watch me see what I can do, when I listen I know what to do*
> *Now I have fun, I have friends, and I like myself a lot*

---

*Teachers began recommending parents to look into a diagnosis so often, and so forcefully, that some states began passing laws that forbade them even to utter the term "ADHD" unless a medical professional had already made a diagnosis.

What some called education, others called shameless propaganda. The more fervently ADHD proponents promoted the disorder and its medication, detractors felt the need to push more forcefully on the other end of the scale. No one was more vehement—and occasionally shrill—than the child psychiatrist Dr. Peter Breggin, whose trenchant sound bites put him on journalists' speed dials. On national television, when told that ADHD children were suffering, he would interrupt, "Who's suffering? These drugs alleviate the suffering of *teachers* in over-crowded classrooms." He would liken kids on Ritalin to "good caged animals." Then he'd drop the hammer, noting that three American adolescents who had recently committed murder were taking Ritalin at the time—a ludicrously unfair point, given how there was no way of knowing if the medication had played even the slightest role in their actions. When told that he was scaring parents, Breggin would stiffen and say, "I want to!"

This was no debate for centrists. The only expert to attempt any real reconciliation of the two sides was a California behavioral pediatrician named Larry Diller, who had been cautiously prescribing Ritalin through the 1980s and 1990s but grew uncomfortable with its overuse, parents coming to his office requesting it, and the ugly debate among rabid ideologues. He wrote a book on the phenomenon and his personal ambivalence called *Running on Ritalin*, for which Bantam Books predicted such a market that they gave Diller a stratospheric $700,000 advance. (It foresaw it as Ritalin's answer to *Listening to Prozac*, the recent bestseller exploring the societal effects of antidepressants.) *Running on Ritalin* was an excellent book, one that examined the Great Ritalin Question through both lenses and weighed the temporary alleviation of a child's school struggles against other health and cultural concerns. This evenhandedness was, as it turned out, commercial suicide; the book flopped, selling only forty thousand copies after its summer 1998 release. At this point ADHD debates had grown so divisive that acknowledging each side only galled both.

Media outlets clumsily covered Ritalin by pitting the Hallowells against the Breggins, whose outlooks were so polarized no one could make sense of either. Two different CBS News segments captured this standoff perfectly. In one, the mother of a difficult twelve-year-old exhaled that the drug had transformed her family's life, that "within twenty minutes of his first dose of Ritalin, I had a child back." In another, the father of a boy who had died of a heart attack while taking Ritalin was asked in an interview, "Are you absolutely convinced that Ritalin killed your son?" The man grieved: "I am absolutely convinced." This back-and-forth made for compelling television but gave increasingly whiplashed parents little sense of how to approach their own family situations.

With millions of children's brains at stake, someone needed to step in and sort ADHD reality from rhetoric. The standoff required an entity with a calm, academic bent, with no allegiances beyond the public good. So in came the National Institutes of Health (NIH), the United States' primary government health agency, which announced that it would gather a wide range of experts in ADHD and child psychiatry to present their outlooks on the disorder. But more important, the NIH would convene an independent panel—doctors and other health care experts with no glaring philosophical or financial biases—to consolidate all of it into some sort of manual that this fractured field could live with. A three-day conference was designed to provide the condition, and Ritalin, a long-needed foundation in science and consensus. And with ADHD affecting such a wide swath of the populace, the forum was made public, too—anyone could sit in the vast auditorium and watch the presentations, even average parents. Everyone involved sensed the stakes: After decades of drug trials, congressional hearings, lawsuits, debates, and confounding media coverage, this was ADHD's reckoning.

The conference convened in Bethesda, Maryland, on November 16, 1998. Every major ADHD figure was there, from well-traveled insiders to infidels like Peter Breggin. (Some started stumping early; interviewed a few days before the event, one emerging ADHD presence with ties to the pharmaceutical industry, Dr. Russell Barkley of the University of Massachusetts, declared to the press that Ritalin soon "will be ranked as one of the leading developments in this century for helping individuals.") Lecture sessions were designed to focus on a wide range of ADHD issues, from the neurological underpinnings of the disorder to whether Ritalin caused drug abuse. Parents would get a chance to address the panel as well.

How to start this pivotal summit? That decision was easy. When the event began at nine a.m. on a temperate autumn Monday, the microphone was handed to the chief architect of ADHD—the man who had started it all, Dr. Keith Conners.

CONNERS DIDN'T UNDERSTAND the commotion. He was now living in Durham, North Carolina, where in 1990 Duke University Medical Center had wooed him to found its first ADHD clinic. The Triangle, North Carolina's central nexus of Raleigh, Durham, and upscale Chapel Hill, was one of America's top growth areas, and someone had to treat all the kids whose parents were reading about ADHD and Ritalin in the press.

Conners was the nation's expert on the disorder and the inventor of the primary checklist doctors used to make the diagnosis. He was the guy who had proven Ritalin's benefits, for crying out loud, and who could all but recite every study on the substance. What Conners had paid less attention to, unfortunately, was Ritalin's use *outside* his practice, in the offices of psychiatrists and pediatricians nationwide. When he saw articles about stark rises in diagnoses and prescriptions, he dismissed them as news media hype. He never saw the PBS documentary disclosing the coziness between Ciba-Geigy and CHADD; and if he had, he probably would have harrumphed at that, too. To Conners, ADHD was as real as the thousands of young patients he had served since the early 1960s.

Now, with this Maryland conference, he had to stand before a panel of non-expert physicians, and even the lay public, to defend his life's work? When the conference began, he strode to the podium feeling, he later recalled, like a medieval witch.

Conners's opening was defensive—almost defiant. He reminded everyone that ADHD behaviors had been theorized as a medical syndrome since at least 1902, when Sir George Frederic Still delivered his lectures on impulsive children to the Royal College of Physicians. He said that the constant changes to the disorder's name and symptoms "should be taken as a strength, not as a sign of unreliability or vague conceptualization." New techniques in brain imaging, he claimed, could very well prove that ADHD brains did in fact have structural and metabolic differences, which could finally put the entire "there's no objective test" carping to rest. And to make sure everyone understood the seriousness of exactly what they were making him defend, he called ADHD a "lifetime disorder"—which is not really true, as at least one-third of diagnosed children have no problems as adults—"that exacts a considerable toll on those suffering from it as well as on the families of those who must care for them."

From there the cavalcade began: Every fifteen or twenty minutes, for two days, a new speaker would take the podium and deliver his or her brick in the ADHD construct. Some described symptoms, others statistics. The disorder was highly hereditary; cost schools and juvenile justice systems hundreds of millions of dollars a year; and, if left unaddressed, would allow these kids' impulsivity to result in car accidents, drug abuse, unwanted pregnancies, and venereal disease. When Ritalin took center stage on the second day of the conference, possible side effects like sleeplessness and growth suppression were only grudgingly acknowledged by the clinicians. Concerns with the medication came mostly from brief messages from the US Drug Enforcement Administration and the National Institute on Drug Abuse, who tried to remind everyone that ADHD drugs could be addictive among teenagers, who were known to trade and sell their pills in school.

To the organizers' credit, they gave time to more than just the typical voices. One Virginia researcher described how close to 20 percent of children in her community were on Ritalin (a staggering figure for the time), while a mother from the Pacific Northwest testified how teachers had pressured her into medicating her fourth-grade son when he had no glaring problems at all. But these were dismissed by the established experts. Conners himself bristled at one point and remarked: "This is a disorder about which there is as much validity as any other medical disorder. And I am afraid that this is going to be used to suggest the continuing argument that after 100 years we really don't have a disorder." The vibe from him and all the ADHD doctors rang loud and clear: *We've studied this, you haven't, so shut up*. Everyone grew more agitated as the drama built.

As for the so-called independent panel of thirteen doctors and researchers drawn from various parts of the medical—but not ADHD—world, they weren't quite sure what to make of all this. Most of them dealt with diseases that could be diagnosed objectively, with a yea-or-nay blood test or an MRI. No matter how many studies the ADHD folks flashed on the screen, no matter how many slides theorized about symptom clusters or dopaminergic pathways, there still was no test for this thing, no blip or biopsy that could objectively say whether a kid had it or not. There was no getting around the uncomfortable fact that the diagnosis derived from opinion, whether of the parent, the teacher, the doctor, or some murky combination of the three. As discomfiting as this was, however, the panel still leaned collegially toward trusting their fellow scientists. The two days ended with the independent panel retiring to deliberate on all the evidence. They would deliver their over-all thoughts to the audience and media the next morning.

With the news cameras rolling and microphones on, the panel's chairman, Dr. David Kupfer of the University of Pittsburgh, delivered some opening remarks before taking questions from the press and public. He steadfastly reasserted ADHD's validity. He dodged issues of misdiagnosis and improper prescriptions of Ritalin. *Nothing to see here, folks.* Matters were reasonably under control until an NPR reporter asked, almost in desperation, for the panel to please just describe what a typical ADHD child actually looks like.

Kupfer tried to sidestep the question. But the reporter didn't let him off the hook. He asked again, remarking that the group sounded like it was resorting to Justice Potter Stewart's description of pornography, "I know it when I see it." Kupfer recoiled, clearly put off by the reporter's insolence. He stepped back from the podium and asked for someone to provide the answer.

The panel went silent.

After several increasingly awkward, crickets-chirping seconds, Kupfer realized that this was not good. He had to just call on someone. He chose Mark Vonnegut, a pediatrician from Massachusetts. Dr. Vonnegut was the son of novelist Kurt Vonnegut who, having endured significant psychiatric troubles himself, took a special interest in children's emotional, as well as physical, ailments. Kupfer picked Vonnegut because he had seen, and treated, ADHD children in his own practice.

But Dr. Vonnegut, caught off guard like a fourth-grader summoned to the chalkboard to reduce a fraction, took a deep breath, waited, stumbled, stumbled some more, and finally bumbled out oratory's longest slow-motion car crash:

> *There . . . [sigh] . . . I think the panel has been frank in, you know, the difficulties here are immense, in terms of, of, of, uh, um . . . these kids . . . I mean . . . [clears throat] . . . aahh . . . it is hard . . . it's very hard to know how to answer this question. These kids, um, in my experience, when you see these kids, um, they are, you know, several standard deviations different in terms of they cannot sit still, they cannot attend their, um, they cannot, you know, even when, um, . . . ahhhhhhh . . . they . . . are as if driven by a motor . . . there are some good clinical descriptions, um, of these kids . . .*
>
> *I think, I mean, these kids do . . . if you spend time around children, and I'm not going to do a lot better than the Supreme Court here, uh, these kids stick out like sore thumbs. And, and they are difficult, they aggravate their parents. Uh . . . But then it's further confounded by the fact there are subtypes of attention deficit disorder where kids have the problems with inattention without the hyperactivity.*
>
> *I think, I don't think the panel is saying anything different, although we've said it in more sophisticated ways, is the diagnosis is a mess.*

The room was stunned. After gathering the field's top experts, and hearing two days of dozens of presentations claiming that ADHD was a serious problem affecting millions of children and causing such suffering that only years and perhaps lifetimes of medication could avert widespread societal harm, the panel couldn't even describe a kid who had it.

The experts went into crisis mode. There was no way to keep Vonnegut's spectacular sound bite—*the diagnosis is a mess!*—out of heavy media coverage. They needed to drown it out with other messages reasserting that ADHD was every bit the problem they had always claimed it to be. One panel member, Lynn Fuchs of Vanderbilt University, told the *Philadelphia Inquirer*: "Parents have to weigh the risk of *not* treating with stimulants," and that "children with ADHD not treated go on to have serious consequences the rest of their lives." Russell Barkley reassured viewers of *Good Morning America* that the pills were "quite safe and effective," "the side effects are benign," and "there's no evidence of any long-lasting harm." (There was "no evidence" perhaps, but at that juncture, long-term effects had not been formally examined.) The experts diverted readers from Vonnegut's quote with enough move-along-people boilerplate that media coverage ended up less skeptical than simply confused.

These were daily newspaper and television outlets putting together reports on deadline, though. *Time* magazine, which had a few days to digest the theater and consider how to handle the event's overall import, decided that the conference—and the topic of ADHD itself—had become so vital to millions of readers that the magazine would devote its cover to this defining, national conference.

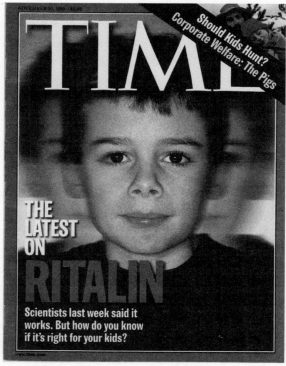

Time, November 30, 1998

To capture the moment, the issue pictured the face of a young boy, maybe ten years old, with Mona Lisa lips, beckoning eyes, and just the trace of a smile. To the left and right were two versions of his head quite fuzzy, as if shaking; the middle one, though, was in calm, pleasing focus. Beside it, the cover's headline:

THE
LATEST
ON
RITALIN
Scientists last week said it
works. But how do you know
if it's right for your kids?

After almost one hundred years of research into children's attention problems, capped off by a three-day virtual jury trial to give the public some clarity on ADHD and its legitimacy, the two most resounding messages that came out of the NIH conference were "The diagnosis is a mess" but "Scientists say Ritalin works." Although seemingly irreconcilable, when it came to the three-decade rise of ADHD, the two messages actually intertwined like the swirls of a candy cane. Doctors still didn't truly know how to define, measure, and then diagnose extreme hyperactivity and impulsivity in troublesome children. But so what? Ritalin sure did help most of them calm down and do better, so why not give it a try?

The magazine was sent to *Time*'s nationwide subscribers a few days later, a significant portion of them parents of school-aged children. Many more grabbed it off the racks in airports and grocery stores. As for the doctors who subscribed to *Time*, the issue naturally made it onto their waiting room tables, sometimes taking center stage.

One of those waiting rooms belonged to a child psychiatrist in suburban Philadelphia named Miranda Seitz. It sat there for almost a year.

And then, on one autumn Thursday, a local family came in with their third-grade daughter. Kristin was vexing her teachers and underperforming on tests. She needed help.

PART TWO

Chapter 5

KRISTIN

I'll be better! I'll be better! I promise!

Kristin wailed as Mom and Dad walked her toward the glass front doors of Dr. Seitz's office building in Haverford, Pennsylvania. It was right there on Lancaster Avenue. Everyone could see! Kristin was seven and a half. She wanted to be normal. But something was wrong with her. Her teacher said.

We'll be back in a few minutes, sweetheart. You just stay here.

Mom and Dad went into the doctor's room. The door thunked shut. She stayed in the small room outside. She played with some toys. A colorful pyramid of rings, some crayons. Too babyish. There were a few kids' magazines. *Highlights.* A stack of old ones for grown-ups. *Newsweek. People.* She liked grown-up stuff. She flipped through them and looked at the shiny pictures on the fronts. One *Time* magazine cover had a big picture of a little boy's face. Neat.

Kristin couldn't hear what was being discussed in the other room. She put her ear against the door. Nothing. Just a dull hum from the whirring tan box down on the floor. She went back to a chair.

After five minutes the door opened. She went in. Dr. Seitz looked serious. Mom and Dad sat on the couch. Kristin sat in the big black chair. It was puffy. Her legs didn't reach the ottoman so she folded them under her and slumped.

Kristin, your parents have brought you here because they're concerned that you're having a hard time concentrating.

I get good grades. Leave me alone!

It's okay, Kristin. We all just want to help you. There might be something to help you.

I don't need help!

Questions about second grade. Homework. Playdates. The arguments with Mom. Dr. Seitz wrote things on her pad.

After a few minutes the doctor took out a piece of paper from beneath her notebook and showed Kristin. It was long. Almost thirty questions. About how she was acting.

The doctor started asking the questions from the sheet. Its title:

CONNERS RATING SCALES

PARENTS THROUGHOUT PHILADELPHIA's well-off northwestern suburbs, known as the Main Line, were pummeled by three big media stories in the mid-1990s: O. J. Simpson, Monica Lewinsky, and Ritalin.

Network news programs reported how the drug was being used to treat more and more children with behavioral and school problems. Talk shows everywhere had Ned Hallowell bubbling about his blockbuster *Driven to Distraction*, encouraging parents to talk with their doctors about the "good-news diagnosis." A *New Yorker* cover showed a teacher scratching "Readin, Ritin, Ritalin" on a chalkboard; *Newsweek*'s cover story, "Mother's Little Helper," dubbed ADHD the nation's "No. 1 psychiatric disorder" and had a Columbia University researcher gushing that "Ritalin is one of the raving successes in psychiatry." Yet another *Newsweek* article had Dr. James Swanson, a psychologist from the University of California at Irvine, tell readers: "If you can have an impact with these kids, you can change whether they go to jail or to Harvard Law School." Prison or Princeton—did parents have a choice?

Ritalin cemented its place in '90s popular culture when television's *The Simpsons* lampooned the craze with its trademark incisiveness. After Bart Simpson, America's favorite ill-behaved and exasperating fourth-grader, finally goes too far—he floods the school gymnasium with a fire hose—he is diagnosed by school officials (not a doctor) with attention deficit disorder. Marge and Homer, Bart's clumsily loving parents, fill a prescription for an alluring new drug called Focusyn.* Bart is imme-

---

*The Simpsons' parody became less funny in 2002, when the pharmaceutical company Novartis released a new ADHD drug called Focalin.

diately transformed: He listens to his parents and teachers, turns into a bespectacled speed reader, and even tutors a classmate. Everyone is delighted. That is, until Bart starts experiencing some of Focusyn's less desirable side effects, including sleeplessness and such paranoia—he's convinced satellites owned by Major League Baseball are spying on him—that he steals an army tank to go and shoot them down.

Some viewers, as one might expect, found this less humorous than others. CHADD and its members lashed out against Fox and *The Simpsons*' producers, claiming—correctly, of course—that the episode disrespected ADHD and distorted the benefits of medication for countless families. Such outrage was predictable. Less so was a spasm of candor in the letter that CHADD president Matthew Cohen fired off to Fox, where he listed his objections but acknowledged that the show did get one thing right: Bart's teachers diagnosing him and then coercing his parents to put him on ADHD medication, Cohen wrote, "may unfortunately reflect what happens in some schools."

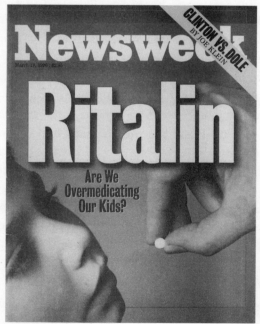

Newsweek, March 18, 1996

Indeed, educators throughout the 1990s were handling more and more students diagnosed with ADHD, but usually for reasons much more valid. Protection for the rights of those with disabilities had been building since the early 1970s. In 1990, when Congress clarified its regulations for how public school systems must accommodate the needs of children with various disabilities, it stipulated that psychiatric impairments, such as behavior disorders and severe anxiety, were to be just as respected as any physical encumbrance. (At first ADHD did not expressly qualify as an official disability—some argued that the fuzziness of the diagnosis would lead to waves of children diverting services and funds away from more impaired children—but after fevered outcry from CHADD and other lobbying groups, attention deficit got folded in.) Changes in other government programs incentivized parents to have their children's ADHD diagnosed and treated. Medicaid had recently expanded to cover far more families than ever before, and households with ADHD children were, through the federal Supplemental Security Income (SSI) program, entitled to hundreds of dollars in monthly payments to offset other costs of care. The rolls of children with ADHD immediately skyrocketed: From just 1990 to 1993, annual diagnoses more than doubled from 900,000 to two million. They kept rising from there.

Of course, there was no way to disentangle which children were actually impaired by severe hyperactivity and distractibility—which only the most inhumane would prefer to ignore—and which were either questionable diagnoses or, at the most cynical end of the spectrum, labeled merely for money or extra services. But either way, ADHD was in the air, all right, drifting across communities throughout the United States. By the fall of 1998, exactly when Keith Conners and the other ADHD experts were convening at the National Institute of Mental Health, it wafted through Haverford, Pennsylvania, and the house of Bill and Kelly Parber. Did their Kristin have ADHD, too?

BILL PARBER WAS a self-made real estate developer. He had grown up only a few minutes south of Haverford, in Newtown Square, lower middle class at best, obsessed with earning his way into the swank and society of the nearby Main Line. The Parber house didn't have air-conditioners, so Bill worked every job he could find—paper route, grocery stocker, tire-checker at a gas station—to earn enough to buy a unit for his bedroom. (A year later, every room had one.) He hitch-hiked his way to Happy Valley and a Penn State business degree. After a stint as a craps croupier in Atlantic City he struggled to find more forward-looking work in New York, sleeping in cars a few nights; he finally caught a break from a friend who not only had a couch, but a bit of a real estate business. Bill thrived there and ultimately settled back in Philadelphia to develop low-income tract housing, and became so suc-cessful that after marrying Kelly Insel they bought a beautiful house in Haverford, one of Philadelphia's most comfortable suburbs, and started living the life they both had always wanted.

Kelly came from a Southern Baptist family in Fredericksburg, Vir-ginia. No dancing, no alcohol, church every Sunday. Kelly grew stun-ningly beautiful, a modeling-worthy blond cheerleader who majored in early-childhood education at Old Dominion University. One day, as she prepared to get off an Amtrak train at Philadelphia's 30th Street Sta-tion, a strapping fellow named Bill Parber—he'd spotted her way back in New Jersey, and strategically sat one row behind her—offered to help her with her bags. Bill was the man of her dreams, six-foot-something, cockily handsome, and with a strong financial future. They married and had their first child, Kristin, in April 1992.

She was perfect. Kristin's halo of blond, fuzzy hair would make a Q-Tip jealous—it might as well have been a tiara. She was smart, learn-ing words and puzzles and numbers earlier than most toddlers. And holy cow, was she active! Darting from one activity to the next, always talking, usually more to adults than to kids, it seemed. When nursery school arrived, the Parbers leaned on Kelly's early-childhood educa-tion instincts and chose a local Montessori school, whose flexible pro-grams would let Kristin be Kristin. She loved kneading and pounding Play-Doh, anything with motion. The little girl spent two delightfully energized years at Montessori, tickling teachers with her enthusiasm for learning and yammering. Sure, she was a handful. But Montessori didn't endure those kids, it enjoyed them.

This was a happy family. Bill provided. Kelly started making her way in Main Line society. Kristin was smart and bouncy and curious. Soon it was time for kindergarten, the on-ramp to her real education.

Bill and Kelly decided Kristin should go to an all-girls private school—girls were more studious than boys, and she was moving from clay to classwork. But beyond that, as he shivered at his own memories of public school, Bill wanted better for Kristin. Haverford's wealthy, even newcomers like the Parbers, sent its kids to private school, pure and simple. The Parbers chose the Agnes Irwin School in Rosemont, a school as stiff as its name. It cost a ton, the Parbers reasoned, so it must be good.

Agnes Irwin's uniformed girls lined up every morning in yellow shirts, white socks, and navy jumpers with the AIS logo. College prep in pigtails. Students had to sit at desks much of the day; recess was minimal, an indulgence, a *distraction*. Enter Kristin. Even though she was a good reader and loved math, she never kept quiet, threw her hand up constantly, blurted out answers, and interrupted the otherwise structured lessons. Even when students were allowed to mill about and work together, giving the teacher a respite at her desk, Kristin would run up and bug her with yet more questions. Some adults nicknamed her "chisel."

Then there was Brenda. With the last name Packett, Brenda was always standing beside Kristin in lines, sitting with her at workstations, and getting under her skin. Brenda would tap her pencil. Shake her foot. Make goofy noises. Kristin's already fleeting concentration span got only shorter. She'd fight with Brenda, exasperate her teachers, and get dispatched to the corner or the principal's office. Parent-teacher conferences got increasingly worrisome. The report cards highlighted Kristin's potential. If she could just slow down in class and stop driving everyone crazy.

But first grade was a dream, at least early on. Mrs. Watson had no problems with Kristin—she delighted in the little girl's spirit and, rather than quash it, chose to cultivate it. (She even sided with Kristin, not Brenda, in the girls' continuing spats.) But then, in January, Mrs. Watson got sick. She wouldn't be back for the rest of the year. No one knew what happened to her.

In came Mrs. Crow, who had no patience for Kristin. The girl was to sit still, not speak unless spoken to. When Kristin broke ranks, which she inevitably did, the teacher took away recess—the one time Kristin and other kids could run around and release their energy. Kristin's was kept inside, percolating.

Kristin didn't explode like a microwaved egg. That actually might have been better. In this little girl, her energy and spirit became so stifled, so increasingly cramped and compressed by the forces around her, that they fused into something else entirely—full-blown anxiety. Everyone hated her, she decided.

Second grade brought Mrs. Beech. Her real name was Marion, but everyone called her "Bing"—she was fun, nurturing, patient. Mrs. Beech only wanted the best for the little jumping bean. The problem was, that jumping bean wasn't thriving. Kristin was getting decent grades, yes, but as schoolwork got harder, she couldn't stay on task nearly as well, and trouble loomed. She wouldn't remember reading passages or complete her math sheets. (These issues were assumed to be the source of her anxiety, rather than the result of it.) At the class musical, as Kristin played the Pied Piper, halfway through the recorder performance she forgot what notes came next. She panicked. She began coughing. Worse and worse. Everyone was looking. She coughed more. She ran off the stage. Kristin never told anyone that she had faked the whole thing—she just didn't want to cry, to mess things up yet again, in front of everyone.

Kristin's angst hit a new high when her parents vacationed in Morocco and got in a car accident in which one of their friends was killed. They returned home covered in bandages. Whatever the projector screen—the blackboard at school or the inside of her eyelids at night—all Kristin would see was Mom and Dad, just driving around town, getting killed themselves in another wreck. Her parents brought her to a therapist.

Everyone was concerned for Kristin—her parents, her therapist, and particularly Mrs. Beech. The little girl had so much potential. She was smart. She was inquisitive. If she could only *pay attention*. Mrs. Beech met with the Parbers to discuss options.

No one quite remembers who brought it up first, but the solution became clear: Kristin probably had ADHD. So many other kids did, after all. It was nothing to be ashamed of. And there was a medicine for it, of course. Ritalin did wonders for other students. It was probably time for Kristin to try it, too. Mrs. Beech didn't diagnose Kristin as ADHD as another teacher might have, and didn't push the Parbers into Ritalin. She cared about Kristin deeply. This solution was just so . . . so obvious. Bill Parber was a weekly reader of *Time*, and he vaguely remembered a recent big thing it had on ADHD and the proven benefits of Ritalin. If that's what Kristin needed, that's what she needed. The Parbers called another local psychiatrist, Dr. Miranda Seitz, to make an appointment.

Kristin already felt different from other kids, constantly in trouble, and being taken to a second psychiatrist only made her feel worse. Mom and Dad and Mrs. Beech said this wasn't punishment. But that wasn't true, Kristin told herself. She was a bad kid.

"Kristin, you can come in now," Dr. Seitz said. Kristin trudged in and, seeing her parents on the couch, sat in the single leather chair off to the side. She was too mad to sit next to them. Bill sat on the side of the couch closer to Kristin; her mother, more distant.

Dr. Seitz explained to the little girl why she was there. Then she pulled out a Conners Scale.

> *Do you have trouble concentrating on one thing at a time, sweetheart?*
> *Do you find it hard to sit still?*
> *How about taking turns?*

Kristin spat out "no" to every one. Dr. Seitz put the forms aside. The decision had been made while Kristin was out of the room, anyway, and her petulance only made them all more confident in next steps.

"Kristin, you're having trouble at school, and you're having trouble at home," the doctor said. "You're having trouble concentrating and finishing your work. I'm going to give you some pills to help you with that, okay? But don't worry. It's just like a vitamin. You'll see, things will be better."

The Parbers filled the prescription for Ritalin on the way home. But they didn't have Kristin take it the next morning. They didn't know what the side effects might be; they certainly didn't want to mess up her school day. They waited until Saturday.

The three of them stood in the family kitchen. Kristin refused even to touch the glass of water.

"We're just going to try it, darling," her mother said. "It's like a vitamin. It's going to help."

Kristin finally stopped crying and swallowed the pill.

THE RITALIN HAD no side effects on Kristin that weekend, at least nothing particularly visible. She seemed less interested in food, but she was never a big eater anyway. Sleep wasn't much of a problem either. The experiment went fine—she didn't sprout horns. So on Monday morning, Kristin took her pill again before school.

The medicine slipped down her esophagus, dissolved in her stomach, and then moved through her intestine, where the molecules of methylphenidate were absorbed into her bloodstream. Her heart pumped them up into her brain. After the chemical reached her prefrontal cortex, the real under-the-hood magic began. Kristin's neurons had always communicated like any human's—dopamine moved across the small gaps between synapses and then was removed. The question was whether she had some differences linked to ADHD. In people with the disorder, various studies suggest, dopamine leaves neurons' synapses a little too quickly, which hampers their communication with each other. When this disconnect takes place in the brain regions that regulate motor control and the seeking of pleasure and reward, it certainly seems reasonable that a dopamine shortage could manifest itself in greater body motion (i.e., hyperactivity and impulsivity) and pleasure-seeking (flitting about from one task to another, essentially inattention). Methylphenidate and amphetamine keep dopamine on the synapse longer, helping the person stay put and persist. Crucially, it does this in all people—more dopamine, more control and focus—but for those with serious ADHD-type behaviors, the results can be more evident.

No one knew exactly what was happening among Kristin's synapses, of course, but the Ritalin did appear to work as advertised, particularly in school. Kristin finally sat still—not catatonic, not at all times, but she stayed calmer and focused on lessons. She didn't talk as much. She didn't bounce around annoying others. She acted a little less bored, too. Definitely better than before, Mrs. Beech and Kristin's parents agreed.

These effects didn't quite arrive until about an hour into the school day, though, which was not optimal. The doctor recommended that Kristin take the pill not at breakfast, but earlier in the morning, so that it began working by schooltime. For the rest of the year, Kristin's parents would wake her up at 6:00, give her a Ritalin pill, and watch her swallow it from a little Evian water bottle. Then back to sleep. By 7:15 the methylphenidate kicked in, she got up, and then headed for breakfast.

Just as people couldn't see exactly how the chemical changed Kristin's behavior, they also didn't see how it made her feel inside. She tried to tell people. "They make me sad," she told her teacher. Every time she went back to Dr. Seitz, and Mom said how well the pills were working, Kristin said she hated them. They asked why. The seven-year-old understandably couldn't put it into words. "I just don't like how it makes me feel" was the best she could muster. Not the most compelling of arguments. The Ritalin remained.

Kristin got good marks in third grade and was less of a problem in the classroom. In fourth grade, she loved math. Her teacher encouraged her, and Dad liked doing problems with her at night. She hated history, though—she could never remember all that reading, and her teacher made her feel stupid for it. But by this time, Kristin understood that it wasn't really her fault anymore. She had attention deficit hyperactivity disorder. Something was wrong with her brain. Those pills helped fix it, whether she liked them or not.

At the end of fourth grade came the standardized tests—ones that really mattered, Kristin was told. The tests you had to start acing to get on the gifted track, to nail the SATs, and then apply to the best universities. On the Main Line, when it comes to college prep, no one starts too early. Yet that pressure wasn't confined to just the high-end Philadelphia suburbs, of course. All across the United States, the college competition was warping childhoods, with students stuffing their applications with more and more honors classes, wedging debate teams and Model UN's into already crammed schedules.

For some kids, their ADHD medications compensated for a legitimate medical problem. But just as Kristin was boarding the Ritalin bus, another population was emerging. This group didn't dislike the drugs. They didn't fight with doctors and parents over taking it. They didn't bristle at the idea at getting diagnosed with ADHD.

No, these high school students didn't have any semblance of ADHD at all. They just made everyone think they did.

Chapter 6

JAMISON

As high school biology labs go, Jamison Monroe's was pretty typical. Microscopes standing sentry along black, wall-length desks. Plastic lungs that opened into full capillarial wonder. Some really unhappy frogs. And, on Monday through Thursday mornings, two dozen freshmen stepping onto high school's moving walkway—grades that mattered, SAT prep, AP classes, college essays. At the end, presumably, the Ivy League. St. John's School was considered the top private high school in Texas, a lavish compound in Houston's wealthy enclave of River Oaks, attracting the area's best and brightest students. And in 1995, few appeared better or brighter than Jamison Monroe.

Blond and blue-blood handsome, Jamison had just graduated top in his class at St. Francis Day, a renowned school itself. He played wide receiver in football. He could run with the studs and mix with the geeks. While other parents had begged St. John's to accept their sons, St. John's recruited Jamison, for goodness' sake. All was proceeding according to plan. Until, a few weeks into the first semester of freshman year, he sat at his bio desk as Miss Taylor announced that she'd finished grading the first test. She walked around the room and handed out the papers. Jamison's, circled at the top: 68.

"How'd this happen? Didn't you study?" Jim Monroe snapped at that night's dinner table. The problem was, Jamison really had studied. At least he thought he had. So for the next month, Jamison hit the books harder—his mom, Kay, woke each day to find her boy zonked out at the kitchen table, drooling into his ribosomes. He'd scramble to get to school by eight, do football practice from three to six, inhale some dinner, and study into the night again. Jamison tried to hunker down. Then Miss Taylor placed the second test into his increasingly sweaty palms. A 75.

It was only late October, and the golden boy was staring straight at a C. What would Dad say? What about *Harvard*? Forget the Ivy League, was he not even St. John's material? It was then, while staring into his microscope, watching some mitochondria flit about like freshmen in hallways, Jamison remembered something he had heard kids talk about at their lockers: Ritalin.

Everyone knew the kids who had ADHD. All through elementary and middle school, they lined up at the nurse each day around lunchtime to get their pills. As they got older, they'd talk openly about Ritalin's effects. Some said it gave them a bit of a "zombie" feeling, dulling them into interest for little but studying. Others called Ritalin their vitamin R, energy that pushed them through overnight test prep. Sounded great to Jamison. That biology grade had to come up, fast. "I used to be smart," he thought to himself.

Jamison didn't have to look far for some vitamin R: His lab partner, Tanner, took it for his ADHD. Hell, he kept the pills in his backpack. He was having no problem with biology at all. So, one day in class, at the back lab tables during some experiment, Jamison brought the topic up.

"How's it work for you?" Jamison asked.

"Pretty good," Tanner replied. "I don't like it much, but my parents make me take it. The doctor says I have ADD so I sort of have to."

"I think I have ADD, too," Jamison said. "Can I try one?"

Tanner hesitated. "I dunno. Seems weird."

Jamison flicked on his made-to-melt charm. "C'mon, man. It's from a doctor. It's not like it's dangerous. I think I really need it."

"I guess it's no big deal," Tanner said. He reached into his backpack, took out the prescription bottle, held it under the desk and twisted off the cap. He jiggled out one pill. Checked to make sure the teacher wasn't looking. Then he handed the pill to Jamison, who swiftly slipped it into his pocket.

Jamison got up and asked Miss Taylor if he could go to the bathroom. He left the room and went straight to the nearest water fountain.

He put the pill on his tongue, leaned over the arc of streaming water, and began the rest his life.

"MAKE HIM DRIBBLE left!

"Jimbo! He can't go left!

"Make him go left!"

Jim Monroe expected his son to run basketball plays just as crisply as he had back in the 1960s, when he played guard at Texas Christian University. Even when he coached Jamison and other six-year-olds in a ragtag beginner's league, Jim designed picks and double-post turn-arounds that befuddled his own players as much as their opponents. "What the hell are you doing?" the irritated other coaches would ask—to which he would respond, "We're running plays, man. What's your problem?" Jim Monroe wanted his first-graders to *win*, and win they did—usually about 35 to 2. He prided himself for being the winningest coach in league history.

By the time Jamison reached ninth grade and the St. John's junior varsity, Jim had moved from the bench to the grandstand but kept yelling at his son, at this point known as Jimbo. Playing defense meant exploiting your opponent's weakness. On this Saturday, that was the kid's ability to dribble to his left.

"Left! Left!" Jim Monroe stood and kept screaming at Jamison, irritating nearby parents. Jimbo angled his feet at the dribbler just as he'd been taught. "Make him go left!" He put his hands up in the ball-handler's face. "Jimbo! Left!"

Then, out of nowhere, Jimbo called a new play. He turned, looked up toward his father, and thrust his right fist under his left forearm and up—an unmistakable and ferocious request that his dad shove it up his ass. The entire gym went instantly silent and fixed its eyes on Jim Monroe. Recognizing which side the crowd was on, Jim didn't bother sitting down. He slinked out of the gym in shame.

But Jim Monroe didn't change—he was who he was, just like his own father. L. A. Monroe, Jamison's grandfather, grew up in Depression-era Arkansas wearing clothes his mom had stitched out of discarded cement sacks. But the boy became a good enough athlete to earn one of Texas

Christian's first basketball scholarships, and starred with the Horned Frogs for three seasons. (He ultimately was inducted into TCU's athletics Hall of Fame.) Known only as L. A. and always a great talker, Monroe parlayed his local fame and connections into a lucrative career in the oil business. So if he could climb out of poverty into wealth, then Jim, his son, could climb even higher. When young Jim scored thirty points in a basketball game, he could have scored forty. When he got an A- in math, it could have been an A. Jim Monroe hated his father for most of his life.

Jim joined the Vietnam-era air force and was serving as a second lieutenant when he met Kay Kehrer, a placid and pretty girl from a small West Virginia town called Sisterville. She wasn't the most assertive of gals, something Jim liked. She had endured scoliosis as a child, and as her spine weakened, painful back surgery left her spending her entire thirteenth year in bed, unable to walk or sit up. She expected to become a teacher, like most of her friends. But in 1967, at twenty-one, as the Mamas and the Papas were "California Dreamin'" on the radio, she sensed there might be more, and flew out to Los Angeles to visit a cousin. "If you decide to stay, I'll understand," her mother said, letting go. Kay took a job as a secretary at Vandenberg Air Force Base; one day in walked Lieutenant Jim Monroe, tall, uniformed, and handsome. Jim and Kay married a few years later.

The Monroes' first child, Leslie, arrived in 1972. Jim loved Leslie—but he loved work more. Having moved his young family to Houston soon after leaving the air force, then putting in long hours as a Merrill Lynch stockbroker, he had little time for fatherhood and eventually little interest. Playing to his strengths as a breadwinner, he began working seventy hours a week. Jim wanted space to pursue his version of success; Kay felt abandoned, and resented Jim's not wanting another child. The tension and distance grew.

Jim became quite successful, working deals with famous and influential southerners—CEOs, oilmen, the football star Archie Manning. Jim and Kay had a cool but convenient marriage through the 1970s. And then, in the summer of 1980, Kay got pregnant. Jim didn't celebrate this time. He focused on work harder than ever, both to benefit his family and to escape from it.

Yet it soon became clear that the Monroes had hit the jackpot with Jamison. Strangers in the supermarket would gush, "You're so handsome! You should be in commercials!" His kindergarten teacher suggested the brilliant boy skip first grade and jump straight to second. (Kay, protective to Jim's pushy, won that argument.) The kid couldn't go a day without overhearing how special he was, how the world would soon be at his feet. He was told he could do anything—except, in his little heart, believe he could ever fulfill such expectations. Asked one day what he wanted to be when he grew up, six-year-old Jamison answered that he wanted to be a weatherman. What? Just a weatherman? A kid like you? Why?

"Because you don't have to be right," the boy explained.

Teachers at Nottingham Country Elementary swooned that Jamison was his grade's smartest kid every year. Increasingly bored, he started to yammer and play the class clown a bit—yet even the strictest teachers surrendered to the boy's inherent charm. As Jim's financial career flourished, the family upgraded to Houston's upscale Tanglewood neighborhood, and similarly upgraded Jamison to St. Francis Episcopal for middle school. Straight A's there, too. Told to take the SAT in seventh grade, just to see how he'd do, he scored alarmingly high for a twelve-year-old. As Jamison became distracted by girls (he'd distracted them for years), he still found school almost uncomfortably easy. He sailed through St. Francis at the top of his class.

As talk turned to high schools, Jamison Monroe did less applying than choosing—Houston's top five private schools courted this breed of smart, athletic, and charismatic kid they could run up their own flagpole. Each school asked that he visit, which meant Jamison missing some St. Francis classes and baseball practices. "Why do I have to do this when no one else does?" he asked Kay while they drove to one school. She replied: "Because you're number one, honey, and they're not." School officials told the family that attending their school could be Jamison's first step toward anything he wanted—Wall Street, medicine, law. One actually mentioned president.

While everyone assumed Jamison would go to St. John's—the top-college feeder school as starched as the boys' button-downs and khakis—Jamison actually preferred Episcopal High. That school tended to be a little less academically pressured, more laid-back. Jamison communicated this feeling not just to his parents over the dinner table, but also, with confident candor, to a rather taken aback St. John's admissions officer during his interview. But if Jim Monroe even heard his son's wishes, he didn't listen. Jim was churning harder than ever to build his own consulting business. And if his firm was going to be number one, his number-one son was going to stay number one. There was really no decision to be made. When St. John's classes began that August, Jamison was sitting in them.

In middle school, Jamison had barely been pushed academically; St. John's was more like a vise. Most of his new classmates were acclimated to this rigor. They'd been there since kindergarten. But Jamison got his new world's message quickly: *Here's your book, kid. Open to page one.*

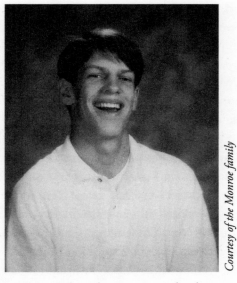

Courtesy of the Monroe family

Jamison Monroe's sophomore year school picture

English papers began coming back with the strangest of symbols: B-, C+. History class brought fifty pages of reading a night. Nowhere did Jamison feel more lost than in biology.

Protective as ever, Kay stepped in. She read Jamison's textbooks so she could test him. She wrote up a study schedule to make postfootball evenings more productive. After he crashed around eleven, she would arrange his notebooks on the kitchen table so they were ready when she rousted him at five to fit in another two hours before school. While most boys ate their cereal over the *Houston Chronicle*'s sports page, he read Crick and Watson.

It didn't work. And definitely not in biology. Those 68 and 75 test scores felt like police floodlights from helicopters he couldn't outrun, at least at his natural speed. With his Harvard future slipping away, Jamison reached out for help, and found it in Tanner's backpack.

JAMISON WALKED BACK from the water fountain unsure of what he'd just done. He knew taking drugs was wrong—"Just Say No" and all—but Tanner took it every day, from a doctor. It wasn't pot or cocaine, for crying out loud. How bad could it be? He walked back to biology class and sat down on his lab stool next to Tanner.

"You take it?"

"Yeah."

"Anything yet?"

"I'm not sure. I don't think so."

"Good luck."

Fifteen minutes later it hit him. Jamison was looking through his microscope at some amoebas when his eyes started focusing differently. They weren't *out* of focus—they went in and out, mostly in. Then he realized it wasn't focus, it felt more like magnification. The cells became crisper. Fuller. He checked to make sure he wasn't turning any knobs. No. This was his lens, not the microscope's. Something was happening, and he liked it.

The bell rang and Jamison zoomed through the hallways' current of students like a jet ski. He got to his next class and never felt so locked in. Took notes like never before. (Not exactly legible, but notes nonetheless.) Didn't even notice that girl in the second row he'd eyed for weeks. The next class went the same way. This stuff was great! Were his sweaty palms and racing heartbeat from the medicine or pure excitement? He didn't know, and didn't care.

It all wore off by football practice. His high turned into horrible lethargy, as if he were wearing thirty pounds of extra shoulder pads—not great for a wide receiver running drills in the eighty-five-degree Houston humidity. He staggered in dehydration toward the Gatorade cups. But Coach never noticed. Jamison was a great actor. And he turned that skill up a notch when his mom rolled up in her Chevy Suburban to pick him up.

"Mom, do you know about ADD?"

"What do you mean?" Kay looked over in confusion.

"ADD—attention deficit disorder," Jamison said, flashing his neediest blue eyes. "I think I have it."

Kay had heard of ADD on the news. Every mother had. And every mother wondered if her kid had it, too.

"I'm having trouble concentrating, and that's why I have a D in biology," Jamison said. "I can't pay attention long enough. You see me at the kitchen table with my homework, right?"

Kay asked questions, but never questioned. Her son would never lie about something like this. Jamison kept quiet through a few traffic lights before casting for what he really wanted.

"You know, there's medicine you can take for it," Jamison said. "You know, Ritalin? It helps you concentrate. Lots of kids take it."

"Well, honey," Kay replied, "if that's what you need."

Mom called a psychiatrist the next morning and pushed for an appointment within forty-eight hours. She scooped up Jamison early from football practice and drove him down Interstate 610 to the doctor. Jamison didn't even hear Kay's small talk as they made their way to the psychiatrist; he uh-huhed and yeahed while reviewing his script in his head. Only an idiot couldn't fake something called "attention deficit disorder," he told himself. *Stare out the window. Act distracted, say "what?" a few times. Say your schoolwork is slipping—that'll clinch it.*

Kay saw the doctor first. Jamison sat in the waiting room for about ten minutes before he was asked to come in. The doctor explained the process.

"I was just asking your mother some questions about what's been giving you trouble," he said as Kay left the room. "I'm going to ask you the same questions. Is that okay?"

"Sure," Jamison said.

Questions, of course, from the Conners Scale. Like so many psychiatrists too old to have gotten any real education about ADHD, this doctor had ordered a stack of questionnaires to help him make the diagnosis. It was the responsible thing to do. ADHD was a difficult thing to pin down, and the pages gave him some reassurance. What they could not do, unfortunately, was detect when a sharp kid like Jamison wanted to game the system.

"For each of these categories, tell me how you would rate yourself on a scale of zero to three—zero being not at all and three being a lot," the doctor said warmly. "Okay?"

"Okay," Jamison said.

"Would you say you're easily distracted?"

"Three—definitely."

"Are you disorganized?"

"Yeah, probably, I guess two."

"Do you sometimes wander off in your mind—kind of daydream?"

"I'm sorry," Jamison said blankly. "What?"

Jamison was the antithesis of Kristin Parber, who up in Pennsylvania answered her Conners questions with increasing hostility. Any discomfort from Jamison was purely for show. He didn't rate himself as a two or three on every category; he wasn't stupid. Jamison answered some immediately, some only after long pauses—either to ponder his answer (conveying sincerity) or to get distracted by something on a shelf (conveying ADHD). If only he could run football pass patterns this well.

Jamison was asked to sit at a computer on the other end of the room and take an electronic test—kind of like a video game, the doctor explained. Numbers, images, or words would flash on the screen, and Jamison was to click the mouse or keyboard when he saw a certain category or color. Children with ADHD tended to do poorly on these types of neuropsychological tests, as their concentration on the screen would wane, or their trigger fingers would fire at answers too quickly. The program presumed that the child was *actually trying*. The test's developers did attempt to guard against questionable effort; glaring delays or implausible results could trip some control-room alarms. But a clever boy like Jamison could easily stay one step ahead. He provided a believable mix of clicks too fast, clicks too slow, clicks just right.

After asking Jamison a few more questions about his school struggles—*I just can't focus, sir*—the doctor asked Kay back in. He said that Jamison had ADHD. Usually it was in smaller kids, but Jamison had been an active child, maybe he always had it. Either way medication would probably help.

"I dunno," Jamison said warily. "I don't want to take pills. I don't want to be one of those kids."

"I know, honey," Kay countered, "but this is a big year for you in school. Maybe we should just give it a try."

Jamison looked even more distressed. Even fidgeted a bit for effect.

"I really think medication would be the best thing at this point," the doctor said. "See if it helps."

He scribbled out the prescription and handed it to Mrs. Monroe. She and Jamison walked out of the office. The doctor called in another family as the Monroes silently walked to the car. Kay wondered what she had lost—her son had just been diagnosed with a mental disorder after all. Jamison focused on what he would soon gain.

They drove straight to their neighborhood Walgreens to fill the prescription. But it actually wasn't for Ritalin. The slip of paper called for a new ADHD medicine being marketed to doctors as even better than Ritalin—more effective, longer lasting, fewer side effects. Even the name sounded like a fresh start.

Adderall.

Chapter 7

ADD FOR ALL

Ritalin's future looked no brighter than in the early 1990s. After thirty years on pharmacy shelves—long enough for the children of one generation to start giving it to the next—the medication had survived the lawsuits that threatened its approval among both society and the crucial news media. Ripped from its scary "brain dysfunction" roots, the ADHD market swelled to include ever more children. Disability and educational law now protected and even expanded the rights of those diagnosed. Ritalin was proven. It was practical. The one thing the drug was not, however, was *profitable*.

CIBA's patents on methylphenidate had expired in the 1970s, ending the company's right to sell the formulation with no competition. As a quintessential blockbuster drug, Ritalin had been an extraordinarily lucrative product—a vial of ninety tablets cost CIBA pennies to produce and sold for about fifty times more, a 5,000 percent profit margin. But when this exclusivity ran out, Ritalin reverted to simple methylphenidate, a chemical reproducible by all pharmaceutical comers, plunging prices and shriveling margins. While doctors were discovering big business in diagnosing and prescribing children with ADHD—some psychiatrists began devoting their entire practices to the steady stream of parents arriving at their doors—the pills themselves went for peanuts.

Fortune beckoned the company that could invent a new drug to treat ADHD, get it approved and patented, then unleash it on the awaiting market. Presumably, this would flow from a well-thought-out, corporate plan. Its scientists would exploit how the brain responded metabolically to the rejiggering of dopamine within the synapses. Its doctors would be expert in the ins and outs of the disorder and the symptoms the medication would need to alleviate (in other words, the Conners Scale). Its salesmen would master why medication was becoming so embraced by parents, educators, and the wider American culture.

Yet that did not happen. What lit the fuse of modern ADHD, the man who made a fortune from it seemingly overnight, was neither scientist nor doctor. He was a sole entrepreneur outside Cincinnati who had barely heard of ADHD at all.

ROGER GRIGGS WAS not a typical pharmaceutical executive. He grew up in postwar Indiana about three miles from the Golden Dome of Notre Dame but ultimately enrolled at Indiana State University, getting a master's in education and using it to become a high school football coach and occasional teacher. Needing a higher income, and always a strong and confident talker, Griggs later became a field representative at Lederle Laboratories in Wayne, New Jersey, extolling various drugs' virtues to hospital personnel. In the early 1990s he decided to start his own drug company, Richwood Pharmaceutical, and looked to purchase other companies with standing patents. One firm, called Rexar, had several intriguing products. Their little weight-control drug named Obetrol, however, was not one of them. That's because Obetrol had one massive pitfall: It was an amphetamine. The few amphetamines doctors had prescribed through the 1980s were typically generic Dexedrine knockoffs that only reminded people of speed's scary and controversial past. Obetrol was just one of many. When Griggs examined Rexar Pharmaceutical's books in 1991, it had only $40,000 in sales. It was a drug about to die.

But something was very strange about those sales. Griggs noticed that a curiously high percentage of prescriptions were being written by one doctor, a pediatrician in Provo, Utah, named Ron Jones. What was this Dr. Jones using Obetrol for, in kids no less? What did he know that no one else did? Griggs flew to Provo to find out.

"I use it for my kids with ADHD," Dr. Jones said.

Griggs didn't want to admit that he had no earthly idea what ADHD was. So he chose his words carefully.

"What situations do you use it in?" Griggs asked.

"I use it when Ritalin fails," Dr. Jones responded.

"How often is that?"

Dr. Jones didn't know exactly, so he went to his patient files and started tallying up cases. About half the time, he said, a child either didn't improve on Ritalin or had to stop because of side effects. But when those kids switched to Obetrol, they improved 70 percent of the time. Why on earth, Griggs asked, would amphetamine be something considered for hyperactivity? Dr. Jones said he didn't remember their names, but some big doctors in the 1960s had found Dexedrine to be helpful in calming uncontrollable children.

Griggs didn't know the ins and outs of ADHD, but he understood a 70 percent response rate. He wondered: Could the United States, with its notoriously short memory, be ready to try amphetamine again? Of course it would—with the right marketing. Griggs flew back to Cincinnati and told his Richwood staff, "We're going to buy Rexar Pharmaceutical, but we're gonna buy it for a totally different reason than I thought."

The name remained a problem. Obetrol—a meld of "obesity" and "control"—made no sense in this new context of child psychiatry. Griggs needed something new. Something catchy that wouldn't scare mothers off. Hyperine? No, hyperactivity wasn't the syndrome's only symptom anymore. Concetrex? Too mind-controlly. At its core, Griggs figured, attention deficit hyperactivity disorder was too amorphous for him to build off anything specific. His drug needed to invite all comers. It needed to be inclusive.

In late 1993, in the conference room of Richwood's headquarters in Florence, Kentucky, Griggs sensed a solution. He started with "ADD" and fiddled with snappy suffixes. Children with the disorder could appear so dissimilar—some distractible, others hyperactive and impulsive, still more with a smorgasbord of symptoms. What word would capture them?

All.

For ADD.

ADD for All.

Adderall.

*　　　*　　　*

"ADDERALL" WAS THE perfect name—agreeable to parents, inviting to doctors, reassuring to everyone. The medication could improve not just some of a child's problems, but all of them. And to anyone still a little spooked about recent headlines and lawsuits, *it wasn't Ritalin.* In sales materials and advertisements in medical journals, Adderall announced itself as a "unique alternative" for ADHD, one more effective and modern than old-fashioned Ritalin. A new product for ADHD's open frontier.

Griggs was so excited, so eager as he pushed Adderall onto the market during the summer of 1994, that he moved too fast for the Food and Drug Administration's taste and almost torpedoed his venture from the start. Within months the FDA informed Richwood, in a decidedly frigid October letter, that (1) Adderall had no data whatsoever to support its claim that it was better than Ritalin, and (2) Adderall *had never been approved by the FDA in the first place.* The government demanded that Griggs halt the marketing and distribution of Adderall immediately.

Adderall had already been prescribed to five thousand children nationwide.* Now their mothers could panic for two starkly opposite reasons: Either their kid had been taking a drug the FDA hadn't approved, or the pills that had so improved his behavior might now be suddenly snatched away. Griggs was forced to write a stunningly embarrassing apology—published as a full-page ad in the same psychiatry journals that had run his advertisements—detailing how many of those ads' statements had no evidence to support them, how the product did not even have government approval, and that it could be removed from the market. The letter closed: "We apologize for any inconvenience we may have caused you."

As it turned out, Adderall's status as unapproved was a relative technicality—Obetrol had been approved as safe at one time, but did not receive updated approval after some FDA regulations changed in the 1970s. Even so, the drug still wasn't shown to work for ADHD, its primary sales claim; Richwood officials admitted to the FDA that its better-

---

*One of them, amazingly enough *that very week*, was a high school freshman in Houston named Jamison Monroe.

than-Ritalin boasts were based not on formal, double-blind studies, but on the flimsy testimonials of clinicians like Dr. Jones. The FDA had the right to remove Adderall from the market altogether, especially because Ritalin remained a perfectly viable alternative for families in need. Griggs thought he had lost everything—the first victim of Adderall withdrawal.

But Adderall had been proven effective in ways the FDA hadn't expected. After more than a year of wrangling with various government agencies and sensing disaster, Griggs was sitting at his Richwood desk, disconsolate, when the phone rang. It was a well-connected Washington lobbyist. As luck would have it, one of those five thousand kids who couldn't get any more Adderall happened to be the son of a senator. The lobbyist told Griggs that the senator "pitched a fit" with a top FDA official.

"You're golden," the lobbyist said.

"Golden what?" Griggs replied. "What are you talking about?"

"Trust me, it's done."

"What's done?"

"You're going to get your approval."

Adderall was officially green-lighted in February 1996. Griggs's marketing department, shackled by the FDA for a year and a half, immediately jumped into action. They flooded psychiatry journals with ads to announce Adderall's return and ability to redefine treatment of ADHD. Richwood sales representatives descended upon doctors' offices to dazzle them with charts and studies and testimonials, usually over an expensive lunch. They gave away logoed pens and notepads, putting Adderall in doctors' line of sight at all times. Griggs also communicated directly to parents by purchasing thousands of CHADD informational booklets that described the seriousness of ADHD and its need for stimulant treatment; sales reps carried stacks of the publications into every doctor's office, but left only some for the doctor himself. Most were placed neatly on end tables in the waiting room, ready for parents' perusal.

Yet that wasn't Griggs's most brilliant idea. Doctors would not prescribe Adderall without first diagnosing ADHD—and some psychiatrists, and most pediatricians, were uncomfortable making that call in the first place. The disorder's name and official symptoms had changed three times in the previous sixteen years. Nasty controversy had cast doubt over the dangers of stimulant medications. And even if doctors were familiar with the disorder and knew some of its characteristics, the telltale signs ("easily distracted"? "forgetful"?) still seemed awfully squishy. If they were going to make the diagnosis, they needed a tool—some would say a crutch—to make it feel more grounded in science, to give the decision an air of medical validity. So, when doctors admitted some discomfort, Adderall sales reps reached into their briefcases and handed over the ultimate ADHD marketing tool: the Conners Scale.

A diagnosis did not always mean a prescription. Many parents were asking their doctors about nondrug options, particularly something called cognitive behavioral therapy, or CBT. This approach focused less directly on the child's behavior than that of the adults around him. It emphasized how parents and teachers could learn how to provide more structured environments for inattentive and hyperactive children, such as set study times and less cluttered workspaces. CBT did not cure attention problems, of course, or alter the child's behavior as directly as medication would; it attempted to place that innate behavior into settings more conducive to learning habits and skills. CBT was relatively expensive, yes, because counseling for parents and extra aides in classrooms cost far more than pills. But both clinical and anecdotal experience had shown that CBT usually did benefit children with ADHD either in combination with medication or, many times, without it at all.

With diagnoses once again growing rapidly, and tension building among clinicians, parents, and the news media about whether strong medicine was truly the best approach for ADHD, Griggs's financial future depended on the crucial question: What's better, drugs or behavioral therapies? As it turned out, Griggs didn't have to lift a finger to prove the case for medication. No drug company did.

The National Institute of Mental Health did it for them. Recognizing the crossroads that ADHD was facing and its importance to millions of current—not to mention unborn—children, America's primary mental health agency stepped in to execute, once and for all, the disorder's most comprehensive clinical trial ever. Top officials agreed that the ultimate ADHD study required far more than just money, probably $10 million, and time, at least six and maybe even ten years. The enterprise needed the most tactical design to answer the drugs-versus-therapy question definitively. It needed complete separation from drug companies to shield the results from bias. It needed the most astute clinicians, the most careful academic scientists, and the most celebrated names in ADHD.

It needed Keith Conners.

WHEN HIS TELEPHONE rang in early 1992, Conners was enjoying one of the more blissful periods of his career. Whereas the Duke University Medical Center had once been unable to accommodate the growing number of parents asking to have their children examined for their attention problems, his new ADHD center served them all.

Conners ran the clinic, seeing kids, diagnosing them when appropriate—he was one of the few clinicians nationwide to use the Conners Scale with caution—and discussing options for medication. (As a psychologist with a PhD, rather than a psychiatrist with an MD, he was not allowed by law to write prescriptions himself.) Part of Conners's work was to collect data on youngsters' treatment response to use in scientific studies—in fact, the clinic ran newspaper and radio advertisements that encouraged parents to have their children evaluated for ADHD. He and his clinical staff would always spend an earnest three to five hours talking with each child, his parents, and teachers before making what became about two hundred diagnoses per year. Conners wasn't paid the largest salary, but his six-figure royalty checks from his scales, plus his steady side income from pharmaceutical companies, made him more than prosperous for Durham, North Carolina.

Conners concentrated solely on his work, living alone only a few miles from the clinic. His professional life had long eclipsed his personal one. He had tried being a family man. He married Patricia Pyper, a high school classmate from back in Ophir, Utah, soon after returning from Oxford. They had four children: Rachel, Anthony, and then twins Rebecca and Sarah. The kids had been born during the first Ritalin trials with Leon Eisenberg, and as Conners devoted ever more time to his career at Johns Hopkins and then Harvard, he and Patricia grew apart. They divorced in 1974. By the time he went to Duke, in 1990, the kids were grown up, leaving him free to devote sixty-hour weeks to the clinic; his little private time got spent listening to opera and learning to paint. His Duke waiting room bustled, his stature never higher.

When NIMH decided to finally identify the best treatments for ADHD, Conners was a clear choice not just to participate, but to oversee the investigation from square one. He had conducted more studies and written more papers on the disorder than anyone in the field. His scales were used to make diagnoses nationwide. He was a Rhodes Scholar who had descended directly from the royal bloodlines of Leon Eisenberg and Leo Kanner. Conners's appeal went beyond his résumé: Pushing sixty and with whiskers increasingly gray, he had a patrician air that was more sturdy than stuffy (except when quoting Aristotle). Conners spoke in steady, cerebral sentences that tended to defuse tension rather than stoke it. So when NIMH selected the twenty-five researchers to conduct its study and convened them in Washington for their initial official meeting, the first order of business was to affirm the obvious: Keith Conners would lead the proceedings.

That was one of the last things the group agreed on. Rival herds tore over every aspect of the study. How many kids were needed? In what age range and from what cities or neighborhoods? Could they have other problems, such as anxiety or conduct disorder, or must they have ADHD only? How long should they get the medications and at what dosage? Who should perform the clinical evaluations, MDs or psychologists? What should be evaluated—school defiance, home relationships—and by whom, parents, teachers, or doctors? Dozens of factors could have dozens of options, each championed by different permutations of supporters. One area that did find quick consensus was that the trial had to be long, preferably five years, because what people truly wanted to know was not which strategy brought overnight improvement, but which helped the kids into adolescence and beyond.

(The politics turned rather bizarre during discussions of which scorecard should measure the children's inattention and impulsivity levels. An obvious choice was the Conners Scale, given that Conners himself was in the room. Then again, so were the psychologists James Swanson, from the University of California at Irvine, and Bill Pelham, from the State University of New York at Buffalo, who had recently developed their own rival questionnaire, called the Swanson, Nolan and Pelham

ADHD Scale, with the catchy acronym SNAP. This checklist rivalry was uncomfortable enough, before considering two of the worst-kept secrets in the room: first, Conners felt the forms were so similar that he considered suing the SNAP guys; and second, far more hilariously, there was no Nolan. Dr. Nolan's real name was actually Logan. They just decided "SNAP" was much better than the alternative.)

The group's most substantive decision entailed pinpointing exactly what Ritalin therapy was going to be compared *to*.* What alternatives might provide similar or perhaps greater benefits over the longer term, leaving youngsters better prepared for middle and high school? The best of these non-pharmacological options, most agreed, was cognitive behavioral therapy, where the skills of parents and teachers were targeted even more than the kids'. This approach often did succeed. The question was how often—and whether it ultimately rivaled Ritalin.

Although NIMH made sure that no drug company had direct input on the study's planning and execution, the investigators—all respected faculty at elite universities—arrived with a decided belief in medication. First, they had seen with their own eyes how rapidly Ritalin could redirect the course of a child's life; there were times when it failed or even backfired, sure, but successes resonated more. Second, a vast majority, including Conners, owed at least some of their professional or financial well-being to pharmaceutical companies, either in the form of research grants or five-figure consulting gigs; chafing those benefactors was not high on their list of career objectives. Yes, a few panel members—most notably Bill Pelham—avidly supported behavioral therapy. But most at least had an emotional, and often monetary, stake in medication remaining ADHD's primary therapy.

The researchers decided to evaluate the effectiveness not just of Ritalin and CBT, but of using neither† (for a baseline) or both. Of course, the group quite reasonably assumed, giving a child the combination—

---

*Adderall was not considered because it was too new and had no track record.

†In actuality, "neither" meant no additional assistance beyond what those children were already receiving from their own doctors—medication, therapy, hypnosis, whatever—because withholding all treatment from an ADHD child would be unethical.

known as multimodal treatment—would be better than just one or the other. After all, the two treatments provided different but complementary help. Ritalin tended to temper and focus the child, creating a less tense and more conducive learning environment for all; behavioral therapy emphasized the learning of long-term skills. A blend would provide both: It gave a hungry family some fish, and then taught them how to catch their own.

The researchers spent two years hammering out the details for the study they called the Multimodal Treatment of Children with ADHD, quickly and mercifully shortened to MTA. The trial was conducted at Conners's clinic at Duke University and five other North American sites, at which groups of twenty-four children aged seven to nine each received one of the four treatments: carefully managed Ritalin; intense behavioral therapy; both of those in combination; or neither. But the lengthy academic rigmarole meant that the study could no longer last five years; it had grown so cumbersome and expensive that the budget now allowed treatment to last only fourteen months. Some worried that this doomed behavioral therapy from the start—hares like Ritalin could be ahead after one year, while tortoises like CBT might catch up and pass them only after three or five. But no one raised much of a fuss. The group had vowed to reach consensus and present a united front.

The MTA team embarked on the most crucial and elaborate clinical trial in the history of child psychiatry. The group spent fourteen months treating the children, several years collating and interpreting and writing up the results, and one day screwing it up forever.

"STUDY OF ATTENTION DEFICIT DISORDER SUPPORTS MEDICINE OVER THERAPY"

USA Today

"STUDY SAYS DRUGS BEST HELP FOR ATTENTION DEFICIT"
ABC World News Tonight

"PSYCHOSOCIAL INTERVENTIONS OF NO BENEFIT"
Clinical Psychiatry News

"Major Study Rebuts Critics of Drug for Attention-Disorder Kids"

Chicago Tribune

The MTA study's results were announced to great fanfare on December 14, 1999, shortly before their publication in one of the American Medical Association's most prestigious journals, *Archives of General Psychiatry*. Because the media and lay public would surely not understand anything so complicated as a scientific study, NIMH made sure to condense the findings into news bites. The lead voice was given to Dr. Peter Jensen, the head of child and adolescent research at NIMH, who declared: "When the best behavioral-management treatment and medication treatments are pitted head to head, medical treatment is a hands-down winner." Other psychiatrists not involved in the study chimed in, too. Dr. James T. McCracken of UCLA told the *New York Times*, "It is still surprising that Ritalin remains as controversial as it is. One hopes that this study will put some of the controversy to rest." The article was headlined: "Study Backs a Drug for Hyperactive Children."

The problem was that these messages weren't quite true. They held some truth—Ritalin had always been, and still was, an effective solution for a lot of families—but were delivered with such tone deafness, with such stunning disregard for how the statements would be interpreted by lay audiences, that they became misleading and occasionally downright wrong. Medication did not win "hands down." Therapy provided far more than "no benefit." In reality, the primary final scorecard for the percentage of children who greatly improved during their respective treatments was:

Medication + Therapy	68 percent
Medication Alone	56 percent
Therapy Alone	34 percent
Neither	25 percent

There were several problems with this chart, not the least of which being that children's behavior is far more complicated and nuanced than some four-line list could possibly capture. Nonetheless, even the innumerate can plainly see that the best performer was combination therapy—just as common sense had suggested. Yes, medication alone did considerably better than therapy alone, a greatly important finding. But each approach provided benefits in its own ways and for different children in different circumstances. They provided them at different rates, with behavioral treatment undoubtedly hampered by the fourteen-month cutoff. This context was completely lost.

But the contortions went so much further. First, almost half of the kids *did not* significantly benefit from just medication, a remarkable finding for a study that was trumpeting the benefits of Ritalin. Second, kids in the "neither" group were not getting *nothing*—they were getting whatever treatments their own doctors were already providing, *which was usually Ritalin*. Therefore, Ritalin, as used in the real world, was doing a pretty rotten job three-quarters of the time, a stunning window into how ADHD was being handled nationwide. And perhaps most important, behavioral therapy's success rate was close enough to Ritalin's that it should still have been presented as viable for families who preferred at least to attempt nonmedication approaches first. But the MTA whispered: *Don't bother.*

In the end, the MTA wrote the ultimate prescription for prescriptions. After three decades of debates, hearings, lawsuits, and other hand-wringing, Ritalin had been vindicated by the field's top experts and the NIMH. Parents could exhale, because the time and expense of behavioral therapy—which they had to undergo, even more than the child—were now no longer necessary. Schools, already under severe financial pressure, could justify cutting aides and other staff who had been brought in to help ADHD kids; after all, the study showed that one-on-one attention didn't work better than a pill. (Any parents who complained about this, saying they preferred not to use medication, were accused of irresponsibly denying their children the *best* treatment.) And it made doctors' lives so much easier. They didn't have to explain the various pros and cons of medication versus therapy. They could avoid the back-and-forths with vacillating parents who clogged up their waiting rooms.

They could put their hands in their lab coat pockets and declare "This is what the most definitive study on ADHD drugs ever found," and move on.

*   *   *

ALTHOUGH THE MTA'S primary message defied logic—therapy was *worthless*? Really?—its resounding endorsement of ADHD medication became a bell impossible to unring. And no group kept ringing it more than the one perfectly positioned to profit most: the pharmaceutical industry, for whom the MTA study became an ultimate, government-sanctioned endorsement.

This outcome would have delighted Roger Griggs, but his estimate of ADHD's growth potential had actually proved too conservative. In 1996, Adderall became the go-to modern treatment for many clinicians across the nation, selling $18 million worth. But the ADHD market still felt a little risky to him: with about 5 percent of children already diagnosed with the disorder, sales had to level out soon, right? How much growth was left? What if lawyers brought another round of lawsuits, this time going after the easier target of amphetamine? What if some other company came along with a better product? Griggs decided not to press his luck—he walked away from the ADHD table as quickly as he'd sat down. A British pharmaceutical company named Shire believed in Adderall and offered to buy Richwood for a positively stupefying $186 million. Griggs took it. It was August 1997. Adderall had been on the market for an entire year and a half.

Griggs was right to anticipate competition that he, and now Shire, would soon face. At the very time he was making his fortune, another pharmaceutical company, a California firm named ALZA, was angling to break into the ADHD business. ALZA's idea was to take the old standby, Ritalin, and merely make it more convenient. All generic forms of methylphenidate still came in only short-acting pills: Kids had to take one in the morning, another during the school day, and sometimes another in the afternoon. One missed dose and a child could turn uncontrollable within forty minutes. Parents and teachers pined for something that kids could function on for the entire day. ALZA set out to invent it.

In October 1999, just two months before the government's MTA study crowned methylphenidate as the best treatment for ADHD, ALZA announced to the medical community that it had found the holy grail: once-a-day Ritalin. The ADHD market would no longer be a two-horse race consisting of short-acting Ritalin and Adderall alone; this new drug formulation, ultimately called Concerta, brought a fresh new thoroughbred to the mix.

For the next four years, Shire and ALZA didn't just fight for larger slices of the ADHD pie. They were going to grow that pie beyond imaginable proportions, through any means necessary.

Chapter 8

THE HIJACKING

Dallas, Boston, Orlando, Santa Fe: If it seemed like Keith Conners was touring like a rock star, that's because he was. His Duke Medical Center ADHD clinic was thriving. He and his expanding clinical team diagnosed and treated thousands of children from central North Carolina and beyond. He contributed to the most cutting-edge clinical trials. He published studies in the most prestigious journals and lectured all over the world. But when pill came to shove, he served more than just a university clinic.

Every pharmaceutical company that wanted a piece of the ADHD business—and they were queuing up quickly—wanted a piece of Keith Conners. His name connoted ADHD like Chevrolet's did cars. In some ways the Conners Scale had gone generic, like Kleenex or Band-Aids; other tests published by competitors, usually condensed versions to make diagnoses even easier and quicker, were mistaken for the real thing. He had even founded a journal, the *Journal of Attention Disorders*, in 1996, which allowed dozens of ADHD studies per year—many of them funded by Big Pharma, naturally—to be published and entered into the forever citable scientific literature. Conners was the epitome of what the industry euphemizes as a key opinion leader, or KOL. But those letters might as well mean "knows our lines." Companies deploy these doctors to spin their marketing objectives into science.

The day back in 1963 when the CIBA representative handed Leon Eisenberg that $5,000 check seemed innocent in comparison. As Americans increasingly reached to the medicine cabinet to cure their varied ills, the drug business had become so profitable, so competitive, that companies were spending billions to get their pills on consumers' tongues. With prescription drugs, which could not (yet) be advertised on television and in consumer magazines, that meant courting the gatekeepers—physicians with prescription pads—to whom Big Pharma had to sell not necessarily the product, but *confidence* in the product and, even before that, the seriousness of the condition it treated. After all, in the drug biz, patients can buy only what their doctors buy into.

Drug companies lavished their KOLs with golf-resort junkets, sports tickets, and cold cash to encourage prescriptions. They staged conferences at which their anointed experts would stand in front of hundreds of local physicians and deliver company-scripted PowerPoints extolling Drug X; afterward, they would all hit the bar for some boozy bonhomie. One company selling antipsychotics handed its KOL a script that outright denied the medication's serious side effects and told him, "We'll give you a thousand dollars if you say this for a half-hour." Even when a company's $50,000 research grant was "unrestricted"—meaning the doctor could run the drug trial unencumbered and report whatever he or she felt appropriate—doctors knew, at least subconsciously, that producing positive results and favorable papers would mean further grants, more published articles, and higher salary. Doctors would contend that all this remuneration was gratitude, not graft, that none of it would ever influence their science or care of individual patients. But it did. Whether they knew it or not, KOLs were not educating, but advertising.

From Shire to ALZA, from Novartis to Eli Lilly, every company courted Conners's expertise and aura to help it build its ADHD operations. His primary function was to fly to conferences where he and other big names in ADHD would teach dozens, even hundreds, of local clinicians to recognize the disorder and treat it, usually with medication. As the most prestigious name on the program, Conners was usually the day's opening act—delivering the overview of what the condition was, how it was widespread and underdiagnosed, and how stimulants could turn patients around.

Audiences' primary complaint had long been that parents didn't like giving their kids two or three ADHD pills a day, and making them line up at the nurse's office at lunchtime. The doctors pleaded: Could someone please come up with a breakfast-through-dinner stimulant? ALZA answered their prayers by launching Concerta in 2000. It was good old Ritalin, essentially, but with a special coating that allowed the medicine to be dispensed and absorbed slowly. Children could take one dose in the morning, from their parents in the privacy of their home. It made life so much easier. And at a time when diagnoses were already increasing 10 to 20 percent annually, it revolutionized the ADHD business.

Concerta's footsteps had been approaching for almost a year—thanks to research buffed to a shine by some familiar names. The safety and efficacy of Concerta was determined by a trial in which about five dozen children aged six to twelve took the drug and had their symptoms improve, a predictable result confirmed by the Conners Scale. ALZA's press release featured a glowing quote—"We are extremely encouraged by the potential role of Concerta in the treatment of ADD/ADHD"—but not from a company executive. It was from one of the principal researchers, Dr. James Swanson of the University of California at Irvine. The endorsement was disturbing enough, coming from an academic, but became more so because Swanson and his primary study collaborator, Dr. William Pelham, had concurrently been working on the MTA study, the supposedly unbiased, government-funded trial that wound up grossly overstating the benefits of—wouldn't you know it—methylphenidate. The MTA results were released a mere seven weeks after Concerta's. For the stimulant business, it was hard to tell them apart.

Once-a-day Concerta was a genuine breakthrough for children with ADHD. But it started a heated rivalry with Shire, which found itself playing catch-up. Adderall's dominance—it was easily the ADHD market leader, selling $250 million worth in 2000 alone—was now threatened by Concerta. Shire scrambled to come up with Adderall XR, as in eXtended Release, its own long-acting form that two years later was launched with the same strategy as ALZA's: Get prominent ADHD voices to conduct studies and spread the gospel, and pay them handsomely to do it.

Conners, meanwhile, assisted everyone. Measured and mannered, he delivered what he considered proper science—published and peer-reviewed facts that, in the appropriate hands, would aid the ADHD children to whom he had devoted his winding-down career. He never lied during his talks, but he also didn't rock boats. When he told his audiences that the MTA study found great benefits in medication, he didn't emphasize how its flawed inner-workings undercut that entire conclusion. When Concerta's prepared speaker notes said little about the medication's side effects, he figured someone else would cover those. Even when a doctor spouted blatant untruths right in front of him, he, like everyone else, didn't call him on it; criticizing colleagues was considered uncouth for academics. A perfect example came during an Adderall XR speaker training session in 2002, when a Colorado psychiatrist and fellow Shire KOL stood at the podium and told the assembled indoctrinates that amphetamines had no abuse potential because, he explained, people who overdose "feel nothing or feel bad"—a patent lie, as if eight espresso shots caused only a tummy ache. Conners was in the audience that day. He sat in his chair, doodled the speaker's face in his notes, and scribbled underneath, "Often in error and never in doubt." He kept this feeling to himself.

Shire appreciated Conners's restraint, no doubt. So did ALZA and all the other drug companies. But even Conners was nowhere near the most profitable commodity for drug companies. For that, they traveled to Harvard University and the most powerful child psychiatrist in the world—the one with the most papers, the most influence, and the most desire to sell it.

DR. JOSEPH BIEDERMAN spoke three languages, and was pompous in all of them.

Born in communist Czechoslovakia just after the Second World War, Biederman entered medical school in Argentina at sixteen, did his residency and fellowship in Israel, and found his muse—child psychiatry—at Massachusetts General Hospital in the early 1980s. He quickly established himself as smart, shrewd, and a tad odd. He was a mousy little character, perhaps five-foot-nine but with a thin frame and wispy hair that made him come off several inches shorter. As he met with hundreds of parents of troubled children and gave countless lectures around the world, Biederman's accent, a squeaky blend of Slavic-laced Spanish and English—*you zee, dee ill-ness iss deefined by deese criteedia*—lent him such an air of old-school erudition he could have been Freud speaking from the grave. The bouquet was savored most by Biederman himself. A full professor at Harvard Medical School, Dr. Biederman was once asked what rank came next. He responded flatly: "God."

Biederman tangoed with dozens of pharmaceutical companies while pumping out studies on ADHD. From 1995 to 2005 he published almost three hundred papers—more than two a month—regarding the disorder, most of them carrying one or more crucial messages: The disorder was widespread and vastly underdiagnosed; children with it met horrible fates; and, lo and behold, such-and-such drug was "safe and effective" in averting these outcomes. (The definitions of "safe" and "effective" were generally left to the imagination.) His work was rooted in empirical research; even cynics stopped short of suspecting that Biederman made up data or knowingly misrepresented his findings. But his interpretations and descriptions of the performance of medication were delivered with such suffocating surety that the words veered from scholarship toward unabashed promotion.

- Study on Adderall XR clinical trial funded by Shire: "These data provide support for the benefit of this novel, once-daily amphetamine preparation for the treatment of ADHD."

- *Journal of Clinical Psychiatry*, 1998: "Family studies of ADHD have shown that the relatives of ADHD children are at high risk for ADHD, comorbid psychiatric disorders, school failure, learning disability, and impairments in intellectual functioning." (Translation: It isn't just that ADHD children face risks, which makes sense. All of their *relatives* are endangered, as well—so they should be diagnosed and medicated, too.)

- Study of pemoline (Cylert) on behalf of Abbott Pharmaceutical: "This trial suggests pemoline is well tolerated and effective in adolescents and may be a particularly useful ADHD treatment for adolescents." He made this statement despite noting elsewhere that pemoline appeared to cause fatal liver damage, and cautioned against its use in adults.

- To *Reuters Health* in 2006, regarding the scholastic benefit of all ADHD medications: "If a child is brilliant but is doing just OK in school, that child may need treatment, which would result in their performing brilliantly at school."

Biederman did not work alone. Several planets revolved around his sun, principally Drs. Timothy Wilens and Thomas Spencer at Harvard and Mass General. The three keynoted drug-company conferences, were saluted at CHADD events, and churned out studies like no one else. A statistical consultant for the group, Joel Adamson, was confident that the doctors always did have children's best interests at heart. But he said they saw that interest as best served by medication—always. Adamson recalls overhearing Wilens say, "If you're not prescribing medication, you're not doing anything." The Harvard group's philosophy, as Adamson put it, was this: "I can't make your home less chaotic, I can't run your school differently, I can't get your parents back together or help you with your homework. But I can give you a diagnosis, I can give you medication."

Biederman's promotion of ADHD, a diagnosis already established, was exceeded only by his enthusiasm for childhood bipolar disorder, a condition previously reserved for adults and occasionally adolescents. His team conducted slews of studies to prove the disorder's prevalence— even two-year-olds could be bipolar, Biederman insisted—and created a market for antipsychotic medications such as Risperdal (from Johnson & Johnson) and Seroquel (AstraZeneca). From 1994 through 2003, bipolar diagnoses in American children increased by *forty times*, with many of them put on potent and expensive medication sold by the corporations subsidizing Biederman's work.*

Biederman tolerated no dissent, shutting down anyone with the temerity to question his findings and interpretations—including Keith Conners, who had been in the ADHD business more than twice as long. While speaking at one conference, Conners discussed evidence that a child's low

---

*Biederman's bizarre rationalization for accepting industry millions in this oft-criticized pursuit: "The more controversial a diagnosis is, the harder it is to get funding from conventional sources."

birth weight and maternal high blood pressure could be signs of future hyperactivity. Biederman stood up from his seat in the audience and told Conners he was wrong, that no evidence supported the claim. (In fact there was, dozens of studies' worth; Biederman simply hadn't read them.) At a conference in Japan on medication's effectiveness on ADHD—co-chaired by Biederman and sponsored by Eli Lilly—Biederman presented his data, then, during the routine question-and-answer period, an audience member politely disagreed with some of Biederman's statements. This wasn't just anyone—it was Leon Eisenberg, the man who had pioneered the study of attention disorders in the 1960s. Biederman harrumphed at Eisenberg's insolence and furiously returned to his seat on the dais, next to none other than Keith Conners. "How dare he challenge me—what does he know about ADHD?" Biederman grumbled.

Biederman eventually made one too many enemies. At the height of the doctor's power, in 2008, Senator Chuck Grassley (R-Iowa) investigated Big Pharma's influence on psychiatric research. Grassley didn't just request documents; he subpoenaed them. The Biederman group became his primary target. And he hit the bull's-eye.

Grassley's team unearthed evidence that showed Biederman had personally accepted more than $1.6 million in drug-company speaking and consulting fees from 2000 to 2007, and had broken Harvard policies by not reporting much of it. His primary collaborators, Wilens and Spencer, had received $1.6 million and $1 million, respectively. Even worse, confidential files revealed the depths of the Harvard group's alliance with Big Pharma—especially Johnson & Johnson, which not only manufactured Risperdal but also, after buying out ALZA to go after the booming ADHD market, Concerta. It wasn't just that J&J had founded a research center at Harvard in 2002 and subsidized it with $500,000 a year. It was how the relationship functioned, according to internal documents.

- The center was a "strategic collaboration" between the two groups, documents said, with a primary goal being to "move forward the commercial goals of J&J."

- A clinical trial would "extend to adolescents positive findings with Concerta."

- The center "will alert physicians to the existence of a large group of children who might benefit from treatment with Risperdal." One trial, before it was ever conducted, "will support the safety and effectiveness" of the drug.

- Regarding both ADHD and bipolar disorder, "genetic and brain imaging studies are needed to show the validity of these disorders as brain disorders that respond to medication [and] are frequently chronic and severely debilitating. Without such data, many clinicians question the wisdom of aggressively treating children with medications."

As the *New York Times* brought these and other audacities to wider public attention, Biederman declined to be interviewed. He responded through e-mail: "My interests are solely in the advancement of medical treatment through rigorous and objective study." Harvard and Mass General apparently agreed. Although Biederman became the public face of conflict of interest in psychiatry, and many colleagues felt he, Wilens, and Spencer should be fired for their actions, their prestige and grant-getting skills were too valuable for Harvard to let go. Their punishment: to refrain from working with drug companies for one year, and to undergo some ethics training.

JOE BIEDERMAN WAS but one of many pharma-subsidized ADHD researchers who churned out papers, delivered countless lectures, and refuted mounting evidence that millions of children were being misdiagnosed and improperly medicated for the disorder. Critics were threatening these doctors' livelihoods. And, even more than Biederman, no one's livelihood depended on ADHD's success more than Russell Barkley.

Barkley, first at the University of Massachusetts Medical School and then at the Medical University of South Carolina, was a one-man ADHD public-relations powerhouse. He not only authored scores of journal papers related to attention disorders, but also wrote and published his own newsletter to lend his voice to various controversies.

His unrelenting message was that people with ADHD, and certainly unmedicated ADHD, were more likely to "drop out of school," "have few or no friends," "under-perform at work," "engage in antisocial activities," "experience teen pregnancy and sexually transmitted diseases," and "have more accidents & speed excessively." (These findings, many derived from Dr. Barkley's own research, were not necessarily false—but they were phrased and wielded to persuade doctors and parents to get any child even suspected of ADHD diagnosed and medicated, or face the consequences.) Dr. Barkley published several mass-market books on the subject, recorded videotapes, and wrote manuals and symptom checklists to help doctors diagnose the disorder.* He lectured to academics and parents in countries from Canada to Kenya, and whenever national television programs like *Good Morning America* and *60 Minutes* did a segment on ADHD, Russ Barkley was ready to oblige. He became the disorder's primary public voice.

Dr. Barkley's ties to drug companies were less front and center. Every year he accepted five- or six-figure sums for industry-sponsored work, accounting for around one-third of his income. But still, and quite movingly, that might not have been his most significant conflict. Barkley had a twin brother, Ron, whose alcohol abuse, traffic tickets, and general life struggles, Russ believed, resulted from ADHD. In 2006 Ron Barkley was killed in a single-car accident in upstate New York. He wasn't wearing a seat belt. Barkley so blamed the underlying disorder that his column about it for CHADD's magazine was titled "I Lost My Brother to ADHD." This was an awful tragedy, of course, and advocates for awareness of many diseases (cancer, diabetes, etc.) are motivated by personal connections. Then again, Barkley advertised himself and his work as purely scientific, while clearly more emotional matters lurked underneath. One of Barkley's colleagues, who asked not to be identified here because he didn't mean it cruelly, remembered: "Whenever I see Russ up there at a podium espousing all his stuff, I can't help but hear him saying, 'It's okay Mom, it's not our fault.'"

---

*Keith Conners remembers Barkley the businessman setting up a sales table at a psychiatry convention with one of the earliest credit-card swipers to accommodate customers short on cash.

Whenever someone questioned whether ADHD diagnoses in children were growing beyond reasonable bounds, Barkley struck back. One prominent case concerned Dr. Gretchen LeFever, a psychologist in the Virginia Beach area who in the mid-1990s began seeing such droves of elementary school kids taking Ritalin that she decided to examine hard-and-fast school records to assess the real rate. It was a shocking 15 percent. (Even some drug companies, which vastly overestimated the need for stimulants, admitted that this far exceeded what could be considered justifiable.) The finding was reported on *CBS Evening News*, CNN, PBS, NPR, and newspapers across the country. Dr. Barkley was often invited to respond. He countered to one newspaper: "Clinical professionals who have experience with this disorder well know that it's not overdiagnosed or overtreated. But that hasn't stopped the press and some social critics from leveling those charges and getting away with it." In 2002, with LeFever and other infidels in mind, Barkley gathered dozens of fellow doctors in the field to publish an "International Consensus Statement on ADHD," which really just presented the consensus of folks who agreed with him. The statement yet again spelled out the connection between childhood ADHD and horrible outcomes, claimed that half of children with the disorder nationally were going untreated, and took a slap at the news media for "purveying the propaganda of some social critics and fringe doctors."

Not long after Dr. LeFever received a significant grant from the US Centers for Disease Control to join a federal study of diagnosis rates in three American communities, an anonymous letter was delivered to her employer, Eastern Virginia Medical School. It accused Dr. LeFever of academic fraud: intentionally inflating her ADHD statistics, using misleading survey language and violating federal protocol regarding research of children. Even though the letter was unsigned, and could very well have been planted by someone with a pro-ADHD agenda, her research was immediately suspended, her computers were seized, and she was placed on administrative leave, providing fodder for local newspaper told-you-sos in which Barkley was, naturally, quoted. "The biggest problem [with ADHD] is under identification and very erratic access to care," he said. "It's not overmedication." Ultimately, a formal investigation into LeFever's research did find a few errors—but they stopped well short of fraud, were described as minor, and, most important here, did not in any way affect the truth of her finding that 15 percent of local children were on ADHD drugs.

Nonetheless, LeFever's career was derailed, as was her willingness to take on the growing ADHD industrial complex. Everyone in the field watched, some in delight and others in horror, the repercussions of those who dared to do so. These conspiracy theories got out of hand. In 2006, Nadine Lambert, a prominent mental health researcher whose studies claimed that ADHD medication led to higher rates of tobacco and cocaine dependence, was killed in California when a truck careened into her car. Some people, including LeFever, feared it was no accident. This was fantastically untrue, as Berkeley police quickly determined that the truck's brakes had failed going down a hill. But the tinge remained among critics of the ADHD industry: Watch your back.

PSYCHIATRY JOURNALS TEEMED with more than a thousand studies on ADHD conducted by Biederman, Barkley, and other pharma-sponsored scientists. The Food and Drug Administration relied upon them when green-lighting medications as safe and effective. Their findings served as the backbone for the lectures that drug companies' key opinion leaders delivered on world tours. The whirlwind created a self-affirming circle of science, one that quashed all dissent. When anyone expressed concern about the path ADHD was on, supporters would always reply: "This is the most studied disorder in the history of child psychiatry," as if volume meant veracity.

Yet the most important pages in psychiatric journals were not the black-and-white papers by Biederman et al. They were the resplendent, full-color advertisements derived from those studies' purported findings. The ads could go way past boring phrases like "symptom control," and provide lightning-bolt messages that married words and pictures to tell doctors, from subliminally to quite literally, that they should— *must*—prescribe stimulants to any kid with a trace of ADHD. Especially if her grades needed a boost.

Adderall XR "Improves Academic Performance," one Shire ad announced, adding that studies had shown that ADHD kids who took it "completed 26 more math problems correctly," whatever that meant. A Concerta ad declared that children on it "improved their math scores nearly one full grade." (Just in case doctors didn't quite catch on, Concerta adopted the slogan "From ABC to GPA.") This math-test improvement might well have been true—but what went unmentioned is that the drugs can have these effects in anyone, not just children with ADHD. This was not only obvious but also had been proven in 1978, thanks to an ingenious maneuver by Judy Rapoport, the young doctor at the National Institute of Mental Health who was at the same time warning, unsuccessfully, that the reformulation of minimal brain dysfunction into attention deficit disorder in the 1980 DSM would cause rampant overdiagnosis. Testing amphetamines' effects on non-ADHD children had always been dismissed by research ethics boards, as having a kid take amphetamine without a medical need felt a little Frankenstein. But Rapoport got around that: She used her own two sons, and twelve other boys of friends in the mental health field who knew the experiment was important, if only to make a point. Each child got a typical dose of Dexedrine. Unsurprisingly, the children hunkered down and performed better on cognitive tests, and the Conners Scale, just like MBD kids.

Adderall and Ritalin could buzz the brains of just about any mammal—but by federal law, drugs then and now can be marketed only to treat a recognized medical condition. So companies positioned their stimulants as effective "for children with ADHD," which of course they were. They did more than boost a kid's GPA, the ad blitz to doctors claimed. They would also:

- Improve personal skills: "CONCERTA helped improve interactions between adolescent patients and their parents," one ad said. Meanwhile, "ADDERALL XR Enhances Social Functioning." Not to be outdone, one ad for Strattera, a new ADHD medication from Eli Lilly, cooed: "What can a child with ADHD gain? Control and Confidence."

- Avert accidents: A Strattera ad showed a child about to skateboard across the street. It asked: "When could ADHD symptoms affect your patients?"

• Give parents peace of mind: Concerta, one ad exclaimed, brought "The Comfort of UNDENIABLE SAFETY."

• Give children a whole new life, by golly: Concerta, with ADHD barely even mentioned, would "allow your patients to experience life's successes every day."

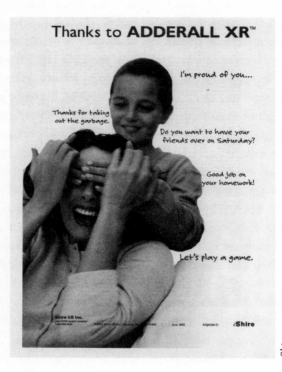

These claims weren't even the most shocking of all. That honor belonged to one of Shire's first Adderall XR ads in June 2002. In it, a mother was shown horsing around with her equally playful son. The headline read: "Thanks to ADDERALL XR, David's mom is learning a whole new language." That language included phrases like, "I'm Proud of You," "Good job on your homework!" "Let's play a game," and "Thanks for taking out the garbage." Adderall XR suddenly wasn't a medicine just for an ADHD child. It was for his mother, too, to make her child less of a pain, to provide her parental satisfaction of a job well done. Thirty years after Ritalin's ads said that the drug "helps the problem child become lovable again," the theme had returned—with the garbage taken out, no less.

Were the statements in these advertisements outright fabrications? No. They did derive from actual data collected by actual doctors in actual trials published in actual academic journals. And the fact that stimulants—known since Charles Bradley's first 1937 trials to calm the hyperactive and focus the distractible—helped many ADHD children concentrate on math tests and become easier to get along with should have surprised no one. Especially when the trials were purposefully conducted on children with the most severe levels of ADHD, so that the benefit would be more detectible. But the advertisements' underlying facts went through so many spin cycles of bias that they emerged barely recognizable.

Decades of research have shown that advertisements affect how and how often doctors prescribe medication to patients, and stimulants were no different. Told that Adderall and Concerta and other ADHD drugs could not just provide relief to a struggling child but also soothe his exasperated parents, doctors obliged like never before. The problem was that a growing portion of children diagnosed with ADHD probably didn't have the brain disorder for which the medications were designed. In 2000, when Concerta took on Adderall, the entire ADHD industry, from doctors to drug companies, agreed and even put in their presentations that the disorder affected about 3 to 5 percent of the child population. Just seven years later, the CDC reported that 10 percent of kids were getting diagnosed by the time they left high school—at least twice that, with no signs of slowing down.

TO ONE COMPANY, print advertisements to doctors were still too dull. Bubbly as the pages could be, they just sat there, hoping the doctor would read them. The field needed something better. Bouncier. And in 2001, Keith Conners and a roomful of other doctors found out exactly what that was.

The meeting had been like so many others. Celltech, a small drug company itching to get into the ADHD market, was developing a slightly tweaked form of Ritalin called Metadate. The firm hired Conners to oversee some of the clinical trials to show how Metadate could control children's ADHD symptoms all the way up to dinnertime, and then gathered all of its medical consultants in a hotel to determine strategy. Conners stood at the lectern to address the group and presented just how the Metadate did, in fact, perform as planned. He sat down and listened to some other speakers.

But then the room grew silent. The lights dimmed. For a few eerie seconds, the audience wondered what was going on.

Suddenly, a man burst through the door and started running around the room. He was in a superhero suit—muscle-bulging blue spandex with red-trimmed boots, a yellow belt, and Metadate's logo emblazoned on his chest. A clown might as well have bounced into a children's birthday party. The doctors sat dumbfounded as Metaman darted from table to table. He finished his act and left.

Conners shrugged and got on with the meeting, having no idea that Metaman was about to change the world of ADHD forever.

Chapter 9

THERE'S SOMETHING
THEY KNOW ABOUT US

Four million readers of *Ladies' Home Journal* flipped through their August 2001 issue, the one with Caroline Kennedy on the cover, to learn what they didn't know they wanted. Articles showed them how to become Queen of the Cookout, how to soothe backaches, and how to use—who knew?—teabags to fill cracks in fingernails. Advertisements trumpeted the wonders of Johnson's Baby Powder, Ziploc bags, and Clorox. But an ad on page 119 was different. A smiling mother draped her loving arms around her freckled eleven-year-old son. She was relieved. He was happy, ready for the upcoming school year. Next to them rang the headline, ONE DOSE COVERS HIS ADHD FOR THE WHOLE SCHOOL DAY. Right above that: INTRODUCING METADATE CD CAPSULES.

This was the first advertisement for an ADHD medication in a consumer magazine—one that shattered the long-understood agreement not to market controlled substances directly to the general public. Way back in 1972, in direct response to drug (and particularly amphetamine) abuse, the United Nations' Convention on Psychotropic Substances had concluded that hawking such medicines to average consumers, rather than only doctors in journals and the like, imperiled public safety. Judicious physicians could see the risks of a drug, the logic went; patients would only crave its benefits. More than 150 countries signed on, including, notably, the rather capitalistic United States. While consumers could certainly benefit from learning the proper medicinal benefits of such products—just as they might, say, Tylenol—these products were more addictive and dangerous than ads could possibly warn, and few even in Big Pharma disagreed.

Drug companies still strived to get around such inconveniences as international consensus by marketing to families more surreptitiously. A perfect example came in 1993, when Sue and Michael Parry, parents of three boys outside Seattle, were summoned to their elementary school to talk about their third-grade son, Andy. Andy's teacher told the Parrys, "unless we get Andy diagnosed and medicated, he probably won't ever do very well in his life." Ritalin was no big deal, the teacher said: Her two twins took the drug, too. The school psychologist handed Mrs. Parry a pamphlet called "ADHD—Attention Deficit-Hyperactivity Disorder and Learning Disabilities—Booklet for Parents." It was written by Larry B. Silver, MD. The passage on medication read:

> *Parents should be aware that these medicines do not "drug" or "alter" the brain of the child. They make the child "normal."*

This claim was ludicrous, a shameful attempt to swing parents into medicating their kids. Whatever their benefits and risks, Ritalin and other ADHD medications unquestionably do drug the brain (i.e., have some sort of chemical enter its mix) and then alter it (provide some sort of, presumably positive, metabolic change). And they do not, then or now, make the child "normal," whatever that might mean. They can help a severely frenetic youngster calm down, be more attentive, and learn, a noble service in many circumstances, but they do not in and of themselves magically turn him into the typical child. But parents don't want to hear that; they want assurance that they're doing a fantastic and safe thing for their child. The Parrys were among them. Heartened by that passage, Andy's parents acquiesced and put him on Ritalin to start fourth grade. He stayed on it for two years—until October 1995, when Mrs. Parry turned on PBS and the *Frontline* exposé on how Ciba-Geigy had infiltrated CHADD and other information outlets to sell more Ritalin.

"Michael! Come here!" Sue cried to her husband in the next room. "You have to see this!"

They watched the rest in horror. When the program ended, Mrs. Parry went to the family desk and started rifling through drawers. She found it—the ADHD pamphlet the school psychologist had handed her a few years before, the one that said Ritalin wouldn't alter Andy's brain, only make him normal. She flipped to the back, and there it was, hiding at the bottom: the logo of Ciba-Geigy.

YES, THE US Food and Drug Administration had, in the late 1990s, loosened some regulations to allow the advertising of relatively benign prescription medications to treat, for example, allergies and asthma. And Congress had never passed explicit legislation to formalize the United Nations agreement on controlled substances as law of the land. But nobody had broken the functional understanding before Celltech Pharma pushed Metadate through the door believed to be latched shut.

The US Drug Enforcement Administration wrote a scathing letter to Celltech officials complaining about the *Ladies' Home Journal* advertisement. Celltech ignored it. The American Medical Association warned that consumers would pressure physicians for unwarranted prescriptions. Celltech kept going. Newspapers and television profiled the alarm over Metadate's ad, along with the response of the notoriously underpowered FDA: No federal law expressly forbade the public marketing of controlled substances, so the government's hands were tied.*

Celltech aggressively targeted mothers with two-page spreads in *Good Housekeeping* and more. Their ads got less subtle by the month, ultimately peaking with the most crude maneuver of all: the launch of Metaman. The determined cartoon superhero declared, "Kids, I'll be there when you need me!" Celltech went so far as to produce five-inch Metaman plastic action figures that sales representatives handed to doctors so that the toys could sit on their desks, preferably played with by children while parents discussed treatment options. (Metamen were not to be taken home, Celltech corporate headquarters said; that would be inappropriate.) Celltech wasn't content with just appealing to parents. It wanted the children, too.

Executives at Shire, whose Adderall had zoomed well into nine figures in sales, and ALZA, which had just about bet its entire future on

---

*Three weeks later came the attacks of September 11, after which government and media focused on other matters.

Concerta, were not going to sit back and watch a piddly upstart like Metadate sneak in and grab what was becoming a $1 billion ADHD market—one that was expected to double every three to five years. Their marketing departments scurried to produce their own direct-to-consumer campaigns. Before long, most women's magazines teemed with advertisements for Adderall, Concerta, Metadate, and others. *Family Circle, Good Housekeeping, Ladies' Home Journal, Parenting,* and *Redbook* had zero pages of ADHD medication ads in 2000; four years later, they had ninety, more than one per issue. The ads leapt onto television, too, always cooing, "Ask your doctor whether [insert drug name here] is right for your child." Their finely tuned messages evolved into misrepresentations, overstatements, and outright lies about what ADHD was and what stimulants did—up to and including Adderall XR's "Thanks for taking out the garbage."

More than any study or news article ever had before, these unprecedented public advertisements for ADHD medications confirmed the disorder as a true consumer-culture phenomenon, one set only to grow even more. Internet sites devoted to the condition, even those with responsible, relatively balanced content, were behind the screens being algorithmically populated with flashing and click-here-for-more-information drug marketing. Just like the Kool-Aid man, the parched and jolly icon appearing in the same magazines and on the same televisions, ADHD ads crashed through a wall and into America's living rooms, informing people just how thirsty they were.

WHILE ADVERTISERS TREAT young men as hedonists howling for sleek cars and beer, mothers have traditionally presented a far different audience—their priorities tend to take a backseat, literally, in sensible suburban minivans, buckled and safe. Mothers want their children's food to be nutritious, their toys wholesome, their well-being secured by mom's knowing oversight. To be sure, women in ads at the turn of the millennium had certainly evolved from the 1950s' happily vacuuming homemakers. They were bankers, lawyers, systems analysts. But that was actually the point. Women were becoming work-and-kids multitaskers in droves, darting between responsibilities whose constant challenges needed quicker and easier solutions.

As this shift occurred, little challenged mothers more than their kids' inability to calm down and stay on task—which a steady stream of newspaper, magazine, and television features portrayed as pure ADHD that must be medicated, lest chaos rule. (Recall *Time*'s 1998 Ritalin cover with the headline "Scientists Said Last Week That It Works.") But even such media reports were less effective than direct advertising would be. For a long time, the best a drug company could do was market the *condition* and hope that sales of its antidote would follow. While developing Concerta, ALZA ran sixty-second cable-television ads on A&E and the Discovery Channel that described the seriousness of ADHD itself; the spots couldn't mention Concerta by name, per the UN ban. But they did tell parents to "talk to your doctor" about treatment options for their children, and to phone a company's toll-free number for more information.

"Make the call that might make the difference," the voice-over said.

This subtlety was rendered downright quaint after Metaman flew into town and unleashed huge marketing opportunities. Recognizing Concerta's blockbuster potential, Johnson & Johnson, the pharmaceutical behemoth, acquired ALZA in May 2001 for $10.5 billion. Its subsequent magazine ads almost flaunted drug companies' newfound freedom. One had a mother gazing proudly at her smiling son and saying: "Better test scores at school, more chores done at home, an independence I try to encourage, a smile I can always count on." Every one of those promises was misleading or simply baseless. Tempering hyperactivity and impulsivity did lead to better self-esteem, some (often pharma-subsidized) studies suggested, but others found that the meds could diminish a kid's exuberance and sense of play, too, undercutting the "smile" promise. Research had shown that less-distractible children did answer more math questions correctly per minute, but that was about all; whether that extended to overall grades, in math or anywhere else, was unknown. Absolutely no studies had indicated any increase in "independence"—or, for that matter, dishwashers emptied. But it all sure sounded delightful to parents. In another print ad,

Concerta transformed a baseball-playing boy who "Can't find glove again," "picks dandelions in outfield," and "annoys teammates" to one who "listens to coach," "focuses during batting practice," and gets "ice cream party with team." The drugs weren't methylphenidate, but pixie dust.

Playing catch-up through Adderall XR, in 2002, Shire targeted fathers. An impish boy, cap turned backward and baseball mitt in hand, declared, "Already Done with my Homework Dad!"—the capital letters in large type cleverly spelling out A, D, H, and D. No study had shown that kids finished homework faster on Adderall XR, but so what? Your boy would be freed to play catch, thanks to these pills. Shire played off Concerta's newness by claiming that Adderall XR "shares a 60-year legacy of safety and clinical experience," a stunning assertion given that Adderall XR was but a year old; the line was based off the product's distant and quite different ancestor, Benzedrine. "Talk to your doctor today," the ad told Dad, "to see if . . . Adderall XR can add new meaning to your child's life."

These ads got even worse. Moving back to mothers, a 2004 Shire ad pictured one hugging her smiling, blond boy, who held a sheet of paper on which was written: B+. "Finally! Schoolwork that matches his intelligence," she exclaimed. In September 2005, Shire paid *People* hundreds of thousands of dollars to wrap that ad around the cover of the magazine, so it was the first thing subscribers would see. Just as school began, mothers were thereby on notice that Adderall XR unlocked children's potential. The messaging was brilliant—what mother thinks her darling, brilliant child's report card "matches his intelligence"? *"He's as smart as you think,"* the ad essentially said, *"and this pill will bring it out for everyone to see."*

Adderall and Concerta became the ADHD industry's Coke and Pepsi, frantically fighting for every scrap of market share. Predictably, the arena did include some Mountain Dew upstarts who tried to nudge themselves into the mix. One of them, a form of Ritalin called Methylin, actually reified the soft-drink analogy—it launched a grape-flavored liquid version engineered to attract fussy kids who didn't like pills. "It's the taste that got his attention," one ad read. One boy spoke straight to his mom: "Give me the grape!"

ADDERALL, CONCERTA, AND other ADHD medications could have sold plenty, made hundreds of millions and fueled their companies' stock value, without distorting what ADHD was and manipulating parents' universal fear for their children's futures. Like so much dangerous marketing, the ads were distantly drawn from truth; for a good majority of severely hyperactive and distractible children, the pills then and now can do wonders—a great service to those families, and something from which the drugs' developers have every right to profit. Concerta and Adderall XR were great advances, removing the embarrassment some kids felt while lining up at the nurse's office. There's nothing inherently wrong with, even, producing a liquid version that children don't detest.

But ADHD medications were hawked like any other consumer product when the companies must have known that they were anything but. Adderall produced intelligence-matching schoolwork as much as Klondike bars whisked you to the Yukon. Concerta was not iced tea, no matter how many smiles it brought to the family. One Concerta ad went so far as to say that it "Reduces conflict with parents." The foot-note to substantiate the claim read: "data on file."

Pushing pills on families naturally meant minimizing and even concealing the risks of what were, lest anyone remember, serious and powerful medications. The FDA mandates that all prescription drug marketing, whether to doctors or consumers, acknowledge the most common side effects—yet, unfortunately, also allows these to be com-municated in type so small and language so oblique that it would be laughable if not so manipulative. ADHD drugs were no different, with their downsides buried in boilerplate text usually only on the flip side of the otherwise glowing ads. Mood swings and anxiety were euphemized as "emotional lability," a term that—perhaps correct in the medical vernacular—conveniently meant nothing to most parents. The terms "hallucinations" or "skin-crawling" did not appear, nor were they required to; however alarming and vital for parents to watch out for, these risks weren't frequent enough to make the "most common" list. Very few ads mentioned in anything but the most minuscule print that Adderall and Concerta, one an amphetamine and the other all but, had the potential for abuse, particularly among kids of high school age.

While almost all other developed nations immediately closed the loop-hole that Metadate had exploited—expressly banning direct-to-consumer advertising of controlled substances, usually through legislation—the United States sat back and let the market take over.* That market behaved exactly as planned: Parents went to their doctors to talk about ADHD and what medications could do for their kids. Of course, diagnoses and prescriptions soared.

In the ten years after Metadate's ads debuted, the number of Ameri-can children on ADHD medication approached two million. Profits became immense for all. Shire's revenue, which crossed the $1 billion mark in 2002 as Adderall XR launched, in only five years tripled past $3 billion. Concerta similarly boosted Johnson & Johnson's balance sheets. Doctors could barely keep up with parents' demand for stimu-

---

*To this day, the United States is one of only two developed nations that allows adver-tising of ADHD medications to the general public. The other is New Zealand, but the practice is rendered unprofitable there by the state-run health care system.

lants. Some communities' drugstores began running out of the medications, harming children who legitimately needed them.

For parents unconvinced by ads' positive images, Shire and Johnson & Johnson used scare tactics. All the money the drug companies had given Joseph Biederman, Russell Barkley, and other researchers to expose the consequences of ADHD—particularly *unmedicated* ADHD—paid off here. One of Shire's Adderall XR Web pages warned parents that ADHD kids were at "high risk for repeating a grade or dropping out." Another said that many children with ADHD can also have conduct disorder, "a condition linked with bullying, physical cruelty, use of weapons and other behaviors that can put them in trouble with the law." Yet another reported that adolescents with ADHD who didn't take medication regularly had four times as many serious injuries and three times as many car accidents. "However," it went on, "ADHD may be successfully treated. Today's ADHD medications, like ADDERALL XR, have come a long way in providing better symptom control."

It stands to reason that being impulsive can lead to injuries, and that distractibility doesn't make for great driving. But there was one problem: The implication that Adderall XR's "symptom control" would lower the risks for injuries or accidents was by no means supported by science. As for Shire's invoking the grim consequences of conduct disorder— the American Psychiatric Association's official term for chronic, violent, antiauthority aggression—Adderall XR had not only never been shown to address those behaviors, the company hadn't even looked into them. Nonetheless, parents got the message: Give your child Adderall or else he could become a car-crashing, felonious psychopath.

By this point, even the FDA had seen enough. Shire and Johnson & Johnson weren't the only companies flouting the agency's already looser rules—Eli Lilly also suggested that Strattera would deter adolescent substance abuse and sexually transmitted diseases. Novartis, maker of Focalin, another form of Ritalin, made similar claims. Alliant, while focusing on how its grape-flavored liquid Methylin would appeal to kids, not only overstated the medicine's clinical effects but went on to declare that 83 percent of children had liked the taste. A clinical study proved it! Unfortunately, the ad did not mention that kids who had answered "unsure" they liked the taste were, alas, counted as if they did.

The FDA sent official "Warning Letters" to each of these companies saying to defend their claims or remove the ads. So the companies removed the ads, knowing that they had already worked as designed. No fines, no meaningful reprimands, no public acknowledgment that they had misrepresented anything. The CEO of Shire, Angus Russell, was later asked by a reporter to comment on his company's third warning letter for false and misleading marketing of its ADHD medications. He shrugged that such inconveniences were merely the cost of doing business: "We are a very regulated industry," he said, "and it is becoming normal practice that from time to time companies of our size or bigger have inquiries from the government."

Everyone in the ADHD business had seen the effectiveness of merely frightening parents into going to the doctor and medicating their kids, FDA or not. Groups beyond Big Pharma, even those with less obvious agendas, engaged in the same fearmongering. The worst example was an advertisement that was so galling, so deplorable, that high-level executives nixed it just before it reached the newspapers, magazines, and even billboards for which it had been designed. But the mock-ups remain, proof of what some people would do to cash in on ADHD.

The ad presented a piece of notebook paper, a ransom note, scrawled with a message.

> We are in possession of your son. We are making him squirm + fidget until he is a detriment to himself + those around him. Ignore this + your kid will pay.
>
> ADHD

The ad was commissioned not by Shire or Johnson & Johnson. No drug company at all. It came from doctors at New York University's Child Study Center—trying to get more patients, squeezing for their spot at the ADHD trough.

GIVE THE ADHD sales force credit: They knew their market. They knew that if mothers were told that their cubs were in harm's way, they would do anything to avert it, driving them to doctors and drugstores alike. A little pill could turn their struggling, difficult kid's grades into A's. (Or, Shire's ad hedged, perhaps a B+.) And with insurance, a year of medication cost less than a few hours of tutoring.

Other costs, however, were more hidden.

The Parber family, back in Haverford, had every reason to believe that they had addressed Kristin's problems. She had ADHD; thank goodness they'd caught it early. Her medicine would calm her down, help her focus, and improve her grades, raising the curtain on her sunny future. The psychiatrist said so. Even if the Parbers had never seen one Adderall or Concerta ad, drug-company marketing had so seduced their community that the point, if not the pills, had all but entered the town's water supply.

As for Jamison Monroe, the boy got what he wanted, too. He had faked ADHD to his parents, beguiled his doctor, and gotten regular supplies of Adderall. This took place in 1995, years before Big Pharma's advertising offensive. Adderall was barely known at the time. But the drugs were still amphetamines. Eventually, that fact became all too clear.

PART THREE

Chapter 10

HIGHER AND HIGHER

Oh, he had it all right.

Within weeks of duping his doctor into prescribing Adderall, Jamison's grades rose steadily through Christmas—particularly that D in biology, now hoisted to a B and heading higher. So, clearly, as far as his parents were concerned, what had been holding back their brilliant son for those horrible opening months of high school was his attention deficit hyperactivity disorder. Poor kid! Thank goodness they'd intervened. With a simple Adderall to correct his faulty brain chemistry, Jamison's five hours of homework a night, sandwiched between football practice and a few hours' sleep, became a breeze. The little blue tablets changed everything, for everyone.

Just like his primary secret—not having ADHD in the first place—Jamison kept Adderall's side effects to himself. Twenty minutes after taking a pill the back of his neck would begin to tingle, before the feeling washed down his body and through his arms. He got horribly dehydrated, particularly in the spring when he played on the St. John's baseball team in Houston's witheringly hot afternoons. So as sophomore year began, he gave up sports and started taking the pills only on the nights he needed to cram. If he had a test on Friday, he could take two the day before, stay up all night, and then pop one in the morning to stave off the crash. For those few precious hours, Adderall animated him like a hand in a sock puppet.

No one around Jamison—his parents, his teachers, even his friends—suspected a thing. His grades merely rose back to their rightful level; a teenager taking amphetamines merely to tackle schoolwork never occurred to anyone. A chronic achiever like Jamison Monroe didn't need to do that, certainly. For him to depend on anything but that brain, rather than a pill that altered it, was simply inconceivable. Amphetamine was abused by speed freaks for the high. But by high school kids for A's? Not a chance.

But there was a chance, one that had been dramatized more than a decade before on one of the most popular sitcoms of the 1980s, *Family Ties*. In a 1983 episode, the show's gifted, straight-laced Harding High brainiac, Alex P. Keaton, played by the breakout star Michael J. Fox, is facing his senior year's fall papers and midterms—his last grades to grace his already overstuffed applications to Harvard and Princeton. Alex coerces his sister, Mallory, to get some of her friend Effie's diet pills (at that time, Dexedrine) so he can work longer and harder. "I'm in trouble," he tells her. "I've got more work to do this week than even I can manage." The pills deliver A's on two papers, a 92 on his economics test, and, this being a comedy, the runneth-over zeal to clean out his neighbor's garage and install an underground sprinkler system in the Keaton backyard. But Alex eventually gets so hopped up on the stuff that his father figures out what's going on, confronts him, and makes him throw the amphetamines in the garbage.

"Dad, they worked! They helped me!" Alex explains. "I've gotten more done this week than I ever thought possible! You gotta admit it, Dad, the stuff works."

"I know what it does!" Mr. Keaton replies. "I took them myself when I was in school!"*

The true lesson arrives the following morning when Alex, his brain obliterated from a week of wiredness, oversleeps and misses a crucial final exam. He maniacally rummages through his trash can to find his pills before slumping away, exhausted, realizing that his plans had boomeranged on him.

"I thought I could handle it," Alex says dejectedly.

"You know how you feel right now?" his mother warns. "Don't ever forget it."

---

*The author of the episode (called "Speed Trap"), Michael Weithorn, had drawn on his own experience at Swarthmore College a few years before, when he bummed a few Dexedrines off a female friend to get through an exam in, of all things, child psychology. "The feeling stuck with me," he recalled, "this feeling of omnipotence."

The credits ran with all in the Keaton house back to normal. But in real life, a teenager's budding drug problem doesn't resolve in twenty-four minutes.

THE MONROES RAISED their glasses to the new couple's happiness. When Jamison attended the wedding of his older sister, Leslie, the summer after his freshman year, he tipped back a champagne flute and enjoyed a strange new feeling. This wasn't his first drop of alcohol—he'd had a few sips of beer over the years, maybe a taste of Mom's wine—but this stuff, now, slipped down his gullet with sweet, bubbly ease. The first glass untensed his body, the second made jokes funnier and bridesmaids curvier. It kept coming, on silver trays from waiters who needed no ID. Before long he'd had five, maybe six, chased with a few glasses of white wine. Yes, he wound up in the bathroom puking his brains out. But he awoke the next morning wanting to do it again.

Champagne was too expensive, of course, so Jamison and three buddies less academic—but far more fun—began heading on weekends to liquor stores for twelve-can boxes of Budweiser. The cashier didn't care that these were clearly high school teens; he asked for their driver's licenses only to satisfy the security cameras. They'd drive to the employee parking lot of River Oaks Country Club, go behind the trees, and get blitzed, first on weekends and then, as the routine ripened, after school. The least drunk would swerve them all home. Scott, Cameron, and Peter would take hours to sober up, sometimes all night. But Jamison had a secret he didn't tell even them. His tried and trusted Adderall—his psychiatrist of course kept prescribing it for his ongoing ADHD—perked him up for three-hour study sessions. Any hangover was solved with another pill. And so the cycle began, Bud for fun and Adderall for A's.

The twelve-packs grew to eighteen and then twenty-four. By the end of sophomore year they became Jack Daniel's and Coca-Cola. Then came the last day of classes, an event all but designed for kids to ditch school and goof off before studying for finals. Jamison and Peter bolted after first period and took Cameron's wheels to McDonald's, not just for the cheeseburgers, but also the cups, lids, and straws to disguise their Jack and Coke from any curious cops. By noon Peter was retching on a curb outside the house of a very disapproving old lady who, when she came out to upbraid the delinquents, watched the white car screech away, leaving only vomit and skid marks. The boys howled as they made their way back to school with one last, hilariously brilliant plan. Their English teacher, Mrs. Morse, was away for the week. Maybe the final exam was in her office.

The door was unlocked—*yes!*—and Jamison found the final in her left-hand desk drawer. Peter gave him a piece of paper to frantically copy down the questions and answers. Then they heard footsteps. Jamison threw everything back in the drawer and they got the hell out of there. Oh well. They were ambling down the hall disappointed yet entertained by the caper, when Peter put his hand in his pocket, found nothing, and froze.

"Holy shit," he said.

"What?" Jamison replied.

"That piece of paper I gave you?"

"Yeah?"

"That was my prom ticket."

Peter's name, Jamison's handwriting. They went back to retrieve it but those footsteps had belonged to a teacher who, sensing trouble, locked Mrs. Morse's office just in case. When she watched from down the hall as the boys jerked the doorknob with increasing and inebriated panic, the jig was up. All three boys never took Mrs. Morse's final or any other. They were immediately expelled from St. John's.

But Jamison's golden reputation—no one knew about his heavy drinking and Adderall abuse—preceded him into the headmaster's office. As Jamison and his mortified parents learned about the punishment, the man almost apologized that a fate this harsh had befallen a kid as smart and good as Jamison Monroe. He was a fine student, after all, with an inner character no doubt hijacked by his more mischievous friends. The headmaster promised to put in a good word with any other school the family wanted to consider. That became Episcopal High, the more laid-back school Jamison had wanted all along. Episcopal was told everything about Jamison's incident and still admitted him gladly. They'd wanted him all along, too.

Jamison made sure to camouflage his drinking better as a junior and senior. Adderall made this misdirection possible—it countered not just the effects of alcohol, but also the lethargy from the marijuana he began to enjoy. But even amphetamine couldn't keep his grades up. His dwindling attempts to study found the pills powerless to prop up his eyes and clear his muddied mind. Jamison's inner smarts still got him a B average at Episcopal, but any hopes for Harvard, onto which his parents held far longer than he did, gradually dissipated.

Because he'd scored a respectable 1320 out of 1600 on the SAT, the University of Texas would admit Jamison if he went to its summer program and proved his worthiness with at least a B in, as fate would have it, biology—the subject that had started his Adderall use four years before. He fooled around all summer, blitzed and baked until the final, on which he needed to get a 98 to raise his D to a B. So for the final week he hunkered down and subsisted on Adderall and Subway turkey clubs. He got a 100. The highest grade in the class. He enrolled full-time at UT.

His relieved parents didn't know that their Jamison, on the outside academically reborn at a darned good university, by this point had baser goals. Texas's summer program had allowed prospective freshmen to rush fraternities, dangling before them fun and freedom that high school never could. Jamison needed no nudge. He chose Sigma Alpha Epsilon because he considered it Austin's most wild party house. Some brothers were just like him, careening through alcohol's down and Adderall's up.

Yet these guys had more experience, more tricks. Sure, they told the young pledge, swallowing a few of the 10-milligram blue pills gave you a buzz, maybe even a jolt. But dude—how about being *electrocuted*?

Jamison's pledge summer taught him a new and improved way to enjoy his Adderall: snorting it. His initiation was officially complete when, sitting in intro bio, he sensed an oncoming sneeze and grabbed one of his Subway white napkins. A split-second later his nose unloaded so furiously into it that he decided to behold just how much mucus had exploded out. He unfolded the napkin and had to choke back his laughter at the goo.

Not the volume. The color.

Blue!

*   *   *

THERE'S A REASON why people don't swallow cocaine. Doing so would force the drug to spend thirty or forty minutes in the gastrointestinal tract before being absorbed into the bloodstream and steadily delivered to the brain, only then causing levels of dopamine—a neurotransmitter that affects energy, cognition, and pleasure—to build up gradually. Sniffing cocaine into the sinus cavity, rather, cascades the brain with dopamine within minutes. The rush is far more intense, the difference between a Ford and a Ferrari.

Most experts agree that the effects of cocaine and stimulants, when snorted, can be remarkably similar, to the point that some call Adderall and Concerta "Diet Coke." It's unassailable that the vast majority of ADHD pills are used properly by people with legitimate medical need; however, when someone (say a grades-crazed, experimental teenager) chooses to grind them into a powder and snort it, it might as well be cocaine. As cocaine became more taboo after its Studio 54 and 1980s heydays, Ritalin and then Adderall became inviting—and as prescriptions soared, increasingly plentiful—alternatives for young people, who could easily score it from doctors or friends at school. These weren't the eight-year-olds in Omaha in 1970 trading pills out of their lunchboxes, figuring they were Tic Tacs. They were teenagers knowing what they wanted and getting it with remarkable ease.

Far beyond Alex P. Keaton, this trend was not exactly a secret. Some local newspapers around the country ran stories about high school students snorting ADHD drugs: a kid from Rockville, Maryland, saying that he did it so "I could do more work. I felt like going to class" (*Washington Post*); a fifteen-year-old boy in central North Carolina who supplied Ritalin to a dozen classmates who snorted it en masse (*Raleigh News & Observer*); and a student in Grand Rapids, Michigan, who got arrested for selling to friends who either snorted the medication or, for an even faster high, injected it (*Phoenix Gazette*). As always, so-called experts disputed these reports of misuse. Two prominent doctors in the *Archives of General Psychiatry* puffed: "There is no basis for such concerns. There is a nearly total absence of methylphenidate abuse reported in methylphenidate-treated children and adolescents in spite of its very widespread application." (This brilliantly sidestepped the point at hand—that these weren't legitimately ADHD kids abusing the pills, but those who got them illicitly.) When Congress held a hearing about the rising number of ADHD prescriptions, a doctor flatly told the committee: "Our experience has been that this [abuse] is not happening." This witness wasn't just some random physician or pharma shill. It was Dr. Richard K. Nakamura, the acting director of the National Institute of Mental Health.

One of the teenagers who apparently did not exist, Jamison Monroe, began placing a credit card over his Adderall pills and pressing down with his palm to crack them, crush them, and ultimately pulverize them into a silky-smooth powder. He would roll up a dollar bill, hold one nostril closed, and sniff it up his sinuses. An instant later he'd get a euphoric rush of clarity and confidence that gave him, he told friends, "a thousand brilliant ideas per second." Jamison's first semester at the University of Texas became a mood-modulating, kaleidoscopic haze of alcohol, Adderall, and Valium. Then came Thanksgiving break.

Back home in Houston, during a binge one night with his old Episcopal buddies, a siren blared and police lights blasted his rearview mirror. Jamison pulled over and failed all six sobriety tests, including simply reciting the alphabet. Five years since being a middle school valedictorian, Jamison Monroe couldn't even say his ABC's.

He was arrested, passed out in jail, and was ultimately bailed out by his parents the next day. A judge required him to be examined by a psychologist, who told the family that Jamison had three options: kill himself in a car accident, kill someone else in a car accident, or go to drug rehab.

As the Monroes walked to their car in the parking lot, Jim Monroe asked his son: "What are you going to do?"

"A and B don't sound so good," Jamison said. "So I guess I'll do C."

Jim Monroe broke down, right there in the parking lot. It was the first time Jamison ever saw him cry.

GRAY WOLF RANCH was like Club Med, only less rugged. Nestled on a wooded peninsula fifty miles north of Seattle, beside the rain forests of Olympic National Park, this was far from the junkie-filled, needle-strewn hellhole that "drug rehab" connoted. The main lodge featured more love seats and coffee tables than a Pottery Barn catalog. The land-scaped grounds teemed with vine maples, native rhododendrons, and sword ferns, all of them ensconcing other amenities like a full basket-ball court, a vegetable garden, and a lily and koi pond. Up to fourteen young men would blend their addiction therapy with outdoor fun to the point that the two became indistinguishable. "There's nothing like cresting a mountain or rafting a river to give you a sense of accomplish-ment and strength," Gray Wolf's promotional literature coos today. "That's what our one-of-a-kind outdoor education regime is all about: pushing your limits, building trust, and having fun along the way."

Between such outings, Jamison talked with therapists about his drug use, his motivations, his fears. He was allowed no alcohol, pot, cocaine, or any other drugs. Except his daily dose of Adderall—after all, his doctor said he had attention deficit hyperactivity disorder. To deny him his pills was to—as the saying went—deny a diabetic his insulin. Even though Adderall was the drug that introduced Jamison to substance abuse and was well known to be addictive, the staff gladly handed him 30 milligrams of amphetamine a day. Jamison rejoiced in their clueless-ness: "A way to get high in rehab!" he said to himself.

Jamison did make some strides at Gray Wolf Ranch, though, and emerged after three and a half months totally sober—except for his continued affinity for amphetamines. He returned to college rededi-cated. He avoided his old UT temptations by enrolling at the Univer-sity of St. Thomas in Houston, where his application essay detailed his bad decisions and pledged a renewed respect for education. Two years later, the kid had backed it up: he made the St. Thomas dean's list three of four semesters and posted a 3.8 grade point average. His parents exhaled; this was the true Jamison, the boy they had always expected.

What they didn't see, nobody did, was that Adderall had a lot to do with it—he was still using the pills to study. After Jamison transferred back to Texas to try to finish his government degree there, he returned to his old cycle of cramming with Adderall—his doctor back home never stopped prescribing it, despite his rehab history—and then com-ing down with alcohol or Xanax. He visited the student-health department to get extra pills, for free of course. Sometimes he road-tripped five hours across the border into Laredo, Mexico, to buy even more. By Christmas he had all but failed out of the University of Texas for a second time. He went back to rehab, his college days over for good.

On the plane out to a different treatment center, this one in southern California, Jamison spoke with one of his new therapists, who was chaperoning him.

"Are you prescribed any drugs?" the counselor asked.

"Yeah. Adderall," Jamison said.

"Do you want to stay on it?"

Jamison thought for a moment.

"No," he said. "I'm fucked up on that, too. It's kinda what got me started in the first place."

This time, therapists pushed Jamison to explore his Adderall use specifically—what originally led him to abuse it, the pressures he felt way back in that ninth-grade biology class. He talked about failing to please his father, going from a middle school genius to a high school nobody. Grabbing at anything to get back on that path to Harvard. Harvard! What a joke now. "After a while I felt like I was living someone else's life," he told a counselor. "Adderall helped me live someone else's life. And alcohol helped me escape that. No one ever asked me what I wanted—what I wanted to do."

Finally, someone did. Jamison's father, needing to consider and reconcile his own role in the circumstances that led Jamison to Adderall and other drugs, flew to California. He joined the therapy sessions and got to know not the son he had expected, but the one actually sitting with him—a flawed, confused yet still promising young man. Jim Monroe asked Jamison what *he* wanted to do.

Jamison hesitated. He didn't know how his father would react.

"I want to open my own treatment center," Jamison said.

The therapy taking hold, Jim Monroe responded: "Okay. Tell me more."

"I've been thinking about this for a really long time, Dad," Jamison said. "I want it to be for teenagers like I was when this all started. I want to help kids like me. I know I can. I've lived it."

Jamison's father listened to his boy for hours. He offered his support, both emotional and financial. He told Jamison that if he learned the ropes by working at some other treatment centers for a while, and developed a legitimate business plan, he would provide some seed money.

In March of 2006, Jamison left rehab for the final time with a purpose he had never felt before. He sold tickets at a southern California performing arts center until a local treatment facility hired him to help counsel a man addicted to Vicodin, a powerful prescription painkiller. Jamison wanted to help people addicted to Adderall, but this treatment center still didn't get it. When he moved up the ladder and began managing the medication window, distributing pills for nausea, cholesterol control, and other ailments, he asked the staff doctors if his giving pure amphetamine to so many substance abusers was a good idea. "Are you a physician?" one doctor snapped at Jamison. He returned to the window and kept handing out the Adderall.

Jamison spent his nights churning out a business plan for his own center, estimating $6 million in start-up costs. He phoned friends who might want to invest. His father also called his wealthier friends and business associates, people who remembered Jamison's smarts and trusted that he had finally turned the corner. They liked how Jamison wanted to provide adolescents not just the treatment and life skills so many programs offered, but formal mental health services too—all while coordinating with kids' high schools back home so they could keep up with their classes under the supervision of on-site teachers. As for the name, Jamison didn't want the cheesy innuendo used by many other southern California centers, like "Promises" or "A Better Tomorrow." It would be something that suggested not just calm, but commitment. Something like . . . Newport Academy.

By April 2008, Jamison had assembled enough investors to start building a girls-only program. He hired a pediatrician and psychiatrist, medical and clinical directors, six therapists and administrative staff—thirty-five people in all. He purchased a private home on three woodsy acres in Orange, midway between Los Angeles and San Diego, and retrofitted it with offices, individual and group therapy rooms, and bedrooms for six young women. He and his team traveled to industry trade shows and spread the word among drug-treatment therapists that Newport Academy would be ready to roll in spring 2009.

On May 12, its first patient arrived—a sixteen-year-old girl from southern California who was abusing tranquilizers and alcohol, and had begun cutting herself to amplify her pain. Another girl enrolled soon afterward. Newport Academy was officially open.

ONE WEEK LATER, a family landed at the Orange County airport and rented a black Chevy Suburban—father and mother in the front seat, daughter and her younger brother in the back. The girl was seventeen, on her way to Newport Academy to get off cocaine and vodka.

They stopped at a strip-mall pancake joint. The girl silently slathered her pancakes with syrup and butter, gobbled them up, went to the bathroom, and promptly vomited them into the toilet.

When they drove up Newport's long driveway, Jamison watched from his upstairs office. Mom and Dad got out first, opened the back door and took a good ten minutes to convince the girl to emerge from the backseat. The boy stayed in the car while his sister, down to ninety-five pounds and wearing a flowery dress purchased to make all this a little less ugly, finally got out and shuffled toward Newport's ivy-covered doorway.

An aide greeted them and led them into a courtyard to meet the founder and CEO of Newport Academy.

"Welcome to California," he said. "I'm Jamison."

The girl, head down, put out her limp hand and shook his without a word.

"What's your name?" he said.

It pained her to even utter it.

"Kristin," she said.

Chapter 11

LESS THAN

Kristin's future began at age nine. That's when fourth-graders nation-wide took standardized tests through which much of secondary education divined the "gifted" children and placed them on the tracks their inner genius deserved. Kristin could be one of those kids, her parents and school thought—assuming her Ritalin kept her ADHD in check and focused her on those test booklets. In April 2001, she joined the other Agnes Irwin girls in the examination room, proctor standing sentry.

She aced the math. Writing: average. Reading comprehension: disaster. Kristin didn't dart around so much or chatter as before, sure, yet her thoughts continued to wander. She still couldn't concentrate. But . . . she was on Ritalin, the focus drug. How could that be?

Kristin was one of the many children on whom Ritalin worked more on the outside than the inside. The medication helped temper the impulsivity everyone around her could see, but only heightened the anxiety they could not. Part of this was metabolic: For some kids, tweaking the transfer of chemicals in the brain only makes them depressed or anxious. Sometimes Ritalin brings the so-called zombie effect. The only way to find out how any kid will react is to try the drug and see what happens. About one in five kids have these or other negative reactions—loss of appetite, trouble falling asleep—enough that most of them go off the medications, no harm done. Most. But not all.

"Kristin's so smart—she's got a really high IQ," her teachers would tell her parents. "A lot of ADHD kids are like that. Give it a chance."

Kristin stayed on the Ritalin. She loved doing math at home with her dad, especially fractions, but struggled at anything requiring memorization: vocabulary words, presidents' names. *What's wrong with me?* Studying really hard for the state-capital quiz bred only worry. *What will Mom and Dad say?* (She failed it.) Fourth grade was the first in which she had a different teacher for every subject—so instead of her disappointing one teacher, now it was three or four. Her stress worsened by the week.

Appallingly, some children have heightened anxiety interpreted not as a side effect of medication, meaning the drug should be reconsidered, but a new condition needing additional treatment. Kristin was a textbook case. To those around her, indeed something else had to be at play—not *other than* ADHD, or a not-uncommon side effect of its medication, but *in addition* to it. Over the next few years, her psychiatrist prescribed Xanax for her anxiety and then Lexapro for depression.* Soon she was taking three pills every day. Three brain defects. Three boxes to check off proving that she was inferior. She spent the rest of elementary school and middle school feeling, as she later put it, "less than." A fraction herself.

KIDS TOLD THAT they had ADHD around this time could get a knowing smile of support through, of all people, Captain Underpants. The wildly popular book series, by Dav Pilkey, depicted the antics of George and Harold, two sixth-grade scamps who delighted in pestering, pranking, and altogether exasperating their clueless, hilariously named superiors. Pilkey wrote: "All of the 'experts' at Jerome Horwitz Elementary School had their opinions about George and Harold. Their guidance counselor, Mr. Rected, thought the boys suffered from ADD. The school psychologist, Miss Labler, diagnosed them with ADHD. And

---

*Unfortunately, Kristin was in good company. Diagnosing young children with several overlapping psychiatric conditions became de rigueur in the 2000s, resulting in what some call a "medication cascade." No doctor was more responsible for the trend than Joe Biederman up at Harvard, who evaluated dozens of drugs on behalf of his Big Pharma benefactors and almost invariably declared them safe and appropriate for children with multiple diagnoses like ADHD and bipolar disorder. Yet neither he nor anyone else ever tested the performance or risks of these drugs *in combination*—no pharmaceutical company would ever sponsor such a study, considering it too risky to their product's reputation.

their mean old principal, Mr. Krupp, thought they were just plain old B.A.D.! But if you ask me, George and Harold simply suffered from I.B.S.S. (Incredibly Boring School Syndrome)." What readers didn't know was that Pilkey believed he had been misdiagnosed as clinically hyperactive himself as a kid growing up in Cleveland in the mid-1970s, and later used his series as comic comeuppance. In a recent interview, Pilkey commented on the handling of difficult kids in increasingly inflexible classrooms: "You're putting a monkey in a cage," he said. "It upsets the monkey, so they say there's something wrong with the monkey. But some monkeys *should* be swinging from a tree."

Kristin's swinging was from one mood to the next. Her three morning pills only reminded her of what people didn't like about her, what they were trying to change. And like any middle schooler she already had her own list, primarily that puberty had skipped her locker; while boys ogled other girls' swelling chests, Kristin's remained so two-by-four flat that classmates called her "Carpenter's Dream." (They also noted that her nose was more curved than her chest.) Resenting her fate and seeking a new identity, Kristin decided to give her parents something to *really* dislike. She stopped caring about grades. She hung with friends who got their tongues pierced and had sex with boys. Kristin did neither of those, alas, but merely putting the thought in her parents' minds felt just as good.

One Friday night, before a seventh-grade dance, Kristin, her friend Heather, and four other girls raided the Parbers' liquor cabinet. The vodka made Kristin shiver in disgust. But as it settled in her stomach and then flushed through her body, she felt a warm, enveloping peace. A hug from inside. Within minutes she was laughing freely, her head dancing and her body wanting to follow suit. After a few more swigs for good measure, the girls bounced into a friend's car to the social. Kristin danced like never before, swinging and spinning beneath diamond-sky lights. Some kids just need a taste of success to find themselves. For this girl, it was a taste of Grey Goose.

"Oh my god, you take Ritalin?!?" Heather asked one night, her eyes shooting open. "Let's go!"

The house to themselves, the girls bounded upstairs to the medicine cabinet. Heather shook a pill from the bottle, took a Visa card from her purse, and began crushing it into a fine powder. She rolled a dollar bill into a makeshift straw. She leaned over the counter and snorted it.

"You wanna try?" Heather asked Kristin.

She didn't hesitate. Fuck Mom and Dad. A few deep sniffs later, two reputations changed forever. Ritalin became fun. And Kristin became cool. Few things boost a girl's popularity more than a steady supply of free blow.

Throughout eighth grade, vodka relaxed Kristin more than Xanax ever did. Her depression dissipated with every sniff of Ritalin. The two substances became Kristin's dials of self-regulation. Ritalin had another benefit, too: It kept her thin. Her appetite shriveled, except for chocolate. She binged on Klondike bars, alone, but simply barfed 'em up.

Kristin kept her substance abuse hidden from her parents. Innate intelligence kept her grades around the B level; her writing even improved. She was moody, yes, going from sullen to defiant and back, but the Parbers, like many parents would, chalked such episodes up to newly teenaged, hormone-raging melodrama. Maybe, they wondered, what Kristin needed was a new high school—a boarding school, where she could reset with new peers and away from family tension. Episcopal High School in Alexandria, Virginia, just outside of Washington, DC, fit perfectly; it had no grades lower than ninth, so everyone entered on the same level, knowing no one, fresh start for all. This appealed to Kristin, too. She loved the idea of living away from her parents.

Kristin's fresh start didn't last. All ninth-graders had to write an essay on what they would change about Episcopal—an odd assignment for kids only a few weeks into a new school—with the best ones to be delivered by the author in a whole-school assembly. Kristin wrote hers on how more than a few classmates kept Confederate flags in their dorm rooms. Teachers loved the essay and chose Kristin to read it to the student body. The kids loved it less. Some booed her. Others shunned her afterward. More than a few times, when Kristin opened her dorm room door, a massive, open Deer Park water container that had been leaned against it would fall over and spill gallons of water all over her floor. Even being a good athlete didn't help—Kristin made the varsity tennis team as a freshman but was begrudged for taking an upperclassman's spot.

With Episcopal an archetypal Ivy League feeder school, slews of kids took ADHD drugs. Administrators were smart enough not to allow the medications in dorm rooms; by 2005, at least some educators had read the articles so many doctors dismissed. Students had to drop their prescriptions at the infirmary and walk there every day for one dose at a time. Nurses would even watch them drink it down. Yet the girls developed another trick: They learned to "cheek" the pill, swooshing it above their back gums and then, when the coast was clear, drying it off and slipping it into their pocket. Kristin did this every day so she could snort the powder later. She twisted herself into knots of stress and shame. By eleventh grade she began using a safety pin to carve "FAT" into her thigh. She weighed ninety pounds.

Over Christmas break, on a ski trip zooming down a hill, Kristin fell so hard that the packed snow broke her nose and almost ripped it right off her face. So much for snorting Ritalin. But after extensive plastic surgery she discovered a whole new drug—the painkiller Vicodin. Doctors of the time prescribed Vicodin and its sibling, OxyContin, even more freely than Adderall, inexplicably ignoring its addictiveness. Kristin loved Vicodin just as much as Ritalin. She got however many she wanted, long after her face had healed and she returned to Episcopal. The one positive from plastic surgery was winding up with the perfect nose she'd always wanted. Yet kids joked that she'd fallen just to get the nose job. *Maybe she should have fallen on her chest*, they snickered. *Then she could get boobs!*

Kristin faked pain to get Vicodin. She cheeked her Ritalin to snort it. She lost all ability to self-regulate her moods, surviving entirely on uppers and downers. She slept through her SATs—twice. When she was caught drinking and got suspended for two weeks, she admitted her Ritalin abuse to her parents and doctor. Rather than heed her stupefyingly obvious addiction to methylphenidate, a doctor instead prescribed a new medication for Kristin's ADHD that Shire marketed as virtually abuse-proof. Daytrana delivered methylphenidate from a patch through the skin, similar to the nicotine swatches that helped people kick cigarettes. No snorting possible. But there were two problems. Kristin broke out in horrible, inexplicable rashes underneath the adhesive. And then, undeterred, she used several patches at once to get high.

Within a few weeks, sick of the rashes and needing her nasal Ritalin buzz, Kristin used cocaine before she got caught. Her parents yanked her out of Episcopal but had no interest in their drug-addicted daughter stay-ing home. She was going to rehab. The Parbers researched different resi-dential programs across the country, their specialties and styles, and got good vibes from a new one in southern California, Newport Academy.

JAMISON SHOOK KRISTIN's wilted hand before walking the Parbers upstairs to fill out paperwork. Kristin sat on a couch with an intake counselor to answer some questions. She said she'd been sober for ninety days, when she hadn't been sober for ninety hours. Had she ever done cocaine? *No.* Did she have an eating disorder? *Absolutely not!* From there Kristin was walked to Bedroom 1, where she watched the counselor search her suitcases for pills. And razor blades.

Less austere were Kristin's new surroundings. No grim hospital, Newport Academy's main, verdant hacienda sat beside a wooded hill with walking trails and a treehouse. Yet it did stop short of being one of the obscenely luxurious drug-treatment resorts popping up all over southern California, which promised the rich and famous a little detox in between tanning sessions. Newport had no world-renowned chef, not even a swimming pool. The comfort it provided merely eased the difficult work Jamison and his team expected.

Kristin was immediately taken off her Ritalin—and during her first extended sit-down with Jamison a few days later, he explained why. He also had grown up in a well-off, big-city suburb with demanding parents and schools. Although ten years older, he knew firsthand just how exhil-arating ADHD medications could be, how abusable they were, how they could cavort with alcohol and other drugs. He had felt the same academic pressure, the futility of meeting expectations. He told her that part of the satisfaction in using drugs was "to say 'fuck you' to my par-ents." Kristin laughed. After she told her own parallel story, Jamison told her, "You're me ten years ago." The connection was instant.

Although being labeled ADHD had shaped Kristin's self-image from a young age, and Adderall had been Jamison's first substance of abuse, neither has ever blamed ADHD drugs outright for landing them in rehab. Nor should they. The question of whether stimulants increase the risk of drug abuse has dogged ADHD researchers for decades.

Adderall and methylphenidate have always been among the most addictive substances in medicine, and they clearly open the door for some people, like Jamison, to reduce any aversion to other prescription pills (hence the term "gateway drug"). Then again, just as regrettably, it is not uncommon for people with serious but *untreated* ADHD to seek relief in anything from black-market Adderall to pot or painkillers (known as "self-medicating"). The many studies seeking to resolve this dichotomy are predictably mixed: Those sponsored by Big Pharma and proselytized by pro-medication advocates such as Joe Biederman and Russell Barkley consistently claim that stimulants protect people with ADHD from later drug abuse.* Other investigations by more neutral parties find little effect at all one way or the other. But even if the *aggregate* effect is zero, stimulants can still work on individual people differently and to varying degrees; perhaps they can dissuade a person from seeking other substances, yes, but also serve as a gateway drug to others, all with little forewarning of which path someone will take.†

Either way, do vast swaths of children have their ADHD diagnoses and drugs so badly backfire as they did with Jamison and Kristin? Of course not. If such horror stories were routine, America would already know. Weird as it may sound, stimulants are dangerous by being not dangerous *enough*—the drugs have found a sweet spot in which their advantages are more common and immediately obvious than their more latent risks, lulling all involved into complacency. The ADHD diagnosis itself has achieved a similar stasis. Enough kids benefit from their problems being given a name, and respect, that children harmed by the label or medications go undetected. Yet no one does studies on them.

"You don't understand—I have ADHD, I need to be on my pills," Kristin told her counselor, a young woman named Mika, when Newport stopped her Ritalin. "I can't function without them."

"I know," Mika said. "Let's just give it a try."

---

*This not-implausible theory is pounded home to so many doctors at industry conventions that some physicians will actually prescribe amphetamines just to keep someone from trying other drugs.

†Misinterpretation of "no effect" studies has led to a popular joke in math circles. Two statisticians, on a hunting trip in the woods, spot a deer and each take aim. One misses three feet to the right. The other misses three feet to the left. They rejoice: "We got him!"

As just the third girl to enroll at Newport, Kristin joined two other teenagers clambering across the rope bridge to sobriety. They spent forty hours a week in various rotations of therapy—with a substance-abuse counselor, a psychiatrist (both alone and in groups), a pediatrician, a family therapist, a yoga instructor. With Newport catering to teenagers, three hours of English, math, science, and other classes each weekday paralleled their courses back home and prepared them for the fall's looming SATs. Kristin's teacher spent extra time showing her how to make flash cards and take organized notes. No one had taught her before.

The most crucial exercise, however, was the Timeline. Every patient at Newport had to sketch out a year-by-year chronicle not of Colonial America or of Key Moments in Science, but crucial junctures in their own lives—the moments that shaped them from as far back as they could remember, both how they experienced them then and viewed them now. A minimum of twenty pages, the common themes rubbing into relief: The death of a grandparent. Being bullied. Kristin's was her being on various psychotropic medications ever since that third-grade afternoon when Dr. Seitz decided she had ADHD.

Writing the autobiography was the easy part. The hardest came the following weekend when the Parbers flew from Pennsylvania for one of their regular family therapy sessions. Kristin, like every girl at Newport, had to sit in a room and read all twenty-plus pages of narrative to her parents—and, crucially, they had to shut up and listen.

"You made me feel different," she read. "Like there was something wrong with me. What about what was wrong with *you?*"

Later: "I feel like you don't think I'm smart enough or good enough. That you're using drugs to change me."

The shouts and tears signaled success, not failure. Kristin and her parents had fought plenty, of course, even in controlled psychotherapy settings. But far more deftly than any suburban shrink, Newport's experts explained to the Parbers how, no, their daughter's substance abuse was not their *fault.* (Any suggestion of blame tends to stiffen and silo parents immediately.) Rather, like so many adolescents, Kristin used drugs and alcohol to soothe an inner pain and emptiness borne of many forces, one of them being the erosion of parental connection. She used drugs as a tool—to feel less crappy and wrest power over her emotional state from parents who didn't understand her. (A common strategy among substance-abuse counselors is to directly ask the child, right in front of the parents, *What does the drug do for you? How does it make you feel?* and force the parents to listen carefully.)

As tempers discharged and cleared, Kristin began to appreciate the patience and commitment that her parents were now showing. They were flying across the country every weekend to do hard work, work as painful for them—quite possibly more so—as it was for her. During their time to speak, they revealed a crucial family secret: that several of Kristin's relatives had also fallen into problems with alcohol and prescription pills. Decades of research have identified substance-abuse disorders as heritable, so Kristin's behavior probably derived in part from genes, not judgment. The Parbers didn't know—had never been told by any doctor—how Ritalin and her other psychiatric medications could interact with those genes. As each weekend of therapy built upon the last, "you" accusations evolved into "we" admissions, rebuilding the inclusiveness of family.

By mid-July, Kristin prepared to go home—not *cured*, certainly, but ready to return to a place where she would feel more welcome than at any time in years. Her parents flew in for her Newport Academy "graduation," a little ceremony held for patients completing treatment. Another nascent tradition was to have graduates paint a ceramic tile with words or images that captured their mind-set as they warily reentered their old world. Today more than a hundred fill the wall, some of them rainbows, others with reminders like "Progress Not Perfection" or "Stay Strong." The third tile is Kristin's, sitting just off the top left corner: "Joy."

The Parbers wanted Kristin to spend her senior year at home, but local high schools didn't exactly fight over a recovering alcoholic and drug addict who could relapse at any time. The only place that believed in giving Kristin another chance was the co-ed Shipley School, whose headmaster empathically but forcefully told her that she would be randomly drug tested, even breathalyzed, to make sure she stayed sober.

"This is your last shot," he said, "but we're willing to give it to you."

Kristin started the school year already behind on the college-application process—after all, her only experience with the SATs had been sleeping through them twice. Her first crack at big standardized tests became the ACT, a similar exam with equal influence on admissions chances. She studied hard, starting at Newport and then through the summer. But she had no idea how her brain, no longer bolstered by Ritalin, Daytrana, or any other ADHD drug, would respond under the pressure.

Kristin made sure to wake up early and get to the exam room at Lower Merion High School by 7:30. She hit the bathroom a few minutes before the test started.

"I'm so stressed," Kristin said to a girl who was fixing her hair in the mirror. "I don't know how I'm gonna do this."

"Oh," said the girl, turning to Kristin helpfully. "You want an Adderall?"

WHEN JAMISON TOOK Adderall to deal with high school pressure in the mid-1990s, he was a bit of a pioneer. Today, misuse of ADHD medications by high school students is far more widespread than most anyone realizes.

About a million high school kids nationwide use Adderall, Concerta, Vyvanse, and others without a doctor's prescription, getting them either from friends or from dealers for a few dollars a pill. This doesn't include the countless teenagers who get prescriptions from doctors under false pretenses, like Jamison did. One girl who recently would sell her meds to fellow students at a high school outside New York City said: "When people take tests, it's immediately, 'Who am I getting Adderall from?' They're always looking for it."

Adderall misuse has paralleled the rising competition for slots at top colleges. Three decades ago, four advanced placement courses, excellent SATs, and maybe some student government would pave your way to a Duke or Stanford; today, with vastly more students scrambling for the same number of chairs, those credentials are effectively sniffed at. Some kids at top public and private high schools take ten AP classes, seek SAT perfection through professional test-preparation services, force themselves to play sports and join a half-dozen clubs, and make darned sure to work at a soup kitchen or old-age home lest the next kid's application has that on there, too. The arms race gets worse every year, with students' hulking college admissions packages reflecting not necessarily who they are, but who the system demands they be.

Days remain only twenty-four hours long, so something must give. The first thing to go is sleep; the medically recommended amount for teenagers is a little over nine hours per night, a cruel joke for these kids. Their average night's rest is only seven hours, meaning that vast amounts of them—particularly those with overpacked schedules—get far less, especially during mid-terms and finals. Decreasing workload is no option. Increasing stamina is. The most efficient method comes through Adderall, a drug many kids consider not a threat to their future, but a means to pursue it. As a student at a prestigious high school in Bethesda, Maryland, put it: "It wasn't that hard of a decision. Do I want only four hours of sleep and be a mess, and then underperform on the test and then in field hockey, or make the teachers happy and the coach happy and get good grades, get into a good college, and make my parents happy?"

Sadly, this common outlook doesn't seem to alarm the grown-ups supposedly devoted to these children's health and well-being. A board of education in one southern California county refused to do a confidential survey of students to assess the situation in their district, because confirming any problem might have made them legally responsible to address it. Similarly, a PTA at one high school in New York's affluent Westchester County (a hotbed of Ivies-or-bust academic pressure) rebuffed an expert's offer to educate the community privately; one reason, a school official later admitted, was that some parents already suspected their kids were taking Adderall and feared their grades would slip if they stopped.

Shire, which has always touted Adderall and Vyvanse as boosting academic performance—"in children with ADHD," the ads wink—has also appeared unmoved by mounting evidence that the drugs' effects are appreciated by normal teenagers, too. In 2012, a company executive claimed there was no "systematic data that suggests there's a widespread problem," and shrugged, "You can always find people who testify that it happens." Perhaps one should expect this reaction from a drug company, but even outside researchers who discover and then publish glaring evidence can be staggeringly obtuse as to what it means. In 2013, a study in a top journal reported that 10 percent of high school seniors had used stimulants illicitly. This presented significant health risks, the researchers wrote, and therefore demanded further investigation. But the authors' explanation for Adderall's high school popularity? The kids were not trying to study harder, they wrote, but merely *self-medicating their undiagnosed ADHD.*

If such reputed experts see ADHD in every stimulant abuser, it's no wonder that, even after all Kristin's parents had learned, they still preferred she stay on Ritalin for her senior year at the Shipley School. Just as Kristin had spent her childhood thinking she had a brain disorder that required medication, they had spent their parenthood thinking the same. That image of Kristin was hard to dispel. Besides, this crucial semester was no time to experiment; she somehow had gotten B's in her three years at Episcopal, and one excellent fall at Shipley could still get her into a good college. But Newport counselors insisted that Kristin stay off all ADHD medications to give her brain a chance to breathe. And so Kristin enrolled in four advanced placement classes—calculus, English, physics, and statistics—with her clearest mind in years.

She made an A-minus average. On the ACT, without any Adderall from that girl in the bathroom, she got a 32, placing her in the 98th percentile nationally. Knowing that her past would discourage top schools, Kristin applied to a half dozen good colleges and only one excellent one: New York University. Because she figured she had no real shot at NYU anyway, when one of its essays asked her to describe her greatest challenge in life, she let it fly. She acknowledged her use of alcohol and drugs. She wrote about the hard work of examining her poor decisions. She concluded: "While I may not have the strongest transcript, I believe it would be beneficial for the NYU community to take a risk by accepting me. At seventeen years old, I learned who I really was and what I stand for—a truly unique thing for an adolescent."

A few months later, after getting rejected by several schools, Kristin was checking her e-mail in the Shipley library and saw something from NYU. She clicked on it. The message said nothing about her application—it was only some boilerplate reminder about how hotel rooms close to campus go fast around move-in day, so her parents should book ahead.

Understandably confused, Kristin called the admissions office. The woman there typed her name into a database. Yep, she was in. Should be receiving materials shortly.

Kristin phoned her dad.

"Are you sure, honey?" he said. "That sounds like a computer glitch."

"It's true, Dad. I called."

Bill Parber was entitled to some skepticism. Kristin's years of lies were hard to forget. She had not only drunk and snorted away her chances at a top school, her NYU essay all but flaunted it! Several lesser colleges had already rejected her. And that e-mail said nothing about her being accepted.

"Forward it to me," he told Kristin. "Let me call them myself."

IN SEPTEMBER 2010, Kristin began classes as a member of New York University's Class of 2014. The fresh-start drive to Greenwich Village in Manhattan took the same three hours as the one to Alexandria and Episcopal High four years before, but couldn't have been more different. North versus south, more than just literally. This time she felt not like an old girl, but a young woman.

Kristin consumed not a drop of alcohol or dapple of drugs at NYU. Her pangs for their buzz and balm remained, of course, as they will forever. A routine helped her stay abstinent and focused: no wild parties, regular Alcoholics Anonymous meetings, dozens of hours a week studying at Bobst Library. A typical formula for success, perhaps. But . . .

Kristin didn't use the Bobst bathrooms. For four years. Whenever the need arose, she would leave her books in a cubicle and walk back to her dorm room.

The sniffing sounds coming from the library's bathroom stalls were too painful, too triggering. Adderall. Again.

What was a relatively new phenomenon within America's high schools—widespread abuse of ADHD drugs—had become almost cliché at colleges nationwide. University officials shrugged at the problem; they probably had popped a few Dexedrines themselves a generation before to get through finals. So they did little about it. Even as kids started dying.

Chapter 12

BRIGHT COLLEGE DAYS

Vanderbilt University fancies itself as "the Harvard of the South," and for good reason. Students on the Nashville campus are just as smart as their high school classmates who go to Ivy League colleges; the school is just as rigorous as any Princetons or Penns up north, often more so. Grading curves breed competition, as only a select number of students can receive the A's—B+ won't cut it—that business and law schools will want upon graduation. Every grade matters. So every test matters, every paper. While the campus enjoys its Frisbees-on-the-green as much as any other, on this beautiful March afternoon, those hunkering down at the Sarratt Student Center can look around and wonder: Is that kid trying harder than me?

In a room down the hall, five undergraduates sit around a conference table and talk about what "trying" means to them.

You take one pill, and next thing you know, the paper's done.

I've known people who have over two hundred pills at one time. One had a jar of like three hundred or four hundred.

I got diagnosed in maybe ten minutes. My doctor is clueless.

Ten bucks a pill, maybe $25 during finals.

It's kind of hard to be like, "Oh, I shouldn't take this." It's like, "Okay I have some shit to get done, and here's a get-shit-done pill."

The pills, of course, are Adderall—medication prescribed to them and their friends for ADHD they don't have, and never did. They laugh at how blithely their doctors use their prescription pads to put thousands of tablets into their college's bloodstream. One student, when he felt a little guilty for having taken and given friends pills since his sophomore year of high school, actually told his psychiatrist back home that he wanted to try weaning off his medication, because his problems weren't so bad anymore. The doctor talked him out of it. She went so far as to insist he take three months' worth of prescriptions—ninety pills of 50-milligram Vyvanse and, just in case he needed an extra boost late in the day, ninety more 30-milligram instant-release Adderalls. He breaks the thirties in half when he needs them, and gives the rest to his appreciative friends.

Three years before, one of those Vanderbilt friends might as well have been a sophomore named Kyle Craig. An excellent student and lacrosse player at a top New Jersey prep school, Kyle had gotten the same rude awakening that befalls so many freshmen: He was no longer one of the smartest kids, just one of the pack trying to keep up. To cram for exams and churn out papers, he got some Adderall pills from a friend. They worked, or at least he thought they did. By sophomore year he went to a doctor, exaggerated ADHD symptoms to get his own prescription, and even told his parents, Chip and Andrea, this was no big deal. ("We all do it at Vanderbilt," he reassured them.) Before Kyle left for a semester studying in Spain, his doctor not only prescribed twice as much Adderall than his supposed ADHD probably needed, but gave him several prescriptions so that he'd never run out.

A few months later, during a Skype call with his parents from Barcelona, Kyle seemed strange, agitated. He wrung his fingers through his hair saying, "I don't know. I don't know. I don't know." After these calls worsened his worried parents offered to fly over, even take him home; Kyle convinced them not to. When he returned in late April and became increasingly anxious and belligerent, they researched the side effects of Adderall—and learned that, particularly in overdose, this kind of behavior was an established possibility. Even Kyle admitted he had a problem and went to a therapist. He was becoming a different person, his brain rewired. He took more Adderall and only got worse.

Less than a month later, on a night when the sky was as dark as his thoughts, Kyle walked to the New Jersey Transit train tracks that ran through his town and stared down the oncoming light.

In a distraught letter to the Vanderbilt chancellor, Nicholas Zeppos, Chip Craig didn't lay blame on the university, but implored it to recognize Adderall's presence on campus:

What we have learned from Kyle's therapist is that he had become abusive in his use of Adderall while at Vanderbilt. In his own words to his therapist, Kyle said, "Adderall ruined my life." As a mature, bright, type A guy, Kyle made bad choices in relation to Adderall and ultimately the downward spiral that followed from that cost him his life. Somewhere in his desire to achieve he lost our voice that only his "best effort" was needed. Again, as he told his therapist, "Guys I knew were getting 4.0s and I knew how they were doing it. I wanted to try what they used for studying."

Three years later, when Vanderbilt's student newspaper did a multipart investigation into Adderall abuse on campus, the university responded with legalese: "We are aware that the illicit use and abuse of prescription medications is an issue on our campus as it is on many other campuses across the country." It claimed that a university survey of students had shown that only 3.1 percent used stimulants during stressful study periods—a number plainly dubious. It didn't mention, although officials clearly knew from Chip Craig's letter, that a recent sophomore had suffered a psychiatric breakdown while abusing Adderall for school.

So, none of the five undergraduates at the student center who misused and distributed Adderall had ever heard of Kyle Craig. They had no idea what their activities could lead to. One was visibly shaken. He said: "They should put posters of that kid all over campus."

ADDERALL'S POWERS AS a "study drug" or "smart drug" are unquestionably exaggerated. Studies generally do not find that stimulants improve people's functional memory or inherent ability to understand concepts. What they do boost, however, is attention and motivation, particularly for tedious tasks like finishing rote math problems or cranking out papers overnight. Not everyone feels these effects—stimulants make about one in five people way too jittery or anxious—but many people will, and those who do are more likely to continue using the pills. Many doctors and researchers, as well as CHADD advocates and pharmaceutical companies, fall all over themselves downplaying these nonmedicinal effects, even denying them outright, by either citing specious short-term studies or simply casting the medications as uniquely vital to those with ADHD, and virtual placebos to anyone else.* This is pure hogwash. Stimulants can often bring *greater* benefits to people with ADHD, but only because there's more room for noticeable improvement; the myth that they do nothing for those without ADHD has been so propagated that some doctors foolishly use improvement on stimulants to confirm a patient's diagnosis.

Dozens of studies since the 1990s have estimated that about 8 to 35 percent of undergraduates take stimulant pills illicitly to try to improve their grades; a reasonable estimate among high-pressure colleges is probably 15 to 20 percent. Most students, of course, don't experience terrible outcomes—if they did, the dangers would already be better recognized. But many do. One 2006 study found that about one in ten adolescents and young adults who misused ADHD medications became addicted to them, with some of those becoming psychotic or suicidal. Unfortunately, those side effects are often chalked up to bipolar disorder or college blues, with the real—or at least exacerbating—culprit ignored. To many college students, the whole topic remains a joke. Some wear T-shirts that declare "ADDERALL—Can't Pass Without It!," while another popular model sports a smiling cartoon bottle of the Adderall, carrying books under one arm on its way to class, with "STUDY BUDDY" above it. Craigslist is strewn with offers to buy and sell Adderall, code-named "study aids."†

Many doctors are absurdly trusting when diagnosing college students,

---

*Vanderbilt, for example, made this mistake in its 2012/2013 student handbook, which relegated its discussion of stimulant abuse to the bottom of page 75. It said only that "some individuals" take the drugs for alertness, but that "They have not, however, been shown to improve academic performance in students without ADD."

†Even Supreme Court justices have snickered at the out-of-control college situation. Discussing a defendant who had been caught carrying Adderall not prescribed to him, Justice Elena Kagan shrugged: "If you go to half the colleges in America . . . and just

who, just as smoothly as Jamison Monroe, can feign ADHD symptoms to get a stimulant prescription with remarkable ease. A 2004 study found that most students were able to fake their way into diagnosis-worthy scores on various symptom tests, including 90 percent who fooled the Conners Scale. One experiment looked at two groups of about seventy students: kids with true ADHD, and others who, given only *five minutes* to research the disorder on the Internet, were promised $45 if they could get themselves diagnosed by a professional clinician. Both groups were run through proper structured interviews, questionnaires, and computer-based tests of attention and reaction time. In the end, the clinicians couldn't tell the groups apart—students wound up getting diagnosed at the same rate.*

Spurious ADHD evaluations often take place not in a private doctor's office, but right on campus, at a college's student-health department. Most of these encounters happen behind closed doors, but one from 2007, at Harvard University, came to light because the kid's family sued and was able to depose the clinician involved. A rising sophomore named Johnny Edwards, one year removed from being the valedictorian of Wellesley High School in Massachusetts and feeling tremendous pressure at Harvard, went to the university student-health center and claimed he was having trouble studying "as much as my friends." He didn't have ADHD, as a child or now, but the nurse practitioner nodded and noted that Johnny had received two minor traffic citations—which to her, quite possibly because of Russell Barkley's research, was a telltale sign of the disorder. When Johnny strategically told her that his father "may have had" ADHD, she took that as further evidence because, she rationalized later, "80 percent of the time, the previous generation will have it."† She

---

randomly pick somebody, there would be a decent chance" they'd have ADHD drugs, too. The courtroom chuckled knowingly.

*In 2013, a young and even younger-looking French newswoman, in a television series on life on American college campuses, went undercover to see how easy getting ADHD pills truly was. She learned of a Manhattan psychiatrist popular among local students, went to his office wearing a hidden camera and microphone, answered a few questions, and walked out ten minutes later with a prescription.

†Her absurd 80 percent claim almost certainly derives from a study by Steve Faraone, a member of Joseph Biederman's group, which declared the "heritability of ADHD to be .76." The number was broadcast throughout the field; problem was, that metric does not speak to the percentage of ADHD kids with ADHD parents.

never talked with Johnny's father or mother, but wrote in her notes, "His parents have also noticed all of his life that it has taken him an unusually long time to do homework." Then came the coup de grâce, when she recounted that Johnny had told her that he liked energy drinks. "The fact that he used stimulant drinks like Red Bull," she testified, under oath, "is always a marker for me when evaluating a youngster or an adult really for attention deficit disorder."

The nurse practitioner prescribed Johnny monthly supplies of Adderall. The fact that he was subsequently given additional psychiatric medications (without ever seeing a physician) that caused him to deteriorate emotionally and kill himself later that year is not the point—no one can know what role, if any, the medications played in his downturn. It's merely how the opening diagnosis of ADHD was handled so recklessly, and then defended by the university. All care that Johnny received at the student-health center, Harvard contended, was "thorough and appropriate."

Adderall use on college campuses has become so common and condoned that some articles in student newspapers openly encourage its use. One kid at the University of Missouri, playing on O. J. Simpson's infamously named memoir, wrote a column called "If I Did It: Academics and Adderall." He snarkily posited that the medication would make him "a scholastic workhorse. If I had Adderall's energy running through my veins with strength caffeine could never match, anything would be possible. . . . If I took Adderall, nothing would feel like work. I'd have a genuine interest in tasks I'd otherwise find repulsive." He closed the column: "If I took Adderall, I'd tell you how great it is. I'd tell you to go out and get some as soon as possible."

In 2013, the University of Miami's student paper, *The Hurricane*, ran an editorial titled "Magic pill can enhance focus, drive," which said that students "shouldn't look down on those who need—and welcome—the extra push" of Adderall. The same day, in a column headlined "Stressed-out students should take advantage of pills," an undergraduate wrote, "With prescription study drugs being handed out like PEZ candies on campus, why wouldn't students take advantage of them?" He urged all students to follow suit: "Medicate, Miami. You've earned it." Once again, the reaction of university officials, the grown-ups charged with educating young minds, was staggering. Miami issued a short press release that said only that the newspaper "does not represent the views and opinions of the university's trustees, faculty or administration."

Some schools and students have found all this less funny. In 2010, Wesleyan University, a liberal-arts school in Connecticut, made the use of Adderall without a prescription a violation of the school's honor code and a form of cheating likened to athletes using steroids, an unfair advantage. The following year, at the behest of frustrated students, Duke University made "the unauthorized use of prescription medication to enhance academic performance" a category of scholastic dishonesty as well. But such relatively symbolic attempts at curbing abuse are rare, leaving many students across the nation either using the pills or feeling tempted.

THE PSYCHOLOGICAL RISKS of amphetamine, spectacularly obvious and scientifically proven since Benzedrine's debut, have been consistently downplayed or even denied by ADHD advocates and pharmaceutical companies. While comparing Ritalin to eyeglasses, CHADD in its early days flatly lied in its literature by claiming, "Psychostimulant medications are not addictive." (Although financially supported by Ritalin's manufacturer, Ciba-Geigy, CHADD and its statements were not subject to FDA guidelines.) Catchphrases to minimize the medications' risks included "stimulants are safer than aspirin," exploiting how aspirin is indeed linked to thousands of deaths a year; problem is, those fatal gastrointestinal bleeds result from chronically high doses in people with heart disease, not the occasional, over-the-counter no-big-deals "aspirin" obviously connotes. Countless clinicians, when prescribing Ritalin and then later Adderall and Concerta, have reassured parents and older patients that the pills are not harmful "when used properly."* True. Then again, so are chain saws.

---

*This disclaimer is common among companies trying to minimize the dangers of their products. The National Football League, during its recent crisis surrounding brain injuries, reassured players that repeated concussions have no long-term effects "if each injury is managed properly."

Yet how true is it? Pharmaceutical companies have always known the risks of the pills, even among patients who use them as directed, but buried that message in documents the public would never see. Some of Shire's US patent applications flatly state:

A user can become dependent over time on these drugs and their physical and psychological effects, **even when the drugs are used for legitimate therapeutic purposes.** *Legitimate amphetamine users that develop drug tolerances are especially susceptible to becoming accidental addicts. . . .* [Emphasis added.]

The word "legitimate" is crucial here: Dependence and addiction can occur not just in people who abuse the medications, Shire admitted, but also in patients who consume them as directed. However, advertisements for ADHD medications were not required to include this detail. Similarly, the (relatively low) risk that the drugs can cause users to hallucinate—see people in rooms, hear voices from the television, feel bugs under their skin—are generally spurned. But that possibility was proven in the medications' original, pharma-overseen clinical trials, of all places. In 2009, some concerned FDA researchers gathered four dozen studies from Shire, ALZA, and others and found that about 1 in 500 patients, most of them young children, experienced hallucinations when using the medication even under the most proper and controlled conditions.* With more than a half a million people starting ADHD medication every year, it's fair to expect that about one thousand of them will experience this reaction— even when they take the pills as directed. To be fair, the side effect is usually transient; stop the medication and the delusions stop as well. But the risk is high enough, and terrifying enough when it occurs, that doctors should at least make parents and patients aware of it. They rarely do, though, either because they are unaware of it or don't want to dissuade anyone from what probably will emerge as beneficial treatment.

---

*The researchers made sure to note, for the inevitable "wait, what about"skeptics, that very few of these kids had any previous psychiatric history that could have caused or contributed to their delusions, and that any child showing an immediate intolerance to the medications was removed from the studies. So 1 in 500, they claimed, was probably an underestimate of the actual rate people should look out for in the real world.

When the drugs are taken in double and triple doses, as with many abusers, the psychological effects of stimulants rise dramatically. So to hand Adderall out to any college undergrad who says he's having trouble concentrating is to abet disaster, particularly among a population notorious for experimenting with mind-altering substances. This problem goes well beyond Vanderbilt's Kyle Craig; recent years have seen several other such stimulant-related suicides. There are undoubtedly dozens or perhaps hundreds more in which the kid doesn't actually succeed.

No case is more instructive and influential than that of a young man named Richard Fee. His downfall from college class president to Adderall addict didn't merely evidence the psychological risks of prescription stimulants. Over three excruciating years, and at every juncture, Fee encountered the carelessness with which ADHD is handled in too many doctor's offices across the United States, particularly among young adults. The story didn't just appall readers of the *New York Times*, when a 2013 exposé laid bare how reckless the attention-deficit business had become. In the end, it made this book possible.

IN AUGUST 2009, Richard Fee walked into the office of the Triad Psychiatric & Counseling Center in Greensboro, North Carolina, the just-down-the-street clinic for students at Greensboro College who wanted prescriptions for Adderall. At the time Richard had everything going for him—academic scholarship, first baseman on the college baseball team, handsome and charismatic enough to have been elected president of his sophomore class. He wanted to go to medical school. Having bummed Adderall pills off friends for a while, he decided to get his own supply by faking ADHD to a gullible Triad nurse. She wrote down his complaints: "poor organization, memory, attention to detail." She gave him an airy eighteen-question survey—not the official Conners Scale, but a descendant of it—and totaled up the zero-to-three scores. Twenty-nine? Yep, ADHD. She arranged for a prescription. The drug worked so well that, a few weeks later, Richard returned to ask that the dose be increased to 50 milligrams. She complied. He soon asked for 60. She green-lighted three months' worth of medication in forty-three days.

Richard Fee on graduation day at Greensboro College

Richard Fee's answers on his ADHD diagnostic questionnaire

Courtesy of the Fee family

When Richard graduated and moved back home to Virginia Beach, Virginia,* to study for medical school entrance exams, he visited a local psychiatrist to get his Adderall prescriptions refilled. Dr. Waldo Ellison listened to the young man's complaints, assumed that his original ADHD diagnosis back in Greensboro had been correct, and began writing Richard regular scripts. Because they met only for five-minute "med checks" once a month the doctor did not notice that Richard was abusing the pills from the start. He would blow through his monthly supply in a few weeks, staying up all night reading and scribbling in notebooks. As amphetamine psychosis took hold, he would climb out his bedroom window onto the roof to talk with the moon and stars. Another side effect of amphetamine abuse is elevated body temperature; Richard would get so overheated that he walked around the house with ice packs around his neck—and, in frigid weather, cooled off by jumping into his parents' fifty-two-degree backyard pool.

Richard's father, Rick, confronted him about his bizarre behavior and whether it had anything to do with Adderall, his son replied, "The doctor wouldn't give me anything that's bad for me, Dad—I'm not buying it on the street corner." When Rick watched Richard grow increasingly violent and heard him complain that his computer camera was spying on him, Rick went to Dr. Ellison's office to discuss the prescriptions. The doctor refused to talk about Richard, citing patient privacy laws. Rick got so frustrated that he yelled at Dr. Ellison, "You keep giving Adderall to my son, you're going to kill him!" Dr. Ellison did leave Mr. Fee with some reassurance, though: This doctor had tremendous experience in this area, he explained, because, "I prescribe more Adderall than anyone in the state." †

---

*This is the same city where Gretchen LeFever had controversially found wild overdiagnosis of ADHD in children ten years before. Ironically, one of the children in her study back then—who went down as a boy *not* on medication, because he never had attention problems—was a fifth-grader at Trantwood Elementary School named Richard Fee.

†Dr. Ellison had shown a somewhat counterintuitive approach to medicine in 1994 when he made a proposal to Philip Morris—one of the tobacco giants that used junk science to cover up the dangers of cigarettes. According to internal documents, Dr. Ellison, who was described as owning at least 3,800 company shares then valued at more than $200,000, said that he supported cigarettes "as something to be used for comfort and stress management." One memo said that Dr. Ellison had, "to help raise the price

When Richard's parents convinced him to see a different psychiatrist, Dr. Charles Parker, they specifically instructed the new doctor not to prescribe Adderall; the doctor understood this so well that he wrote in his chart "no meds" with a box around it, as well as noting Richard's anxiety and suicidal thoughts. And yet, not long afterward, Dr. Parker gave Richard a prescription for Adderall, and eventually a huge dose of 80 milligrams a day. The doctor later recalled that Richard had seemed so sincere about his needing the drug for ADHD—an aspiring medical-school student wouldn't lie about something like this, would he?—and didn't exhibit any outward signs of abuse during their occasional appointments. Richard's delusions returned so severely that he spent a week in a psychiatric hospital.

When he got out, and needing his amphetamine fix, Richard returned to Dr. Ellison. After only six minutes in the office, Richard left with not one, but three thirty-day prescriptions for Adderall: one for that day, and one each for the next two months, so that he didn't have to schlep to the office for more. When Richard's father returned to Dr. Ellison to ask what in God's name he was thinking, it was too late— Richard had his three-month supply. By the time those pills ran out, Richard became so violent that his rages forced calls to the police. He moved into his own apartment and became despondent, withdrawn, and suicidal anew. He didn't recover. His life and psyche in tatters, he hanged himself in a closet.

The Fees held a gathering in Richard's memory afterward. His old college friends recalled how they, too, had used Adderall in college—to cram, just like Richard did—and realized Richard's fate could have easily been theirs. A baseball teammate later recalled: "It's so prevalent and widely used, people had no idea it could be abused to the point of no return."

Still grieving as the anniversary of Richard's death approached, Mr. and Mrs. Fee noticed in the local paper that a new documentary called "ADD and Loving It?!" was being screened at a nearby auditorium,

---

of the stock," strongly encouraged the company to "conduct a study to determine what motivates people to smoke cigarettes. Dr. Ellison believes that the results of this study will show that the psychological benefits of smoking may outweigh concerns raised by anti-smoking groups." Philip Morris officials convinced Dr. Ellison to drop his idea.

followed by a panel discussion among experts. They decided to go. It was being hosted by CHADD, whose emcee opened by thanking their sponsor for the event: Shire pharmaceuticals. The hour-long movie was of the Ned Hallowell genre, casting ADHD as a humorous, and often positive, condition; afflicted spouses giggled about misplaced keys and forgotten appointments, while doctors recalled the "enthusiasm and excitement" their patients had felt upon diagnosis. It closed by examining several "myths" about stimulant medications, with doctors praising their efficacy and safety, mentioning no risks. Hallowell himself said the pills were "safer than aspirin," while another clinician was even more reassuring. "It's okay," he said. "There's nothing that's going to happen."

Rick Fee seethed silently. After the movie ended, during the expert panel Q&A, he rose from his fourth-row seat to ask a question. The panel was moderated by a local clinical psychologist named Jeffrey Katz, who also happened to be chairman of CHADD's public policy committee.

"What are some of the drawbacks or some of the dangers of a misdiagnosis in somebody," Rick Fee asked, "and then the subsequent medication that goes along with that?"

Dr. Katz took the question.

"Not much—the medication itself is pretty innocuous," he replied. He explained that people without ADHD would see no benefit from Adderall and stop on their own. Dr. Katz concluded, as if puzzled by the question: "If you misdiagnose it, and you give somebody medication, it's not going to do anything for them. Why would they continue to take it?"

REACTION TO THE *Times*'s profile of Richard Fee was as polarized as ever, with critics of the ADHD explosion being generally drowned out by those most invested in the disorder's continued popularity. CHADD's president blogged that Richard's death was clearly tragic, but "stimulant medications that are taken as prescribed are highly unlikely to lead to addiction"—avoiding the issue at hand, which was the not uncommon circumstance when they are prescribed, and taken, *improperly*. An official from the Child Mind Institute, a New York clinic devoted to diag-

nosing and treating children with ADHD—and whose president, Dr.
Harold Koplewicz, had been involved with NYU's "Your Kid Will Pay"
ransom-ad marketing campaign—took the standard route of claiming
that the Richard Fee story only "verges on the kind of fear-mongering
that is unhelpful to parents trying to provide the best support and care
to struggling children." The most befuddling response came in a *Times*
Letter to the Editor from Martin J. Drell, the president of the American
Academy of Child and Adolescent Psychiatry, whose journal had long
survived on glowing reviews of ADHD medications and pharmaceutical advertising. Dr. Drell emphasized that the millions of Americans
with ADHD were at risk for "accidents, injury and substance abuse,"
but that "fortunately, effective treatment is available."

One doctor, though, read the story of Richard Fee and had a reaction all his own. The events didn't take place in his office, and he had
never met or spoken with the patient or doctors involved. He didn't
write the prescriptions—and, in fact, still deeply believed in the benefits of ADHD medication. But as he put down the newspaper, having
soaked the ghastly story in, he felt a unique sensation. He didn't feel
particularly sad. He wasn't angry either. No. It was something different,
more personal. He felt *embarrassed*.

That Sunday morning, Dr. C. Keith Conners decided that ADHD,
whose Manhattan Project he had so enthusiastically helped lead, had
clearly melted down. Not just on college campuses, but everywhere.
His questionnaire, for which he was now annually getting $600,000
in royalties, and others were making false diagnoses for lazy doctors
nationwide. The medications he had championed were being as over-
prescribed as antibiotics. As he recalled all his work for pharmaceutical companies—from CIBA to Abbott to Shire to ALZA to Lilly
and more—he feared that his career had strayed from medicine to
marketing.

After disregarding four decades of gathering clouds, Conners
decided to get up and see just how bad the situation had become. He
quickly found it worse than he even feared. Drug companies had grown
unsatisfied with the population of children that he himself had discovered. Those kids were now growing into adults—and as they did, Big
Pharma wanted to keep their business.

Chapter 13

AND NOW,
A WORD FROM OUR SPONSORS

Now *this* would be a great show.

The audience lights dimmed. The cast took their spots. The cameras rolled. The stage was ABC's Chelsea studios in New York, a 2012 taping of *The Revolution*, yet another self-improvement hour in which hundreds of clapping audience members and millions more at televisions learned what was wrong with them and how to fix it.

And the host! Out ran Ty Pennington, the peppy, goofy, self-deprecating former star of *Extreme Makeover: Home Edition*, the hit reality show that from 2003 to 2011 had deployed Pennington, a carpenter so handsome he'd done some J.Crew ads, to plank-by-screw rebuild houses for wowed and appreciative Janes and Joes. Now, in *The Revolution*, he would show people how to rebuild themselves—extreme makeovers for the soul. This was one of his first episodes, and the still-learning host chose some very low-hanging fruit. He made it clear from the open.

> **TY (to camera)**
>
> I have ADHD. Today, I'm gonna finally show you what it's like!

Pennington's co-host, a lab-coated and Barbie-blond gynecologist named Jennifer Ashton, gravely told the cameras, "Eighty-five percent of adults"—she paused for effect—"*undiagnosed*. That is a lot of people having trouble in their day-to-day life and not knowing why." To tell everyone why, they brought onstage the perfect man to explain:

Dr. Ned Hallowell. Hallowell was more than just a vending machine for bubbly quotes on all things ADHD. He had become the field's Energizer Bunny, tirelessly beating its drum.

NED

Undiagnosed, this condition can ruin your family life, ruin your school life. Among adults [it] leads to underachievement. The prison population is full with people with undiagnosed ADHD. The divorced, the unemployed, the addicted. [But] it's a good-news diagnosis, because then you can skyrocket, you can soar, you can achieve your goals. . . . Go get this diagnosis!

TY

It affects your relationship, whether or not you can communicate with your partner, it affects your job, whether or not they're going to hire you to get the job done, it affects everything.

NED

Eighty percent of adults don't know they have it. That drives me crazy! If only they knew they had it!

This got worse. Fast. Asked to name ADHD's primary symptom, Hallowell replied, "Unexplained underachievement." He went on: "You may be a straight-A student. You may be a Nobel Prize winner. But you know you could be doing better." Ty took over to demonstrate what ADHD felt like: He had Jennifer and another co-host struggle to play Ping-Pong with two balls at the same time. The audience was asked to stand and clap and yell to distract them. For good measure—and theater—Ty then tossed some brownies on the table, bounced a few more balls at them, and shouted at Jennifer, "Recite the alphabet backward!" She flailed and giggled and finally surrendered, as the crowd howled approvingly.

AND NOW, A WORD FROM OUR SPONSORS

TY

Welcome to my world. But that's really what's going on out there.

JENNIFER (to camera)

If that's what your day-to-day life is, you can see how difficult it can be. So when we come back, is undiagnosed ADD or ADHD hurting your kids or even ruining your job or marriage?

OTHER CO-HOST

We'll also tell you what everybody should know about diagnosing yourself, or your kids.

After the commercials, viewers were spoon-fed the best way to, indeed, diagnose themselves. They met Alicia, a young, perky everywoman in the audience who wondered if she, too, had ADHD. She explained that she jumped from task to task at home, with e-mail distracting her from laundry. Jennifer, still in her lab coat, shook her head and somberly offered, "How many moms feel exactly the same way you do?" Ty revealed that the show would now present a six-question quiz to see if Alicia had ADHD. Hallowell, making sure to mention that the test was devised by doctors at Harvard and NYU, served as doctor.

NED

Do you have trouble wrapping up the final details of a project?

ALICIA

Yes. [Laughs]

NED

Do you have trouble getting things in order?

ALICIA

Yes I do.

NED

Do you have trouble remembering appointments or other obligations?

ALICIA

Yeah.

NED

Do you delay getting things started or procrastinate?

ALICIA

Yes. There's a picture of me next to that description, for sure.

NED

Do you fidget or squirm when you have to sit still for an extended period of time?

ALICIA

I think so. [Laughs]

NED

Do you feel overly active as if you're sort of driven by a motor?

ALICIA

Yes.

NED (excited)

So you passed the test. Welcome to the illustrious club [of ADHD]! It's a good-news diagnosis. Don't be afraid of it. The worst is over.

Viewers were left wondering: *I clearly have ADHD, Dr. Hallowell, but what can I do about it? What can transform this job-hampering, marriage-ruining, jail-inviting scourge into the brighter days you promise?*

The segment was running out of time, so Hallowell hurried up. Better diet and exercise, he said. Better time structure.

                    NED

```
And then there's medication, which people are so
afraid of, but they shouldn't be. Medication works
about 80 percent of the time. And when it works it
works like eyeglasses!
```

                    TY

```
Right. Yeah. [Nods]
```

                    NED

```
You can suddenly see! [Starbursts his fingers as if
magic] . . . Very safe, very effective. It shouldn't
be feared as it is feared. See a doctor who knows what
he or she is doing, and it's safer than aspirin.
```

Hallowell smiled like a politician at his applauding and appreciative audience. Ty wrapped up the segment. He thanked Dr. Hallowell for his great insight, and thanked Alicia for sharing her life trials.

What Ty did not do, not once during the eighteen-minute puppet show, was mention to anyone that he had spent several years as a paid celebrity spokesman for Shire and Adderall XR. In print ads and YouTube videos, he had crowed that Adderall XR "literally changed my life" and "gave me the confidence to achieve my goals"—marketing that had gotten formally condemned by the Food and Drug Administration for being false and misleading. He had hosted Shire's telephone hotline in which adults could call 1-888-ASK-ADHD to learn about the wonders of the ADHD diagnosis. Of course, he was paid handsomely for this endorsement of Shire's lifeblood combination, ADHD and Adderall.

More than a million Americans watched that episode of *The Revo-*

lution nationwide, and countless more via online streaming. One of them was a Shire sales representative—someone who had handed out Pennington-brand Adderall marketing materials to countless doctors over the years—who, after seeing it, shook his head in disbelief.

"Holy shit," he thought to himself. "That was better than anything we'd ever paid for."

EVER SINCE THE minimal brain dysfunction days in the 1960s, doctors suspected—and Ritalin makers hoped—that the syndrome affected more than just young children. When asked publicly, most experts said that kids grew out of it; the suggestion that kids might take speed the rest of their lives would not have gone down very well. (A primary example of this reassurance came during Cornelius Gallagher's testy congressional hearing in 1970, when the architects of MBD testified that children would magically have no problems by age twelve, ending any risk of their abusing Ritalin or Dexedrine.) But many doctors knew better. They knew that some adults struggled to stay on task just like youngsters did. They knew full well what amphetamine could deliver to adults, its boost in focus and zest for the tedious.

The first to promote attentional difficulties among adults as a full-fledged syndrome was Dr. Paul Wender, the firebrand who also claimed that not treating MBD children with stimulants constituted malpractice. Wender spent most of the 1970s pushing his theory of adult attention deficits. As the American Psychiatric Association began rebuilding its *Diagnostic and Statistical Manual*, and sensing a chance to cement his legacy, Wender fought not just to have an adult type appear in the catalog, but that it be placed in the Adult Disorders section for fear that doctors would resist prescribing for what still felt like a child's problem. The *DSM* committee ultimately compromised. A nod to grown-up attention deficit disorder appeared in the child section of the 1980 book but was called a "Residual Type" of ADHD—essentially, symptoms that remained after childhood. The construct was so jerry-built that the next *DSM* edition, in 1987, removed it.

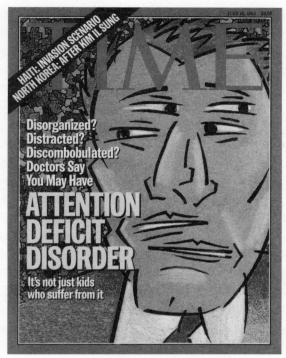

Time, July 18, 1994

But the concept had entered the zeitgeist, growing to the point that in 1994, *Time* magazine provided the most valuable advertisement of all, a cover story with massive lettering: "Disorganized? Distracted? Discombobulated? Doctors Say You May Have ATTENTION DEFICIT DISORDER. . . . It's not just kids who suffer from it." (The cover featured an alarming, Picasso-like illustration of a suit-and-tied businessman so uncontrollably jittery that he had four eyes, two noses, and two mouths.) Parents and professionals recalled how their difficult childhoods must have derived from unrecognized ADHD, and how after getting diagnosed they blossomed into better workers and wives. "Many adults respond to the diagnosis with relief," the story read, "a sense that 'at least my problem has a name and it's not my fault.'" Russell Barkley claimed that 40 percent of ADHD kids had a parent with the problem, as if it were a fire around which the whole family could gather. A box next to the article pondered some famous folks whose company they could all join: Ben Franklin, Winston Churchill, and, of course, Albert Einstein. They might have had ADHD, too.

Exposure like this became free market research for Big Pharma. Adult ADHD wasn't even formally recognized by the American Psychiatric Association, but it became too tempting a diagnosis for doctors and patients to resist, or the media to cover as a medical/cultural happening. (A 1997 feature in the *New York Times* led with a woman who declared appreciatively, "Being diagnosed with ADD gave me my life back.") The potential sales were immense. Five percent of children having ADHD—the generally accepted prevalence estimate in the 1990s—translated to about three million customers. Adults, who were less resistant to take medication themselves than to give it to their children, could become two or three times that. As Shire (Adderall XR), ALZA (Concerta), and Eli Lilly (Strattera) began developing their new-and-improved products as the millennium neared, they did so with the stated intent to serve children. But behind the boardroom doors they were also targeting an adult market vastly larger.

The manufacturers' first order of business was getting doctors nationwide to believe that ADHD in adults was real and common— then, hopefully, best treated with their product. So, just as they had long done with childhood ADHD, companies reenlisted their legion of "key opinion leaders" to evangelize all things *adult* ADHD. Forget the brand of drug—the primary goal was to convince as many adults as possible that they might have ADHD and need drug treatment of any kind. (After all, getting half of a $2 billion market pales to splitting $5 billion three ways.) Getting there required more than just crass advertising, though. Companies had to get creative.

Eli Lilly built a mechanism not for money laundering, but what might be called message laundering. It gathered most of the top experts in the field, primarily the Joe Biederman group at Harvard, and bankrolled the founding of the National Alliance for the Advancement of ADHD Care.* The organization sounded to the naked ear like a rea-

---

*Keith Conners was not an officer of the group, but served on its "faculty" and gave lectures on its behalf.

sonably independent medical association; in practice, it functioned as a Lilly front group of well-paid spokesmen whose sole purpose was to teach primary-care physicians how to diagnose adults with the disorder—and then, wink-wink, prescribe Strattera.

The group held medical education conferences across the country, some simulcast on the Internet for optimal reach, titled "ADHD in Adults: The Often Missed Diagnosis." They explained how adult ADHD was real, and that perhaps ten million Americans were afflicted with it. They demonstrated how the condition ran in families, so that doctors could diagnose parents right along with their kids. They flashed brain scans of ADHD and normal brains, slides whose tiny, abstruse differences in color splotches beguiled audiences with the sheen of science. One such meeting, at Cincinnati Children's Hospital, was hosted by doctors who had been funded to conduct some of Lilly's Strattera trials. The hospital's psychiatry director remarked to the local business journal: "We're only seeing the tip of the iceberg if adult ADHD is going to be readily accepted like erectile dysfunction was."

Keith Conners conducted some of Eli Lilly's first clinical trials on Strattera, and served on its Global Advisory Board, being paid thousands of dollars per lecture. In them, he explained (quite reasonably) that Strattera was a positive development in ADHD care—it was not a stimulant like Adderall or Concerta, but an altogether different chemical, called atomoxetine, which didn't appear to have the same risk for addiction. This was the good part. Less good was its effectiveness. After one lecture, an audience member raised his hand and asked Conners: "How well does it work?" With characteristic scientific dispassion, Conners replied that Strattera hadn't been pitted head-to-head with Adderall or Concerta yet, but early returns suggested that it might be a little less effective than conventional stimulants.

Later that night, in his hotel room, Conners's phone rang. It was Doug Kelsey, a Lilly executive who had arranged for Conners to speak at the event. Conners recalls Kelsey saying: "What were you thinking, Keith? That was way off-base. You shouldn't have said that."

"What?" Conners replied.

"Saying Strattera is not as good as the other drugs."

"That isn't incorrect," Conners said. "It has a smaller effect size."

"If you stray from what we ask you to talk about," Kelsey said, "we won't be able to use your services anymore."

Conners stiffened. "I just told what I thought was scientifically the fact."

"Well, I'm sorry, Keith, but you have to understand we can't allow you to say things off-line like that."

Conners's name was removed from Lilly's consultant list. He would never speak for the company again.

FOR THE DOCTORS who didn't attend conferences or watch videos online, Shire sent the show to their mailbox. These installments didn't peddle Adderall XR specifically. The company sold adult ADHD itself, knowing that prescriptions would follow.

Few were more eager to help than Dr. William Dodson, a psychiatrist from Denver who had already assisted with many Shire projects. In April 2002, he stood before an audience of seventy doctors at the Ritz-Carlton Hotel & Spa in Pasadena, California, and delivered a Power-Point presentation titled "ADHD and the New Standards of Care." One slide told doctors to "educate the patient on the lifelong nature of the disorder and the benefits of lifelong treatment"—despite science then and now showing that as many as 30 to 50 percent of ADHD kids do not retain symptoms past childhood (and that little was known about the safety or efficacy of long-term stimulant use). In 2004, aiming to build the grown-up ADHD market, Shire commissioned Dodson to author a booklet called *Faces of Adult ADHD*. It would be distributed to doctors nationwide, with a cover that promised to "help clinicians recognize and diagnose adults with ADHD." Give Dodson credit: He got right down to business.

"We know now that about 10% of adults have ADHD, which means you're probably already treating patients with ADHD even though you don't know it," the first paragraph ended. That 10 percent figure was a gross misrepresentation. The two studies Dr. Dodson footnoted to back it up, which surely no one ever checked, were papers regarding children, not adults; no credible national study before (or since) has ever estimated an adult prevalence as high as 10 percent.

Dr. Dodson continued, "I promise you: the improvement you will see in a properly treated adult ADHD patient—and the gratitude that patient will demonstrate—will be among your most satisfying clinical experiences." The message to doctors: Stimulants would feel as good to you as the patient, who would keep coming back for more. To illustrate, Dr. Dodson described some success stories. "Daniel," a scatterbrained underachiever, went to a doctor who "decided that a trial of medication for ADHD could be worthwhile"; both rejoiced when it "helped him concentrate on his many business activities." (Supposedly, Daniel had since become CEO of a large commercial real estate company.) "Melissa" was no longer overwhelmed as wife and mother, thanks to her diagnosis and prescription. And fear not, doctors, amphetamines aren't addictive at all. Just listen to a patient named Scarlett, who reassured them: "If you give me a drink or a drug, I'll abuse it, but not this medication. I don't consider it a drug. Drugs get abused. Medication helps people have satisfying lives."

None of this baloney could be touched by the Food and Drug Administration; even though the booklet was funded by Shire, the manufacturer of Adderall, it didn't discuss Adderall itself, and therefore did not officially qualify as product advertising. All it was selling was adult ADHD.

As much as Big Pharma tried to prove how much people benefited from taking medications, it focused even more on the dangers awaiting those who did not. (Call this the equivalent of negative political ads— it's easier to depict others' faults than to prove your own strengths.) Shire commissioned a telephone survey it coyly called "Capturing America's Attention," in which adults who had been diagnosed with ADHD were asked about how their lives were unraveling. The results: People with ADHD were twice as likely to be divorced or separated; less likely to graduate from high school or college; more likely to be arrested; more likely to smoke or abuse drugs; and more likely to be depressed with a negative self-image. This was all quantified and written up in scientific verbiage for a paper published in the *Journal of Clin-*

ical Psychiatry. But Shire made sure to jump the gun with a press release in May of 2004, headlined "Survey of Adults Reveals Life-Long Consequences of Attention-Deficit/Hyperactivity Disorder." It described how "ADHD may prohibit adults with the condition from reaching their full academic and occupational potential, and limit their satisfaction with themselves and their relationships." If anyone didn't want to take Shire's word for it, Harvard's Joe Biederman himself provided the press release's money quote, one sounding awfully like something scripted by the company: "The compelling results of this survey," Biederman said, "reinforce the fact that ADHD is a serious medical condition causing significant, life-long impairments."

The following May, Biederman stood before a huge audience at the American Psychiatric Association's annual meeting to describe how he had computed just how much ADHD cost American households: $77 billion. The disorder, he said, "may be one of the costliest medical conditions in the United States," an inane assertion, akin to saying that West Virginia is one of the largest states in the union. But the survey worked perfectly: The figures, and Biederman's statements, were reproduced on medical websites, included in CHADD materials, and cited by slews of other scientific papers.

But how should a doctor diagnose adult ADHD, when a few of *DSM*'s official criteria, like "runs about or climbs excessively" and "has difficulty waiting turn," sounded so, well, so *childish*? Could there be a better way? Lilly took the lead here, enlisting some Biederman team doctors and Dr. Lenard Adler—an emerging adult ADHD specialist at New York University—to translate the *DSM* symptoms into an eighteen-item checklist for grown-ups. (For example, "Often leaves seat in classroom" became, "How often do you leave your seat in meetings?") But even that became too inefficient for doctors wanting to make the diagnosis. Less than a year later, having decided that "An 18-question screening scale is too long for many purposes," the team announced a better way to fit ADHD appraisals into doctors' busy schedules: a checklist of only six questions:

1. How often do you have trouble wrapping up the fine details of a project, once the challenging parts have been done?

2. How often do you have difficulty getting things in order when you have to do a task that requires organization?
3. When you have a task that requires a lot of thought, how often do you avoid or delay getting started?
4. How often do you have problems remembering appointments or obligations?
5. How often do you fidget or squirm with your hands or your feet when you have to sit down for a long time?
6. How often do you feel overly active and compelled to do things, like you were driven by a motor?

Respondents checked off whether they experienced those problems "never," "rarely," "sometimes," "often," or "very often." For questions 3, 5, and 6, any "often" or higher counted for one point; questions 1, 2, and 4 got a point for something as weak as "sometimes." Four total points signaled ADHD. So if you occasionally had trouble finishing tasks, were disorganized, and forgot some appointments, you were three-quarters there. An "often" on anything else put you over the top. The developers of this screening tool, in a tradition stretching back to Keith Conners's first scale in the 1960s, cautioned that doctors shouldn't rely on this sheet alone, that a score of 4 meant only that "further investigation is warranted," as they put it. But in the same breath—literally, the same paragraph—they wrote that passing their test meant "the patient has symptoms highly consistent with ADHD." They got the quiz endorsed by the World Health Organization (WHO), an imprimatur that forever obscured its Big Pharma roots.

Naturally, Eli Lilly then assembled a veritable all-star team to measure (and undoubtedly expand) ADHD's adult market. The study was led by the Biederman group, Russell Barkley, and Len Adler. Using the streamlined six-question questionnaire as one of their tools, the researchers determined that 4.4 percent of American adults, about ten million, had ADHD.

"Efforts are needed to increase the detection and treatment of adult ADHD," the paper concluded. Guess who was ready and waiting, advertisements cocked and ready.

*   *   *

SHIRE FIRED FAST. One was a picture of a wedding-day bride and groom in which the bride was airbrushed out, "DIVORCED" stamped across it; another in the series featured a woman's driver's license blocked out by "REVOKED." One ad told doctors, "Adults with ADHD were 3x more likely to be unemployed. The consequences may be serious. Screen for ADHD." Of course, to back up these statements and reassure folks that they were grounded in science, the advertisements footnoted the studies by Barkley and Biederman—studies spawned in pharma's own boardrooms.

Shire was betting on the growth of adult ADHD more than most people realized. With Adderall XR's patent protection expiring soon, slaughtering the company's yearly $1 billion cash cow, financial analysts started downgrading Shire's stock rating and forecasting a dire future. Shire had to come up with something new. So it worked with a small firm, New River Pharmaceuticals, on a slightly tweaked form of Adderall called lisdexamfetamine dimesylate, and in 2007 paid New River $2.6 billion to gain exclusive rights to what became Vyvanse. (As opposed to Adderall, the name had nothing to do with ADHD—its first syllable merely evoked "vitality," and its entire name was strangely similar to the "Vivarin" caffeine pills long sold over the counter.) Vyvanse launched in July 2008, with Shire unleashing its top spokesman, Ty Pennington, on a media tour that turned more surreal than his talk show.

Pennington swiftly appeared on the radio program hosted by the conservative personality Glenn Beck, which reached about six million listeners daily. His audience had every reason to expect a standard chummy chat about *Extreme Makeover*. But right from the start, for the first ten minutes, they instead giggled about their mutual ADHD. Beck had long celebrated overcoming his mental disorder to attain celebrity and national influence. But this episode went much further.

"Once I was put on lasting medications like Vyvanse, next thing you know, *bam*—it's like somebody gave me glasses and all of a sudden I could see," Pennington raved.

Beck later: "The first time I took ADD medication, I wept because I played with my son on the floor for forty minutes and I had never done that with any of my children. It was . . . it was night and day."

Pennington never mentioned he was a paid spokesman for Shire and its Vyvanse launch. Neither acknowledged stimulants' abuse potential and addictiveness, particularly among adults.

The FDA couldn't jump on these shenanigans because the Glenn Beck show (somehow) didn't qualify as a Shire advertisement. But the feds did send Shire a cease-and-desist letter for a video of Pennington the company posted on YouTube, in which Pennington repeated his Vyvanse chorus. "Once I got on the medication, it's just amazing the transformation I made," he said. "It literally changed my life and gave me the confidence to achieve my goals." The FDA had to remind Shire that Vyvanse had never been shown to change lives and give people confidence. Shire's explanation: The video was supposed to remain internal, but some employee goofed by putting it online. The company took it down. The spot had been up for months, watched by countless consumers.*

Adults who wondered if they also had ADHD were bombarded by the six-question quiz that Eli Lilly had paid its doctors to devise, which, because of the WHO endorsement, any company could now use to drive people to their doctor. Johnson & Johnson struck first to push Concerta. It brilliantly leveraged Biederman-group studies that assessed how ADHD ran in families in pamphlets titled "Like Parent, Like Child?"—which told adults, "If your child has been diagnosed with ADHD, you may have it too." The booklets, complete with the quiz—and the answers that would lead to a diagnosis conveniently *highlighted yellow*—were placed in piles in doctors' waiting rooms by sales reps. Parents bringing their kids to the psychiatrist would learn that "ADHD is a highly heritable disorder," take the quiz, reconsider

---

*For some reason, the FDA did not come down on Shire for its revamped magazine ads that depicted suburban parents describing how Vyvanse had worked on them. A man lounged on the family couch eating popcorn with his adoring wife and daughter, saying he was now "able to sit through my child's favorite movie." One mother thanked Vyvanse for helping her get dinner ready for the kids so she could spend time with her husband.

their own forgetfulness and procrastination, and all but diagnose themselves. Efforts like this led a company that evaluated pharmaceutical marketing to rank J&J's Concerta campaign "Genius."

In perhaps the creepiest maneuver of all, Shire literally drove the quiz directly to adults. During the summers of 2008 and 2009, it commissioned a massive tractor trailer to rumble into state fairs nationwide, inviting folks to hop on board and get screened for ADHD. Almost 100,000 people broke away from the prize pigs and volleyball tomatoes to get evaluated.

Shire soon ditched such old-school methods and focused on the most powerful distribution system around: the Internet. The six-question quiz began appearing on dozens of websites. One was everydayhealth.com, a prominent portal of supposedly unbiased psychiatric information that under the hood had significant elements sponsored by Shire—including the questionnaire for users to assess their own ADHD. But crucial aspects of the quiz had magically changed. Hidden to all, someone altered the test's back-end scoring system; any symptom rated "sometimes" or above got overweighted to artificially raise the user's final score. Those results were then explained in language styled to seduce. People with low scores were told "ADHD Unlikely." Those in a narrow midrange section were told "ADHD Possible," that it would be "advisable and likely beneficial for you to seek further diagnosis." And then, stunningly, everyone else was told "ADHD May Be Likely." Now, everything "may be likely"—the question is whether it is or isn't, and to what extent. But this was a brilliant construction, as its hedge ("may") was immediately overcome by the real message ("likely"). Users were instructed to visit their doctor for an evaluation. In the end, about half of people who took this quiz were told they might have ADHD and were encouraged to consider treatment.*

Prescriptions predictably soared among young adults in their twenties and thirties. Scripts for ADHD numbered 5.6 million in 2007; only five years later, the total had almost tripled, to 16 million. It kept

---

*In 2013, even after correcting for the misweighted scoring system, the *New York Times* administered the quiz by phone to more than a thousand randomly selected adults. Forty-nine percent landed in the "possible" or "may be likely" categories.

going higher from there. Shire's chief executive, Angus Russell, took to Bloomberg TV to tell investors just how great the company's bet on ADHD was: "The fastest growing segment of the market now," he said, "is the new adults who were never diagnosed."

By this time, Shire had moved past Ty Pennington and sought a new face of ADHD, someone higher on the popular-with-everyone scale. The company teamed with CHADD and another advocacy group to form a campaign they called "It's Your ADHD—Own It," whose title clearly signaled their Hallowellian strategy to get potential patients not only to accept their problem, but also to take pride in it. Shire and its allies needed a celebrity for this push, so it chose one of the most universally admired among the coveted eighteen-to-thirty-five market—Adam Levine, the dreamboat lead singer of Maroon 5. In magazine ads, Levine told readers, "I remember being the kid with ADHD. Truth is, I still have it." But video was where the charismatic Levine would shine. His "ADHD—Own It" testimonial, which aired more than eight thousand times nationally in the second half of 2011, was run specifically alongside Levine's appearances on the *Today* show and *Saturday Night Live*. It appeared not just on television but also video streams from MTV, ABC, Fox, and Hulu, where it was viewed 40 million times.

"I didn't outgrow my ADHD—did you?" Levine asked reassuringly. He described how he was "stuck" writing his first album because he couldn't organize his thoughts: "So many amazing songs, so many amazing ideas, just fall by the wayside." So he went to the doctor, he said, and was now encouraging you to do the same. The spot wrapped up with a female voice telling viewers, "If you were diagnosed with ADHD as a kid, you might still have it. Find out more—take a quiz at ownyouradhd.com to recognize your symptoms." As it turns out, ownyouradhd.com wasn't a stand-alone website—it instantly sent people to the Everyday Health questionnaire sponsored by Shire, the one with the rejiggered scoring system and absurd "ADHD May Be Likely" messaging. More than half a million people took the quiz.

Not long afterward, the Letters section of CHADD's magazine, *ADDitude*, featured a note from "Mark" that sounded an awful lot like a television ad:

ADHD is Cool?

Finding out that Adam Levine, of Maroon 5 and The Voice, is challenged by ADHD gives me the inspiration to try and manage my own symptoms. . . . I've been diagnosed, but I haven't started medication. Adam's experience with ADHD medication will get me to talk with my doctor about whether it is right for me.

The fairy tale continued. A few months later, *People* magazine named Adam Levine its "Sexiest Man Alive."

Chapter 14

AWAKENING

Everyone called her Puppy. Conners had originally named her Annie, for his mother back in Utah, but the little brown Labradoodle was too spunky for something so matronly. The pooch bounded after squirrels, slobbered on visitors, and enlivened the days of this old doctor pushing eighty, enjoying his well-funded retirement. Conners had his hobbies—painting, exercising, watching baseball on TV, and rereading Great Books, from Plato's *Dialogues* to more contemporary stuff, like Galileo. But his true passion was Puppy.

One morning, as they walked down Colony Road near their home in Durham, Puppy sighted some friendly-looking passersby and jumped toward them, frantically entangling Conners in her leash. He fell hard to the pavement, shattering his left femur. Conners was whisked away by ambulance, wailing in agony as his leg swelled to the size of a watermelon, to a Duke University Hospital operating room.

Conners awoke from the anesthesia in terrible pain and incredibly thirsty. When nurses explained that it was too soon after the surgery to drink anything, he was so disoriented from the drugs that he thought the people standing over him were Taliban soldiers keeping him prisoner. So he tried to escape. He leapt out of bed—almost shearing the sutures in his reconstructed leg—and punched the closest person square in the face. A nurse. He was tied to his bed and sedated until the psychosis passed.

When Conners finally came to, his doctor explained that he was lucky to be alive, that only one in three people his age survive his injury and the surgery that followed. Conners knew this was no exaggeration—his beloved friend and mentor, Leon Eisenberg, had, only a few years before, slipped on ice, broken his arm, had a seizure, and died. During Conners's six weeks in the hospital and then ten more bedridden months at Hillcrest Convalescent Center, he had plenty of time to ponder his own mortality.

He did have someone to ponder it with. Carolyn Cofrancesco, a young child psychologist even more sweet than beautiful, had worked in Conners's Duke University clinic for a few years before his retirement. They were fond of each other but kept their distance until he left. She phoned Conners and asked him to dinner. They married the next year; she was thirty-five, he seventy-two. Carolyn's spirit so invigorated Conners that he had begun lifting weights and running ten miles a day. Then, his broken leg rendered him an old man forever.

On February 3, 2013, Super Bowl Sunday, Conners lay in bed when a nurse arrived with his weekly treat—the Sunday *New York Times*, the polymathic beast with book reviews, travel essays, and the tortuous crossword. But he started with Section A, Page 1. A huge photograph at the top showed a handsome, cap-and-gowned college graduate looking off into the future like so many classmates. Underneath it, the headline:

DROWNED IN A STREAM OF PRESCRIPTIONS
Addict's Parents Couldn't Halt Flow of Attention Deficit Drug

It was the story of Richard Fee. As Conners kept reading the sprawling, operatic tragedy, each paragraph more horrifying than the one before, it shook his soul unlike any other reader's. He felt almost ashamed. He felt . . . *complicit*.

The article presented pictures of the actual zero-to-three Conners-esque symptom questionnaire on which Richard had strategically circled numbers in his first waiting room: *Do you make a lot of mistakes in school or work?* (1); *Do you have trouble paying attention when watching movies, reading, or during lectures?* (3); *Do you have trouble sitting still?* (2). Conners saw the nurse's scratch marks adding the scores up to 29. Then, on the chart, in script, "ADD, inattentive type." He could almost see it unfolding, as if in real time. Conners wondered to himself: *Is this how my scales are being used?*

Conners watched the prescriptions and doses increase, hallucinations scramble Richard's brain, and his psychiatrists pay no attention. *Did I help pharma cover up the dangers of these drugs?* He saw Richard's hometown doctors never check Richard for ADHD at all, just take the kid's word for it. *This is what doctors are doing?* Conners didn't feel as if he had killed Richard Fee. But the system he had helped build sure did.*

Then came the voice of Leon Eisenberg, who had years before developed serious misgivings about his own role in the explosion of ADHD and Ritalin. Shortly before he died, Eisenberg wrote an essay titled "Were We All Asleep at the Switch?" in which he accused psychiatry of letting itself get commandeered by Big Pharma. In an interview, he said: "Drugs are being prescribed . . . for kids that don't have reasonable ADHD. They are being prescribed without any kind of monitoring at all. Schoolteachers call the pediatrician, the pediatrician finds it the easiest way to deal with it. I think it's dreadful." During a conversation with Conners, Eisenberg asked his protégé, with a whiff of paternal disapproval, "How much have you made off your rating scales? Is that why so many kids are being misdiagnosed?" Conners resented the implication.

But the Richard Fee story became Conners's smelling salts, shuddering him alert to a problem he had so comfortably ignored. He told Carolyn that the feeling was like one of those illusional sketches that can appear to be two things at once, depending on how you look at it—two faces or an urn, swimming fish or flying birds. He couldn't get out of his mind the well-known drawing that could be either a young, beautiful woman or, just as easily, an old hag. For five decades, Conners had seen the worlds of ADHD and Ritalin as noble. But he saw something different now. Something shady.

---

*Conners's dismay worsened when he came across a Letter to the Editor in the *Raleigh News & Observer*, his local paper that reprinted the Richard Fee article. A Durham child psychiatrist exonerated the string of doctors who had so clearly mistreated Fee, and instead blamed insurance companies. The clinicians "could not afford to spend adequate time with patients," he wrote, because of "inadequate reimbursement for mental health services." The letter was signed Dr. Scott H. Kollins of the Duke University ADHD Program, whom Conners had hired thirteen years before.

A few days after the Richard Fee story appeared, a Duke student visited Conners in the hospital.

"I have to ask you something," Conners said from his bed, fearing the answer. "How easy is it to get Ritalin on campus?"

The kid almost laughed.

"If I asked three guys," he said, "two of them would be able to give it to me on the spot."

Conners decided to learn more. Ever the scientist, he didn't want to rely on anecdotes, even those as moving as Richard Fee's. He wanted hard data. How many children are actually being diagnosed? How old are they? What percentage are put on medication?

Those statistics would tell Conners the state of ADHD in America. He went after every figure he could get. What he discovered was a numbers game just as disturbing, and misleading, as everything else.

IT BECAME A catchphrase, an industry talking point learned at conventions and repeated in interviews, distorting discourse as brilliantly as "Guns don't kill people, people kill people." As concern rose in the 1990s and 2000s that too many children were being labeled with attention deficit hyperactivity disorder, advocates deployed the line with such alacrity that dissent could only nod, downright charmed.

"ADHD," they would say, "is overdiagnosed and underdiagnosed."

Who could argue with that? A concession to the undeniable—obviously, some kids were being mislabeled and medicated—took an immediate right turn into a notion just as compelling or more: that some kids with untreated ADHD were still out there, suffering. The ADHD lobby used the overdiagnosed-underdiagnosed line not just while addressing the public, like CHADD executive director Leslie Roth in a Florida newspaper in 1996; doctors used it among themselves, too, in such publications as *Clinical Psychiatry News*. It was repeated so countlessly that journalists began parroting it verbatim as established and unremarkable fact. The magic sentence still pervades discussions about ADHD, clouding conversation from the start.

At its core, this issue is rooted in simple numbers—diagnosis rates kept since the days of minimal brain dysfunction. When MBD stood trial at the 1970 congressional hearing, experts estimated that perhaps 2 or 3 percent of children nationally had the condition—a forecast that, even without any studies to support it, was not particularly blasphemous. As the American Psychiatric Association repurposed MBD into attention deficit disorder in the 1980 *DSM*, it declared that the condition was "common"—that perhaps as many as 3 percent had the disorder. By 1994, the new edition of the *DSM* inched its estimate upward to "3%–5% in school-age children." Today's *DSM*, relying on hundreds of studies that have assessed how often children truly show the symptoms of ADHD, has settled on this flat benchmark: 5 percent.

That is the level that the experts, after great, consensus-building deliberations, have decided is a fair approximation of how many children truly have the life-altering psychiatric condition. If there were a telltale blood test or magic X-ray to give to every child—which there isn't, of course—that is how many would probably qualify. The question then becomes: What is actually happening in actual doctors' offices? Regardless of whether a child's behaviors really do fit the approved criteria of ADHD, how many are still being *diagnosed*?

The US Centers for Disease Control and Prevention (CDC) examines this crucial distinction not with stethoscopes, but telephones. The agency regularly surveys tens of thousands of parents nationwide regarding the health care of their children, asking simple yes-or-no questions about various medical conditions they might be diagnosed with, from those that have definite diagnostic procedures (such as cancer) to more murky matters like ADHD. In 2003, the CDC found that 7.8 percent of children had been diagnosed with ADHD—with about half of them currently taking medication.

Mental health experts dismissed those figures out of hand. Dr. Peter Jensen, who helped run the infamous MTA study that oversold the benefits of Ritalin, claimed that such surveys were meaningless, because studies had shown that parents gave inaccurate answers 30 percent of the time. His response was disingenuous, for two reasons. First, to suggest that so many parents don't know whether their child has been diagnosed with a serious problem as to throw the numbers way off (in either direction) is silly. Second, studies by none other than the Joe Biederman group at Harvard had concluded that mothers were indeed quite accurate and reliable in describing their children's often subtle and nebulous ADHD symptoms.* During criticism of the CDC survey—which Biederman himself joined—the assumption that these women suddenly couldn't remember whether their child had actually received a diagnosis or not went unexplained. One doctor from central New York who regularly diagnoses children said of the 7.8 percent result, dead seriously: "I don't believe those numbers. The CDC cooks their books just to get more funding."

Seeking a more thorough consideration of which diagnosed children really had ADHD, the CDC interviewed a representative group of parents nationwide about their child's hyperactivity and inattentiveness to estimate whether they met the disorder's official criteria. Eventually published in 2007 by researchers at Cincinnati Children's Hospital Medical Center, those data suggested that at most 8.7 percent of children had the condition—a rate close enough to the CDC's 7.8 percent of real-life diagnoses to seemingly vindicate how the ADHD system was operating. Moreover, only half of those 8.7 percent with real ADHD had ever been diagnosed; the other half, millions of youngsters, were surely struggling without treatment. Drug makers rejoiced. Shire broadcast the findings in their marketing materials as peer-reviewed, indisputable, CDC-sanctioned proof that the problem with ADHD was not *overdiagnosis* but, just as the experts had said all along, *under-diagnosis*.

What went unnoticed, then and ever since, was that some alarming numbers elsewhere in that study's data set had been rather conveniently ignored. First, 3.3 percent of children aged eight to fifteen—or almost a million in that age group alone—were found to be taking ADHD medications *despite not having diagnosis-worthy symptoms*. Now, this was not necessarily some smoking gun. The whole point of ADHD kids taking medication, the study authors noted quite reasonably, is to improve their behavior; so these prescriptions could once have been justified and simply be working as expected. But there remained a

---

*Biederman et al.'s exact words: "clinicians and researchers can have confidence in diagnoses derived from maternal reports of psychopathology in their ADHD children . . . reliability and recall accuracy over a 1-year period are very good."

problem that went unaddressed. If those 3.3 percent had in fact been correct diagnoses, they would join the 8.7 percent of children who were still presenting diagnosis-worthy symptoms. That meant *12 percent* of American kids would suddenly have ADHD, a completely indefensible figure that begged some explanation. It got none. In the end, anyone who would have cared to look deeper at this fact and others lurking in the Cincinnati paper and elsewhere would have had no choice but to realize that perhaps as many as two million children across America were taking stimulants for ADHD *they did not have*. But no one took the time to look.

The CDC's next survey, released in 2010, raised the national estimate of ADHD diagnosis in children from 7.8 percent to 9.5. The next one, only three years later, went up to 11—more than twice what even the American Psychiatric Association's official manual said was proper.

And yet the situation was even far worse than those numbers indicate. A crucial distinction in these conversations is roundly misunderstood not only by the ADHD cognoscenti, but by many government health officials as well. It follows logically, unassailably, from experts' longtime and passionate contention that a person's ADHD is *innate*— something that regardless of when it's diagnosed had always been, and always will be, part of a person's inherent brain chemistry.

The CDC's 11 percent came from the entire population of 56 million children who were aged four to seventeen. The problem is, in right-now snapshots like these, most of the younger children hadn't reached the age (ten? eleven? fifteen?) at which their hardwired ADHD will become visible, recognized, and diagnosed. They must count in the totals, too— because what we truly want to ask is how many of these 56 million specific human beings will, at whatever point before they become adults, be told they have the lifetime condition. This approach considers each child as a self-contained, evolving individual—which, after all, is the point of psychiatry itself. What happens to the numbers then?

The answer is shocking. The CDC's data unmistakably show that 15 percent of all American children today—one in seven, now *triple* the APA's stated appropriate rate—will be diagnosed with ADHD. Among boys, the figure is a whopping 20 percent, or one in five nationwide. In many Southern states like Arkansas, Kentucky, and South Carolina, almost 30 percent—one in three!—of boys get diagnosed, most of them put on medication at some point. The data are so staggering that the *New York Times* article that revealed them appeared in the top-right corner of the paper's front page, a spot usually reserved for wars and government corruption.

But yet again, with these numbers reaching heights no one had ever imagined, the industry's level of denial somehow kept pace. The American Medical Association simply harrumphed, claiming that yes-or-no surveys "overestimate true prevalence" of medical conditions. Dr. Sanjay Gupta, CNN's brainy physician-on-call, flatly declared to Anderson Cooper: "There's not a lot of value in these studies." Dr. Peter Jensen reappeared to say that "single-question surveys based on a yes-no parent report are notoriously inaccurate. You simply can't make scientific statements based on them." None of these commenters either recognized or admitted that the CDC's results had been validated by numerous other studies, and thereby held far more truth than they preferred.

The most obtuse response came from Dr. John Walkup of Weill Cornell Medical College in New York, a prominent voice who was given three pages in child psychiatry's top journal to chime in on the findings. He highlighted that the CDC had found that only two-thirds of diagnosed children were taking medication—creating, sure enough, "a pattern of undertreatment of ADHD, not of overtreatment." (Roughly translated: *Diagnose as many kids as you want, just make sure they're medicated.*) But not all was lost, Dr. Walkup wrote. These high numbers were actually all good news.

His conclusion: "It appears that we are getting close—after more than 2 decades of advocacy—to identifying and treating a majority of children and adolescents with ADHD."

CONNERS READ THE comments from Walkup and others with whom he had long schmoozed at industry and Big Pharma events—Russ Barkley, Joe Biederman, CHADD—and pondered the role he had played in all this. He always knew that his Conners Scale was misused from time to time. But it, and its descendants, had clearly gotten in the hands of doctors who couldn't handle them, like a manic fire hose.

The news kept getting worse, sometimes head-slappingly absurd.

One day, Conners clicked on a web article about a new study headlined, "Drug Therapy for *Parents'* ADHD Improves *Kids'* Behavior" (emphasis added). Apparently, a researcher had determined that thirty-eight men and women with ADHD who took Vyvanse showed better "ability to help their children do homework and . . . interact with their children in a more positive, nurturing way," which made them more obedient. The message: Treat your ADHD with Vyvanse and your kids will act better too!* Only after the two-page article concluded did it acknowledge that Shire had paid for the study.

The *Times* profiled a doctor in rural Georgia who prescribed Adderall and Concerta not because children had real ADHD, but merely to help them in what were financially strapped, subpar schools. "I don't have a whole lot of choice," the doctor explained candidly. "We've decided as a society that it's too expensive to modify the kid's environment. So we have to modify the kid." Perhaps even more amazing, several experts conceded that this approach was not necessarily rare. They agreed that, because class sizes have consistently increased while physical education and other services waned, doctors were indeed being forced to rely on medication to keep some kids from getting sucked down failure's whirlpool. Stephen Colbert, on *The Colbert Report*, discussed the phenomenon while coining his own term for it: *Meducation*.

There was the Harvard nurse practitioner who said she diagnosed kids because they drank Red Bull. There was a study from Oklahoma and South Carolina that found that only about one in three children taking ADHD medications there actually met criteria for the disorder. Then there was Richard Fee.

Conners decided to push back, at least in a way that behooved a Rhodes Scholar.

Conners had already agreed to serve on the board of directors of a relatively new association of doctors called the American Professional Society of ADHD and Related Disorders. The group claimed to be devoted to promoting research and understanding of the disorder; its very existence depended on the continued growth of the ADHD

---

*This was a spooky reincarnation of Ritalin's old claim that it would make children "lovable again."

industry. (A slide during one of its meetings played off an old American Express slogan by telling the audience: "ADHD: It's Everywhere YOU Want to Be.") Its cofounders were Dr. Len Adler of New York University, who helped develop the six-question form to screen adults while receiving great institutional and personal funding from Big Pharma, and Dr. Anthony Rostain of the Hospital of the University of Pennsylvania, a clinician who, like Adler, liked to brush aside rising rates among children with the vapid "overdiagnosed and underdiagnosed" cliché. Conners was starting to see all this nonsense in a new light. When he was asked to deliver the closing address for the group's 2013 conference in Washington, DC, he accepted with intentions no one foresaw.

Conners hobbled to the podium slowly, neither physically nor emotionally the man who opened the National Institute of Mental Health conference in 1998. His permanently damaged leg left him using a cane on which he leaned heavily. He received a standing ovation from an audience that clearly sensed this might be their last chance to honor the father of their field.

Conners went through the steady climb of national diagnosis rates among children—the incipient group of kids with minimal brain dysfunction, the 2 to 3 percent believed to exist in the early 1970s, the 3 to 5 percent in the 1980s, the 5 to 7 percent in the 1990s, and then the explosion to its current 11 percent. He contended that this was scandalously high, that studies involving proper and careful evaluations of kids suggested that the true number was probably 2 or 3 percent, 5 percent tops. He discussed how the entire field, himself included, had turned a blind eye to the situation, and the time had arrived to do something about it.

The current state of ADHD, he closed, was a "national disaster of dangerous proportions."

The audience didn't know what to make of that final remark. Had they heard Conners correctly? No, there it was on his PowerPoint slide. Was his mind as wobbly as his leg? Didn't seem like it. They sat silent for an awkward few seconds before realizing that they had to clap as Conners returned to his seat.

No one asked him about his statement afterward. They ignored it, preferring to chalk it up to a spasm of senility that would be rude to question. Conners was eighty, clearly disconnected from the modern field. Old news. He was not a player anymore.

Conners was furious. Academics trained to weigh alternate hypotheses—to reconsider their own longtime beliefs—heard what he said and were too arrogant even to consider it. They thought Conners would just fade away.

He didn't. While researching for his talk, Conners had noticed that North Carolina, his adopted home state, owned the dubious distinction of having the nation's highest rate of kids diagnosed with ADHD. He had probably played some role in that, with his Duke clinic serving more children than ever since he'd left.

So when an opportunity arrived for him to see the mess with his own eyes, in one community just down the interstate, he got in his car to investigate.

TIM SUTTON WAS a commissioner of Alamance County, in the dead center of North Carolina. In many ways Alamance could be any rural area in America, a cluster of small, spread-out towns whose best textile and manufacturing days are behind them—and whose metropolis is Burlington, population fifty-one thousand. Residents aren't Andy and Opie Taylor rubes of Andy Griffith's fictional television, but they like their church, their traditions, and not being told how to raise their children. But Sutton resolved to shake things up.

For three years, Sutton had heard how his grandson's elementary school was pushing to have the boy evaluated and medicated for ADHD, so he investigated further and found just how common such strong-arming might be. Almost 16 percent of North Carolina's children, about one in six, had already been diagnosed with ADHD by a medical provider, leading the nation. Among those of high school age, more than 20 percent had been given the label, most of them taking medication at some point. Although further digging revealed that Alamance County's rates were probably a tick lower than the rest of North Carolina, they were still way too high. Sutton called a school superintendent from another part of the state to ask his reaction to these statistics; the superintendent grew increasingly unnerved, as *two of his own kids* were currently on Adderall at their school's suggestion. If a school official could be pressured into this, what chance did the average family have? Sutton phoned the state's Board of Eduction and got stonewalled. So Sutton chose to flex his county-commissioner muscle. In May 2014, he called a meeting of Alamance's school board to ask them questions directly, in the hope of finally getting some answers.

Having read in the *Times* about Keith Conners's growing distaste for the ADHD industry, and realizing that the man lived less than an hour away in Durham, Sutton invited him to come and contribute some insight, to tell everyone what ADHD was and was not. Conners, aware that some of these Alamance kids might very well have been diagnosed at his Duke clinic, gladly accepted the invitation and drove west to the 10 a.m. meeting. He sat down in a standard-issue, municipal-building conference room far removed from the luxurious, backslapping venues of his past. Here, he was an outsider. To the Alamance school superintendent, other county officials, and a few state folks making the trip from Raleigh—Sutton's ruckus had gotten some big cheeses' attention—Conners was less than welcome.

It did not go well. Sutton took the floor first and, in his best Southern Gentleman, thanked the officials for their time and attention to the matter. He never accused the school system or teachers of pushing parents, at least not knowingly; but something, whatever it was, was leading to so many children in the community being diagnosed with ADHD, with a vast majority being put on stimulant medications. He wondered how any of this might result from subtle incentives from the state—schools get extra funding for every child with a learning disability, and teachers can receive raises and tenure when their classes score highly on standardized tests. "I have a hard time believing that this many kids have a psychiatric disorder," he said. "When I talk with parents, ADHD is coming out in every corner. It's almost like I'm at an ADHD convention."

After twenty minutes, the state officials responded. One questioned the purpose of the meeting itself, because, after all, Alamance County's rates appeared lower than the North Carolina average—dopily ignoring that the rates were still indefensibly high. (He did later say, "If there's a problem, we're at the forefront of a solution," without offering any details about this solution.) A different official questioned what all the fuss was for; his own son had been diagnosed with ADHD, and the medication had really helped. Meanwhile, the Alamance superintendent, Lillie Cox, said nothing. She spent most of the time checking and pecking on her two mobile devices, rarely even looking up.

She didn't when Conners finally spoke, either. He offered his history in the field and said that no community, let alone state, should have anything close to one in five teenagers diagnosed with ADHD. "That's pretty scary—there's no way," he said. "A vast proportion of [kids] on medication received an incorrect diagnosis." He laid a good deal of blame at the feet of doctors who made swift and sloppy evaluations, but also questioned what role school systems play. "Testing and funding is at stake and nobody wants these kids dragging down the numbers," Conners said. "School systems have developed some secret process—teachers have a way of talking to parents. And it's not just teachers either; it's school personnel. There's a roundabout system because the incentives are for the school system to deliver better test scores, more end-of-school graduation rates."

When the superintendent was asked to look up from her cell phone and join the conversation, she refused to address what might be causing so many students in her district to be diagnosed with ADHD.

"That sounds like it's a question for physicians," she said. "Because they write the prescriptions."

Asked why so many parents were going to their physicians in the first place, she huffed: "That's a question for the parents."

Was it of concern to her that this was happening?

"Our responsibility is educating those children whether they're diagnosed or not."

Her verbal gymnastics continued, growing so inane that Sutton realized that the meeting had run its course. He had gotten nowhere with the people in charge of educating his community's youngsters—no explanations, no thoughts for doing better. He closed almost begging: "Please stop it the best you can here locally. *Please?*"

Everyone got up. Not one of the five school officials made small talk or even shook hands with Sutton or Conners. They all ducked out the room's back door, never to be heard from again.

*   *   *

DISMAYED MORE THAN ever, Conners wanted to check out the upcoming annual meeting of the American Academy of Child and Adolescent Psychiatry, the primary jamboree for child mental health professionals. He had gone for decades. But his leg kept him from flying to San Diego. It was just as well.

In room after room, experts stood before podiums and sat behind microphones teaching the current and next generation of clinicians about various syndromes, medications old and new, and other strategies to help children in need. This was all fine and perfectly admirable. Until you visited the ADHD seminars, which included some remarkable scenes:

- One session used a cell phone app to quiz the audience on basic ADHD issues, and then had a panel of experts discuss the answers. One question concerned a longtime debate regarding ADHD medications: Do they suppress children's growth? Less than half the audience gave the correct answer, which was that the longer a child stays on stimulants, the more his height can suffer.* (One doctor said he reassures parents that Michael Phelps, the buff Olympic swimmer who has ADHD, took stimulants as a kid—and became a national hero.) A case study involved a seven-year-old boy who, after two years on Concerta, abruptly became irritable and anxious—and began hallucinating. What was probably going on? Most of the audience answered correctly, that the Concerta had likely begun backfiring and causing serious side effects well known to occur occasionally. But then, Harvard's Tim Wilens, the Joe Biederman associate who had made millions of dollars working on behalf of pharmaceutical companies, said that he actually disagreed—that he "would have been concerned with an emerging disorder" on top of the ADHD.

---

*It's vital to note that while this growth suppression appears real, the effect is probably less than an inch on average—important for kids who actually lose two or maybe three, but not necessarily something to scare parents away from treating a truly impaired ADHD child.

His first instinct was not to heed well-known side effects, but to assume something new was wrong with the kid, often requiring another medication. (Which is what happened to Kristin Parber.)

• An academy committee that focused on medications— disquietingly titled the "Pediatric Psychopharmacology Initiative"—discussed its new guide to various ADHD meds. The book would be especially valuable for pediatricians to deal with parents, one attendee said, because "when you're in a busy primary-care practice and you don't have an hour to do an evaluation and go over side effects, it's a nice resource to have." The committee was not just ignoring but endorsing the greatest problem with ADHD today—quick-and-dirty diagnoses and prescriptions.

• A session devoted to the issue of college students abusing ADHD medication discussed a survey that found 30 percent of collegians had used them without a prescription, a figure that most people would find rather alarming. But one speaker explained that some estimates have been as high as 60 percent, so the problem really is not so bad. "Seventy percent are *not* using prescription stimulants," she reassured the audience. Only at a child-psychiatry convention can someone be heartened that only one in three college kids abuse amphetamines.

Conners was not required to go to the AACAP convention. He had no official role with the organization; his absence raised no eyebrows. Conners was expected, however, a few months later at the annual Washington, DC, meeting of APSARD, the American Professional Society of ADHD and Related Disorders, where the year before he had made his "national disaster of dangerous proportions" remark that everyone brushed off. He still served on the group's board of directors, a Mount Rushmore of ADHD that included Joe Biederman, Steve Faraone, and other luminaries. Conners had been to more than a hundred events like it. But this time, he arrived at the opulent Mandarin Hotel prepared to view the affair more skeptically.

At the board meeting, members discussed matter-of-factly that the convention had been almost entirely subsidized by Eli Lilly and Shire. A media consultant described how the association should start a Facebook campaign to grow its presence and market what he called its "product," a word that made Conners squirm to the point that he spoke up. "We're not selling cars," he said. "If fifteen percent of children have parents buying the 'product' of ADHD, then something is wrong, not right." The cofounder of APSARD, Dr. Len Adler of NYU, later remarked, "ADHD is both overdiagnosed and underdiagnosed. That's why we're having a session on prevalence rates—to talk about that." There it was again: *overdiagnosed and underdiagnosed*. The meeting devolved from there.

In one seminar, adult ADHD was compared to "erectile dysfunction of the mind." A room in which posters explained the results of soon-to-be-published studies had a few doozies, too. A poster presented new data on the wondrous effects of Strattera, manufactured by Eli Lilly, the convention's primary financial sponsor. Three of the five authors were Lilly employees; the others were Adler and Dr. Oren Mason of Grand Rapids, Michigan, who operates a clinic called "Attention MD" and has been paid almost $200,000 by Lilly as a consultant and speaker. Then, in the most delicious Lilly-related moment of all, APSARD gave its annual lifetime achievement award to an Eli Lilly employee. Not just any employee. It was Doug Kelsey—the same man who, a decade before, had scolded Keith Conners after a Strattera talk for not accentuating the product's positives.

Conners sat in the second row for the session he anticipated most: "Measuring ADHD Prevalence—Controversies About Overdiagnosis." The opening speaker fittingly came from the CDC, who explained where all of their percentages came from. Two longtime ADHD researchers, Dr. Jane Costello and Dr. Kathleen Merikangas, prattled on about the inner workings of various studies without meaningfully addressing how millions of children were being diagnosed well beyond what the *DSM* suggests.

When the question-and-answer portion opened, the first raised hand belonged to the old man in the second row. Conners wrenched himself to his feet and leaned on his cane. Everyone knew who he was. More than four hundred eyeballs fixed on him.

"When I see these prevalence rates going up to fifteen—almost twenty percent in the adolescent male population—I can't believe that represents real cases of ADHD," he said to his longtime colleagues. "But how does that get there?"

Costello did share Dr. Conners's concern. But she also reminded him how detached he might be from current realities, where one should not expect a child to be examined as thoroughly and carefully as in his day. This was a new world.

"It probably costs somewhere around $10,000," she explained, "to make a state-of-the-art diagnosis by the time you've interviewed the kid, interviewed the parent, gone to the school and had repeated assessments at school, and done this, that and the other and ruled out this diagnosis and that diagnosis. It's a very expensive process. And one can see why it doesn't happen."

Later, Dr. Costello was asked by another doctor whether all this talk about overdiagnosis should affect how he evaluates children for ADHD. She said no, because the disorder is, somehow, still *underdiagnosed*.

"My message to you," she answered, "would be this kid is very lucky to have gotten as far as your clinic. For every one you treat there are probably three or four out there who are not being treated. And what are you doing about them?"

CONNERS LEFT THE convention aghast. As he flew back to North Carolina, he realized that ADHD's power structure would never, at least in his remaining years, allow its momentum to be slowed. Too much money was at stake. Doctors who had rooted their mind-sets (or careers) in the disorder needed to keep their waiting rooms filled. Drug makers needed to sell—what was it again?—*product*. After decades of commanding ADHD's rocket as it lifted off on its remarkable journey, Conners now was its old fuel tank, disconnected and drifting into space while the spaceship zoomed away. No one heard him anymore.

If the grown-ups wouldn't listen, maybe young people would.

After a career of meeting kids with legitimate ADHD, Conners decided to sit down with the group he had only just begun to recognize: children *without* the disorder but diagnosed and medicated anyway, burned in the brushfire whose match he had struck so long ago. Some would be youngsters whose real problems were mishandled by doctors too quick with the ADHD label and prescriptions. Then there was the other group, the high school and college kids under such academic pressure that they faked the condition to get Adderall. The Richard Fees who lived.

Taking what would be one of the last airplane rides of his life, and unable to drive anymore, Conners flew to New York and got driven up to the perfect spot for such a summit. It was a Connecticut mental health center for adolescents run by two young people who had lived through ADHD's darker side, and populated with kids who knew it, too.

Two hours later he arrived in Bethlehem and shook hands with his hosts: Jamison Monroe and Kristin Parber.

Chapter 15

CONNECTION

Kristin graduated from New York University in 2014. She had stayed sober and drug-free for all four years, a nifty trick for any undergrad, let alone a recent addict. Her A-minus average would have attracted plenty of top graduate schools and employers. She wanted neither. Feeling that Newport Academy had probably saved her life—and that her story mirrored those of so many other young people—Kristin spent her junior and senior summers working for Jamison learning the ins and outs of running a treatment center. She joined full-time immediately after graduation. Her primary responsibility was to explain the treatment process to mothers and fathers, families as skeptical and scared as hers once had been.

One challenge surfaced consistently: convincing parents that the ADHD medications their kids had taken for years might actually be part of the problem, and needed to be stopped in order to assess the child's full range of substance and emotional issues. The morning that Keith Conners arrived in Bethlehem, Kristin was speaking on the phone with a mother who insisted that her alcoholic daughter stay on her Concerta during treatment. How else could she function or do her schoolwork? Kristin explained Newport's policy of giving all kids a clean slate, and how she herself had gone through the same uncomfortable process; perhaps this girl really did have ADHD and need stimulants, but now was a good time to find out. The mother stood firm. After several back-and-forths, Kristin finally said they'd continue the debate later. She had a visitor.

Conners wobbled worse than ever as he walked toward the main

Newport building, the gravel driveway crunching beneath his cane. Carolyn held his elbow lest he crash to the ground again. He arrived in an untucked checkered shirt, dark blue corduroys, sneakers, and good spirits. Jamison and Kristin greeted him at the door and led him into their meeting room, a cozy octagonal rotunda with tall bay windows and a ring of six leather chairs. Conners maneuvered his way toward one and plopped into it. He broke the ice with some small talk—about pot, of all things. "I wonder if a cat on marijuana thinks it's human," Conners wondered playfully. He described a conference with Leon Eisenberg decades ago at which an MIT woman brought a batch of oven-fresh hash brownies. "It was a fun get-together," he smiled. "It wasn't as stuffy as usual."

Nursing half-globes of coffee, the three soon began talking ADHD. Conners shared the early days of the field, his first efforts in the 1960s to identify and help all those seriously hyperactive children long labeled with rotten little kid syndrome. He described his satisfaction in discovering Ritalin's often transformative effects on many such kids. Kristin went next: that first appointment with Dr. Seitz, her experiments with mind-altering substances to find herself in middle school, her own stay at Newport. Jamison told Conners about his original biology experiment and then faking ADHD to get more Adderall. "I wonder if you were taking my scale," Conners said, lips pursed.

"In my office," Conners recalled, "I would get medical students who wanted a prescription: 'I know I have ADD, if you could just get me some medicine I'm sure I could get through medical school.' If you talk to people like that about what's really going on, pretty soon they tell you the truth—'Unless I get this medicine, my father's going to kill me because I'm not going to do well.'"

Kristin: "I think also, especially with the girls, there's a lot of anxiety of coming off their ADHD medicine because it's suppressed their appetite for so long. I think that for a lot of the girls it expedites and assists with their eating disorder. With me, it was always linked to that desire to eat less."

"Part of the ethos at Newport Academy," Jamison added, "is to figure out why kids are reaching outside of themselves in order to alter reality—as simple as that. Then we're healing those reasons, those causes. One place I went didn't even ask questions about why you're taking medicines: 'You're depressed so we should probably put you on antidepressants.'"

Conners talked about child psychiatry's direction: "There are some good people in the business who are trying to do it right and correct the problem—but the vast majority of the industry is latched on to the quick buck. There is a group of researchers who are aligned almost entirely with Big Pharma. They get their research money from pharma and you never know how valid the results are. One of them, I saw, was getting a patent on something to prevent the abuse of stimulant drugs. It's like a pyromaniac inventing a new smoke detector."

As much as Conners clearly lamented his role in the ADHD explosion, and offered his regret sincerely, to him this meeting was less apology than opportunity. Jamison and Kristin could very well have been his patients fifteen or twenty years ago; how often does a child psychiatrist get to see how the kids eventually wind up? These two had evolved as strong, responsible, and confident as any parent or doctor could want.

But he knew there was more to see. He wanted to learn all he could about what they had overcome to get there—through the current Newport patients going through it now.

THREE TEENAGED GIRLS walked into the room and filled the remaining leather chairs. Only one had been officially diagnosed with ADHD, at age seven. The other two assumed they had it because, you know, like, they couldn't focus sometimes and lost things a lot. All three had taken Adderall or Concerta on their own to either feel good, study harder, or eat less. They had abused plenty of other drugs as well, and they landed in rehab for many additional and more complicated reasons. But they were all learning during their stays at Newport about stimulants' contribution to their problems. Now came their chance to learn from the doctor who in some ways started it all.

They weren't shy—particularly one in a T-shirt five sizes too big that draped past her knees, which she held tight, cross-legged.

"Have you ever done it?" she asked.

Conners smiled and said yes, he had—and told the story about the night in the late sixties when he popped a Ritalin to withstand the boring monkey-doctor lecture. He admitted how fantastic the subsequent hours felt, but explained that he understood the pills' addictiveness and never tried it again. He looked compassionately at the girls and said, "I don't think children know—and even if doctors told them, which most don't, they are just trying to get through what's happening in their life. Kids like you have so many emotional and family problems they're trying to get through. Amphetamine and Ritalin make you feel good, and maybe more makes you feel even better. At some point you find that you need to increase the dose in order to get the same nice effect."

Every girl recalled how she had been a discipline case in elementary school, and that several teachers at various junctures recommended her parents get her tested for ADHD. Conners claimed that educators actually can be important sources of information on kids' behaviors—after all, his first scale, released in 1969, was for teachers to offer data for doctors to consider. ("It was minimal brain dysfunction then," he noted, getting less reaction from the girls than he expected.) But he also told them that decades of ADHD spin cycles had left teachers' evaluations far less valid. As knowledgeable and caring as they can be about their students, teachers vastly overestimate ADHD symptoms; a 2001 study found that teachers' Conners-type questionnaires support a diagnosis in 16 percent of children, and more than one in five boys. A different study found that teachers suspected ADHD far more often in elementary school children whose birthdays made them one of the youngest in their grade—just a tick over six, say, when the rest of their classmates were nearing seven. Therefore, many kids were being diagnosed merely because they were born in the wrong month: "The youngest children in fifth and eighth grades," it concluded starkly, "are nearly twice as likely as their older classmates to regularly use stimulants prescribed to treat ADHD."

Looking at Conners, showing no emotion whatsoever, one girl said, "My parents, since I got diagnosed with ADHD, feel like they've accomplished their biggest goal—like, 'Now we know why our kid is so messed up her whole life.'"

"Does your doctor have any knowledge or skill about other things going on?" Conners asked. "There are behavioral therapies that can help you. The problem is both internal and external. It comes from within but there are things in your environment that make a difference. This environment [at Newport] makes a difference for you, because you get individual help and individual recognition and attention. It requires more than just the drug."

The girl asked Conners if he thought she had ADHD.

"How much time have we had? Ten minutes?" he said, taken aback. "That's not enough. You're describing things I've heard many, many times from patients. I've heard patients that would've sounded very similar. You can see the distress, how hard this is. But I'd need to sit here for a few weeks before I could have any real insight into what's going on with you. ADHD, or whatever you want to call that set of problems, it takes a while for anyone to really get to know the whole story, to unravel what it is. Some of it's obvious and some of it is not obvious. And that's not what's happening today in too many settings."

About twenty minutes later, a Newport counselor knocked on a doorjamb gingerly. The girls had to go—they had classes to stay on track with their schoolwork back home.

"I wish I could stay. I wish I had more time," Conners said, unable to rise from his chair. "I enjoy listening to you so much."

One girl extended her hand.

"It's nice to listen to you, too, Dr. Conners."

JAMISON, KRISTIN, AND Conners shared some Newport-kitchen salads before taking a walk around the grounds. Most of the facilities were in small buildings on sixty-five acres of green hills and surrounding woods. The classroom had six kids doing research on computers; Conners poked his head in and gave a little wave to one of the girls he had met earlier. A barnlike building had yoga mats and free weights for exercise when rain soaked the basketball court. Conners was most taken with the simple beauty of the place. Carolyn held his shirt as he took pictures of the pond with his iPhone. "Thank goodness for Big Pharma," he sighed. "Where would you be without them?"

Newport tends to keep its male and female patients separate during therapy, hence Conners's meeting with the young women first. Now he wanted to see the boys. As Carolyn and Kristin excused themselves to chat elsewhere, Jamison walked Conners into another building with four teenagers eagerly awaiting their visiting celebrity.

"Hey man, are you the Conners Scale guy?" one gushed. "I took that thing!"

The boy, now a sturdy six-foot-one and two hundred pounds, had been abusing Xanax and snorting cocaine throughout ninth grade when his worried parents took him to a psychiatrist. The doctor listened for a while and decided that the young man probably had ADHD, and was merely taking the wrong drugs to treat it. The psychiatrist prescribed Vyvanse. "That's ethically . . ." Conners said, searching for the right word. "Unusual." The boy liked his Vyvanse to the point that he started getting dozens more pills from his friends. "I can get it as easily as I can get food," he said. "Anyone at my school who wants it can get it within twenty minutes."

They sat in a makeshift circle on folding chairs. A younger boy, a pale and sullen fourteen-year-old, grumbled that he believed he really did have ADHD. "My mom kind of diagnosed me with it," he said. "I was just out of control with my anger." His mother kept his Focalin prescription in the family medicine cabinet, allowing him to pull back the mirror to take as many as he wanted, leading to his addiction. Sitting between that boy and Conners, a high school junior said he got diagnosed just because his grades were dropping; like the first boy, his parents preferred the explanation that his drug use derived from ADHD, something due to fate, not fault. They never considered other explanations for his lack of concentration—his substance abuse or their incessant fighting, for starters. "My dad's a doctor," the boy explained. "He wanted to put me on something. He said my abusing substances brought my ADD out."

"Do you have ADD?" the blond boy blurted at Conners, clearly hoping the answer was yes.

"I never did," Conners answered. "I lucked into the whole involvement with it, pure chance. I grew up a normal kid out in the West with strict rules like no coffee, no tea, no alcohol, no drugs, and that was a good thing. I was lucky to be born into a system that protected me."

Before anyone had to ask, Conners described the one time he took Ritalin back in the 1960s—not just entertaining the boys but, on a more subtle level, admitting to them that they were not crazy for liking the stuff.

"I'm having two feelings listening to you now," Conners said. "Each of you can probably attest to the fact that, with some people who are struggling against the way their brain is configured, [Adderall] can feel like it's making a big difference. But we have to avoid the deadly path when it's inappropriate. You probably wouldn't be here if there weren't unfortunate consequences, too.

"You're vulnerable," he continued, before wafting his finger across them. "The one thing you learn from this place is that you will and can get better—you'll look back and say, 'That's not the same me, I'm different now and my brain is different.' Adolescence is a very unfortunate period that you have to go through."

Conners talked less than he listened, pinning the boys' stories on his mental corkboard so he could consider them later. Carolyn walked in at two o'clock, angstily reminding him that their flight back to North Carolina left in four hours. Hustling had left Conners's repertoire years ago, so Carolyn grew more insistent that he wrap things up. He said good-bye to the boys. Three of them shook his hand; one offered the more hip fist-bump, at which Conners was understandably nonplussed. He learned the move cheerfully. Some therapy is best unspoken.

Jamison and Kristin guided Conners down the driveway this time as Carolyn hung back. Kristin hugged him farewell. "Thank you so much for coming," she said, pressing her head into Conners's thick shoulder. Jamison gave a hearty handshake. All said they hoped to keep in touch.

The next day, back in Durham, Conners sat at the computer in his upstairs study and typed out an e-mail. It was to a fellow child psychologist with whom he had paved ADHD's highway. He offered no grand epiphanies, no self-flagellating penitence. But this one Connecticut afternoon, Conners wrote, would inform his worldview for the years he had left.

My head is buzzing from an exciting visit to see a new substance use facility. What made it of special interest to me was the fact that the two dynamic-duo founders of the program had both received an early diagnosis of ADHD and treatment with a stimulant drug.

Kristin, the young woman, apparently had enough of a rebellious streak, at least in the eyes of her well-intentioned parents, that her physician prescribed the stimulant medicine. Jamison recalled faking answers to my scale in connection with a diagnosis of ADHD.

They invited me to meet with several of the residents, all teenagers. Many of the young women were very frank in feeling that ADHD did not explain their problems, most of which seemed to them to grow out of family conflicts, not necessarily medical problems needing a drug therapy. One handsome young man (God, the beauty of youth) felt that their addictive behavior and personality came first. One cited the problems caused by a depressed mother & how he used the drug to rouse him from apathy. And so on.

A constant theme was the brief and casual way in which parents and physicians seemed to latch on to the diagnosis, with little attempt to sort out the complicating specific problems in their life. Similarly, no attempt to try a treatment other than medication. This small group experience was clear in showing how substance use appears as a risk not just of ADHD itself, which we already know, but the label *of ADHD, whether the diagnosis is correct or not.*

I learned so much from this experience. Many intersecting pathways to ADHD diag., some legitimate, some intertwined with stimulant effects and family dynamics, etc. Complicated as making diagnosis is supposed to be. As Gordon Allport, one of my Harvard teachers, always said: "Beware the simple & sovereign explanation."

All the best,
Keith

PART FOUR

Chapter 16

THIS IS YOUR BRAIN ON CAPITALISM

"It's been a while, Professor Brown. Now that we have your blood pressure under control I don't see you as often. What brings you in today?"

The lab-coated, stethoscoped doctor clasped her hands and peered into the patient's sunken eyes. The fortysomething man explained that his work had slipped. His boss was getting annoyed.

"I just need to focus on getting things done," he groaned.

"Do you find it difficult staying on a task without wandering off onto something else?" she asked.

He did.

"I'm just not organized and I don't understand how people get so much done," the man explained. "I really have no patience to sit for long periods of time. These are usually important meetings—I just get bored and lose track."

"I'd like to explore this with you further," she said. She handed him an adult ADHD rating scale, almost certainly the six- or eighteen-question sheet devised by the Harvard and NYU doctors, and asked him to fill it out. Afterward, she reviewed his answers and grew serious.

"You indicate that you interrupt conversations and have trouble waiting in line," the doctor said. "I'm concerned about your difficulty with procrastinating, missing deadlines and making careless errors. . . . You've never been diagnosed with ADHD. Has anyone in your immediate family been diagnosed?"

The man perked up.

"Well, actually, yes," he said. "I was surprised when my son was diagnosed before he went to college. He's on medication now, and he's doing well, especially with schoolwork."

"Well, that is interesting," she said, her eyes widening. "Because if you have ADHD—*which I believe you do*—family members often respond well to similar medications."

Her lips cracked into the slightest of knowing grins.

"*Would you consider giving that a try?*"

It took an entire six minutes for the doctor to diagnose her adult patient with ADHD, and to recommend some of the most addictive substances known to medicine. No discussion of their risks. No talk of what other factors might be causing his work distress, if in fact he really was distressed in the first place. Just a few boilerplate questions, a check-off-some-boxes survey, and—*voilà!*—another patient off the ADHD assembly line.

A spoof by antipsychiatry zealots? A snarky How to Score Free Blow Internet script for college students? No. Precisely the opposite.

These scenes came straight from an ostensibly serious video series that aimed to teach today's physicians how to diagnose adult ADHD. It was part of doctors' Continuing Medical Education—the small courses that states require providers to take so that they stay abreast of new medical developments (and keep their licenses). The videos and Web pages, often absorbed in an hour and ending with a remarkably obliging multiple-choice quiz, have become a primary means by which psychiatry is taught after medical school. But while other professionals, such as lawyers and hairdressers, generally pay to fulfill their fields' requirements, drug companies often foot the bill for doctors. Symposia held by major organizations, such as the American Psychiatric Association, or more niche groups, such as APSARD, are heavily subsidized by drug makers, who can fund classes and other events that amount to free promotion, to great audience appreciation. A psychiatrist once gazed at the lavish digs at an APA convention and said that without industry money, "We'd be sitting in the basement of the YMCA."

The title of the outrageous video described above didn't mince words: "Unmasking ADHD in Adults." Few would ever notice the small type on the Web page:

Supported by an independent educational grant from Shire.

*　　　*　　　*

WHATEVER THE MOTIVATION, the medical and pharmaceutical push to understand adult ADHD over the past decade has undoubtedly done good. Men and women so scattered and impulsive as to threaten their jobs and family life really might have persistent ADHD that deserves medical consideration. One middle-aged woman from suburban New York who began taking Adderall in 2010 spoke for countless adults when she discussed her recent, and legitimate, ADHD diagnosis: "We always felt that it was something for children. It's almost a relief to be told there's something you can do to help."

Problem is, as high school and college students well know, amphetamine can help anyone—particularly those at jobs that demand concentration and stamina. This boost in workplace productivity has been known since Benzedrine hit the scene in the 1930s. A scientist proclaimed to the *New York Times* that amphetamine was a "high octane number gasoline" for the brain that allowed it to "hit on all cylinders." One study discussed how the pills increased adults' initiative and efficiency, while another found that young hospital workers who took it became eager to work longer hours. One of them raved: "Nothing seemed impossible."

Today, growing numbers of adults are using ADHD medications as a performance-enhancing drug; Adderall misuse has graduated from college into the American workplace. A woman in her twenties, who started her own tech company in New York, has taken Adderall to sleep only three and a half hours a night and claims it's "necessary for survival." One of her employees keeps Adderall in an Altoids case in her open purse for anyone to grab as necessary—like the take-a-penny, leave-a-penny bowls in a 7-Eleven. "For people like me," she said, "not using Adderall is like trying to play tennis with a wood racquet."

Bartenders keep it in the cash register for double shifts. Newspaper reporters and editors pop Vyvanse to push through late-evening deadlines. A survey of Wall Street traders found many taking it to get a break-of-dawn jump on the competition. It's not just for typically high-pressure jobs either: people acknowledging the habit have included a beer-warehouse stacker, a yoga instructor, and a glass blower, all of them adding that coworkers use Adderall for the same purpose. Some professionals who know the risks of addiction more than anyone else—doctors, dentists—have been known to prescribe it to themselves in order to see more patients. Truck drivers. Poker players. Even video gamers, whose professional circuits have resorted to drug testing because so many competitors use it for an unfair concentration advantage. As for the intellectuals who report and analyze these issues, they are not immune either. Two University of Cambridge scientists in 2007 wrote an article on misuse within academia in the journal *Nature* with the slick headline: "Professor's Little Helper."*

People who take Adderall to improve their work production merely take advantage of the sloppiness depicted—some would say encouraged—in that Continuing Medical Education video by telling their doctors of concentration problems, then walking out minutes later with a prescription. Some do get the pills from friends, and occasionally dealers, but today's most prolific drug distributors don't set up on street corners. They wear lab coats, conditioned to diagnose conditions like ADHD or chronic pain at the slightest of signals.

One Houston attorney counted thirty-five friends in his firm and across the city who take Adderall regularly to bill hundreds of extra hours in the race for partnership. He recalled the conversation with a psychiatrist that got him his regular supply: "I pretty much just said, 'Look, I'm a lawyer, I work a lot of hours and I feel like I'm falling behind and I can't concentrate. I need some help.' So he gave me a script of Adderall, sixty milligrams a day."

Did the doctor ask any questions to determine if this was really ADHD?

"No."

Did he ask any questions?

---

*This phrase obviously plays off the Rolling Stones' 1966 song "Mother's Little Helper," whose "little yellow pill" is never identified. Some speculate that the pill was Dexedrine, but it was almost certainly Valium, which came in small yellow tablets. The best rock-and-roll reference to amphetamine is probably the Beatles' song "Doctor Robert." Researchers believe the song celebrates a Manhattan psychiatrist named Dr. Robert Freymann, who was popular among the rich and famous, including rock stars, for freely prescribing them speed.

"I told him that I previously had a prescription. But other than that he didn't ask me squat."

Did he ask for proof of this old prescription?

"No."

Did he ask for the previous doctor's name?

"No."

Just took your word for it?

"Took my word for it," the lawyer said, before laughing: "All you have to do is wear a suit."*

Because the trend is relatively new, no study has formally estimated the prevalence of adults abusing stimulants to improve work performance. The National Institute on Drug Abuse has acknowledged the growing problem and is looking into possible research. It's indisputable, however, that prescriptions to adults have exploded. The population of American adults taking ADHD drugs is moving past five million, with no signs of slowing down. Prescriptions among young adults (ages twenty-six to thirty-four) are the driving force. But there's no way to know how many of those were legitimate—the reasonable result of greater awareness of adults truly having ADHD—and which materialized from dishonest patients or lazy doctors. It is obvious, though, that abuse has helped cause the occasional shortages of medication in pharmacies nationwide, including one in 2011 that found the FDA and the Drug Enforcement Administration quite at odds. The FDA, more of a treatment-promoting agency, wanted production increased for bona fide patients. The DEA, more of an abuse-deterring agency, responded tersely: "We believe there is plenty of supply."

It's clear that as more people take stimulants, more abuse them and can become addicted: One study found that about one in ten people who took prescription stimulants for improper reasons wound up becoming dangerously dependent on them. Very few get sucked into Richard Fee's perfect storm of medical carelessness and die. But the number of people entering drug rehab specifically for abuse of Adderall and other ADHD medications has risen substantially. Estimates are

---

*The Onion's report on this trend: "Physician Shoots Off A Few Adderall Prescriptions To Improve Yelp Rating."

almost certainly low, too: Many patients who enter treatment for addiction to prescription painkillers like oxycodone or opiates like heroin
began using those substances to counteract the buzz of stimulants.

One of them was the Houston lawyer mentioned above: He got so
hooked on Adderall that he required Xanax to sleep, then Adderall to
wake up, and so on. The cycle intensified over months to the point that
he spent six weeks in drug rehab. "It all fell apart on me," he explained.
"You become so dependent on it that you don't think you can succeed
like you used to without it. I lost sight of the fact that I graduated in the
top two percent of my class out of law school without it. It's a crutch,
and it becomes a crutch immediately."*

In the meantime, as one might expect, employers rarely discourage
employees from working harder and longer. A few years ago, it looked
like some might: The National Business Group on Health, which
advises large companies on health care issues, published a three-page
report titled "ADHD Diagnosis and Stimulant Medication Misuse: Five
Things Employers Can Do." This sounded encouraging, until it focused
almost entirely on reducing employers' insurance costs for the growing
number of unnecessary prescriptions. The "misuse" so promisingly featured in the report's title was not discussed. An executive of the business
group explained later, with perfect-circle logic: "I certainly wouldn't
know that a person is misusing it for quote-unquote job enhancement.
That wouldn't be on my radar screen if they're doing a good job."

Well beyond the more obvious high-wire settings of Wall Street and
law, homemakers have trouble getting everything done, too—and Shire
has stepped in to show them a better way. The company has run ads in

---

*Some people skip rehab and go directly to jail. A young man from outside Philadel-
phia, Ken Mazik, started abusing Adderall while at the University of Delaware and
kept doing so after graduation to improve his focus as a business analyst. (He wore
a suit to his doctor.) He grew increasingly dependent on it and, running out of his
prescription early, started bumming some pills off friends. One morning in 2012, having spent three straight days awake on the stuff, he grew psychotic and paranoid, and
hallucinated that secret agents were trying to kill him. Mazik grew so terrified that he
jumped in his Jeep and sped to the Philadelphia international airport to escape them.
When he got there, he rammed through a locked gate and accelerated along the run-
ways up past 100 miles an hour, trying to take off. He was arrested and served eleven
months in federal prison.

Good Housekeeping and other women's magazines for Vyvanse, each nomi-
nally mentioning ADHD but dangling so much more. In one, a blue-
eyed, toothy, and beaming blond extolls the all-day virtues of her pills:

> 7:00 a.m.–Ate breakfast and took Vyvanse.
> 11:00 a.m.–Organized the family photo albums.
> 5:00 p.m.–Focused on getting dinner started for my kids.
> 9:00 p.m.–Was able to spend time with my husband.

Ads like this one have helped ADHD medication sales increase
more quickly among women than men. Greater medical and societal
recognition of female ADHD has fueled much of that rise. Another
part can be ascribed to women's greater likelihood to use amphetamine
as an appetite suppressant. Distasteful as that theory sounds, Shire has
made it indisputable.

A few years ago, Shire's stable of key opinion leaders helped convince the American Psychiatric Association to place a new medical
condition—binge eating disorder—into the most recent *DSM* manual.
The malady is marked by someone eating uncontrollably at least once
a week for at least three months. Of course, appetite suppression is a
long-understood effect of all amphetamines, notably Vyvanse's direct
ancestor, Obetrol. So while lobbying the APA and government health
officials to create the syndrome, Shire paid university-affiliated doctors to conduct studies to prove the obvious, that amphetamine would
in fact make people eat less. (One well-funded researcher nonetheless
declared, "We were a bit surprised by how positive these findings were.")
Shire set up the website BingeEatingDisorder.com. Then it convinced
the FDA to approve Vyvanse, which already had almost $1.5 billion in
ADHD-related sales in 2014, for binge eating, too.

Monica Seles, the former tennis star, was one of many women heartened that her overeating had been reified as a medical condition. She
immediately hit *Dr. Oz, Good Morning America*, and the rest of the
talk-show circuit to describe her own struggles with binge eating disorder.

"It took a while until I felt comfortable talking about it," Seles told
the readers of *People* magazine. "That's one of the reasons I decided to

do this campaign: to raise awareness that binge eating is a real medical condition."

People's article did not mention that Seles was a paid spokesperson for Shire, its new Ty Pennington.

AS WE'VE SEEN, about every fifteen years, doctors and pharmaceutical companies steer ADHD toward an older demographic—what started with elementary school children moved to adolescents and then adults. The justification is always the same: Whereas the disorder was once thought to affect only ages X through Y, it actually is now found in Z-year-olds, and they need treatment like anyone else. Some undoubtedly do. But the pattern begs consideration of when the age spectrum's final frontier—the elderly—will be visited by the ADHD medication cart.

Early results are mixed. Although aging Baby Boomers are becoming the most profitable demographic in the history of pharmacology, the prospect of widespread ADHD diagnoses and medications in that population appears unlikely, at least in the near future. Certainly, a seventy-five-year-old can have ADHD—although getting a parent's or teacher's appraisal of childhood symptoms could prove tricky—and can consider using medication. But two forces will work against this. First, many senior citizens dismiss ADHD as modern malarkey; their more hardscrabble generation survived just fine without it. Second, even more already take dozens of pills for their heart, kidneys, and more with little idea of how all the drugs truly interact; adding stimulants to this mix, especially in anyone with cardiac issues or high blood pressure, is generally considered a risk best avoided. The primary even experimental use of such medications in the elderly is methylphenidate (essentially Ritalin) for people with mild to moderate Alzheimer's disease. The therapy aims not to improve their cognition or memory, but to roust them out of what's formally termed "apathy"—a sluggishness toward tedious daily tasks, such as brushing teeth or cleaning dishes.

(The elderly have long been quite capable of misusing ADHD medications for the same purposes their grandchildren do. For example, Paul Erdős [pronounced AIR-dish], widely considered the most prolific mathematician of the twentieth century, spent his sixties downing prescription amphetamines to work nineteen-hour days and maintain his renowned productivity. In 1979, a concerned friend bet Erdős that he couldn't stop taking the pills for a month. Erdős accepted the bet and did abstain for those thirty days, but found little solace in victory. "I didn't get any work done," he complained. "You've set mathematics back a month." Erdős resumed his amphetamine regimen immediately.)

But some pharma-connected clinicians have begun to evangelize senior-citizen ADHD. David Goodman—a Johns Hopkins psychiatrist who also oversaw the continuing education six-minute-diagnosis course sponsored by Shire—runs a private-practice ADHD clinic in Maryland where he has diagnosed many over-sixties and encourages other doctors to do the same. The symptoms are not hyperactivity, generally, and not even impulsivity, but more so the cognitive decline experienced by so many elderly. In a *New York Times* article, Dr. Goodman described a seventy-three-year-old widow who continually lost her pocketbook and struggled to follow or remember conversations. This wasn't due to early-stage Alzheimer's disease, Goodman surmised. Because the woman recalled doodling and drifting in classrooms some sixty years before, and had symptoms of inattention through her life, she probably had ADHD. The clincher came with the revelation that her daughter and granddaughter had both been diagnosed as ADHD a few years earlier. (A different doctor explained the up-the-generations thought process here: "A child had been treated, then a parent, then everyone started looking at Grandpa, and saying, 'Oh my gosh.'") Dr. Goodman prescribed Vyvanse, and now reported that the woman no longer misplaced her keys and was more focused on conversations. "That is a very liberating experience," Dr. Goodman said, "even if you're 65, 72 or 83."

Mental invigoration has tempted humans of all ages for at least five thousand years. The ancient Chinese discovered caffeine by placing tea leaves in boiling water and drinking it; subsequent caffeine-delivery innovations have included coffee, chocolate, Coca-Cola (named after an original ingredient, cocaine), over-the-counter NoDoz pills, and Red Bull energy drinks. Caffeine stimulates brain activity much as amphetamine and methylphenidate do—it is the most consumed psychoactive substance on earth—but at conventional lattelike doses poses nowhere near the health risks and therefore is sold freely. (One could argue that nicotine, tobacco's primary selling point for centuries, is a stimulant whose addictiveness ranks between coffee's and cocaine's.) Then there's ephedrine, a chemical from the Chinese ma huang plant that was sold over the counter in the United States as a weight-loss supplement—with bonus stimulant effects, similar to Obetrol—until a Baltimore Orioles pitcher dropped dead from it in 2003. It was subsequently banned by the FDA.

The seduction of some magic pill to awaken mankind's inner intelligence is so relatable that a movie and television series, both called *Limitless*, dramatize it. In the 2011 movie, Bradley Cooper plays an author under a crushing deadline whose friend happens to work for a pharmaceutical company that is developing a "smart pill" code-named NZT-48. Cooper takes one, quite obviously Adderall's successor, and is instantly transformed—he not only writes prolifically but also finds himself retaining information and analyzing financial data so astutely that he scores big in the stock market. (He also learns proficient piano in three days and, in a nod to college students everywhere, frenetically cleans his apartment.) Although Cooper becomes so addicted that he begins injecting himself with the drug and licking his own blood to enjoy more, the movie actually ends with the sunnier notion that Cooper could use the drug to become president. Toning down the fantasy a tad, *Limitless* the television series has the main character merely solving crimes for the FBI.

Recognizing the allure of intelligence through chemistry, drug companies are racing to produce something with Adderall's punch but coffee's safety. Provigil, a pill sold by Cephalon, is designed to treat narcolepsy and excessive fatigue caused by long, nighttime work stretches, a condition the American Psychiatric Association has officially named shift work disorder. (Advertisements specifically target professionals like firefighters and nurses.) Cephalon's promotional activities have gone far further, though, including a claim that the pills also treat generic "fatigue," "tiredness," or mere "sleepiness." The company wound up paying $425 million to the FDA to settle complaints for improper advertising.

The money was probably well spent. Even though Provigil is addictive and shares many of amphetamine's side effects, overworked professionals started going to their doctors for prescriptions some call

"Adderall Lite" or "Brain Viagra." ABC's *Nightline* profiled the phenomenon with a segment called "Provigil: The Secret Success Drug?," in which an Internet executive took a pill on camera and reported that his brain came alive—comparing the sensation to the moment when *The Wizard of Oz* magically went from black-and-white to color.

The man couldn't have known how appropriate, and sad, his analogy was. In 1939, when Judy Garland tiptoed into Oz's Technicolor paradise, she was almost certainly wired on Benzedrine. Metro-Goldwyn-Mayer studio executives during that period put Garland on generous portions of the amphetamine to keep her waistline trim and invigorate her during brutal shooting schedules. Whether Dorothy had binge eating disorder remains unknown.

VYVANSE'S NEW INDICATION for binge eating will probably make the company more than $2 billion. First, the company itself projects prescriptions for the disorder to generate $250 million a year until 2023, when its patents on Vyvanse expire. Given the drug's new purpose, though, the company could also apply for a patent extension, keeping its market exclusivity even longer. The maneuver brilliantly, and legally, has exploited cracks in America's policies regarding pharmaceuticals. Similarly, some doctors' push to reassign the cognitive impairments in millions of aging Baby Boomers from early Alzheimer's to ADHD will only expand Vyvanse profits.

Adults are clearly the new ADHD growth market. Competition has slowed for the children on whom the industry was built; with 15 percent of kids already getting diagnosed with ADHD by the time they leave high school, their rise will level off somewhere. Whether the percentage settles at 17 or 19 or 21—the inconceivable now inevitable—climbing much higher seems unlikely.

As it turns out, the next frontier need not be a new drug at all. Not when you can invent a whole new attention disorder.

Chapter 17

COMING SOON TO
A DOCTOR NEAR YOU

At the current rate, in 2017, half a million American children will be taken to their doctors and be newly diagnosed with attention deficit hyperactivity disorder. Many of them will receive thoughtful and reasonable evaluations and benefit from medication. Another sizable number will be seen by casual clinicians who either bypass the child's real problems or give in to his frustrated parents and teachers. Some of the adolescents will be faking ADHD just to get Adderall for themselves or others. Whatever the actual breakdown, there will be 500,000 new diagnostic visits, millions of follow-ups, tens of millions of pills, and hundreds of millions in sales. Lots of business for everyone.

Apparently, though, this market must expand. The same folks who built today's ADHD machine—the same doctors, the same drug companies—are already working on tomorrow's. A new disorder is being buffed and burnished as you read this. Its name: sluggish cognitive tempo, or SCT.

It's kinda like ADHD, but not *quite*. Sluggish cognitive tempo, as currently conceived, is a syndrome marked by daydreaming, lethargy, and "slowed thinking or behavior," according to one journal's primer on the subject. Kids with SCT are anything but hyperactive: Rather than move faster than we would prefer, they move slower. They're not *slow* in the crass, intelligence sense; they just don't seem to concentrate in constructive ways, their thought-to-action connections a little fritzy. One of SCT's mechanics, Keith McBurnett of the University of California at San Francisco, explained it thusly: "These children are not the ones giving adults much trouble, so they're easy to miss. They're the daydreamy ones, the ones with work that's not turned in, leaving names off of papers or skipping questions, things like that, that impinge on grades or performance. . . . Someone who has a son or daughter who does this excessively says, 'I know about this from my own experience.' They know what you're talking about."

In January 2014, the *Journal of Abnormal Child Psychology* decided to throw SCT a coming-out party. More than one hundred pages of papers described the condition and pondered exactly how it afflicts children. Although no formal definition or roster of SCT's symptoms were (or have yet been) decided upon, the journal authors were remarkably confident. Several claimed that debate over sluggish cognitive tempo's existence "seems to be laid to rest"—even though the vast majority of psychiatrists, let alone the wider medical community, had never heard of it in the first place. After reading these papers, doctors outside the SCT cabal were horrified. Dr. Allen Frances, a prominent psychiatrist who worked with Keith Conners at Duke, recoiled and said, "This is a public-health experiment on millions of kids." One top government health official, after reading the journal, said in disgust: "It almost looks like an April Fool's issue."

Some SCT researchers claim that they are simply trying to resolve some long-standing confusion about ADHD, whose name has been more than clumsy since "hyperactivity" arrived in 1987 and was monkeyed with again in 1994. (No wonder, a few years later, Dr. Mark Vonnegut couldn't even describe what ADHD looked like and finally announced, "The diagnosis is a mess.") Sluggish cognitive tempo attempts to rename the merely inattentive children who have never quite fit the ADHD construct anyway—which is not such a terrible idea.

But SCT advocates have set their sights so much higher. Some say that as many as three million children have the disorder—half of them already diagnosed with ADHD (and merely getting reclassified), but the other half receiving a new psychiatric label they wouldn't carry otherwise. The result: At a time when ADHD rates are pushing the obscene, at least another *million* children would be told they too have a brain disorder, one charmingly named sluggish cognitive tempo.

No researcher is more invested, both intellectually and financially, in the success of SCT than Russell Barkley, whose decades of research in ADHD have resulted in hundreds of papers, a dozen books, seven hundred speeches in sixteen countries, and countless dollars from appreciative drug sponsors. Dr. Barkley's marketing of SCT is anything but sluggish. He has proclaimed in lectures and educational videos that sluggish cognitive tempo "*has become* the second attention disorder" (emphasis his). Barkley has been an impassioned editor of SCT's Wikipedia page, adding material to support the disorder's construct while deleting dissent. He has written a textbook chapter on SCT, and devised the first Conners-like symptom checklist for doctors to diagnose adults—even though the condition has never been recognized by the American Psychiatric Association or anyone else beyond, well, him. Perhaps more will if Barkley succeeds in another crucial effort: He is lobbying for SCT's name to be changed to concentration deficit disorder, or CDD, much as minimal brain dysfuction rebranded itself as ADD almost forty years ago.

Anyone who gets diagnosed with SCT will find help ready and waiting—thanks to Eli Lilly, which has already enlisted Barkley, McBurnett, and other doctors to investigate how Strattera would treat SCT, too. This was a riskless bet; in many ways SCT is merely a wing of ADHD, so it stands to reason that Strattera would provide benefits there as well. McBurnett led a study, funded and designed by Lilly, whose results appeared in a 2013 journal paper. "This is the first study to report significant effects of any medication on SCT," the paper concluded, referring to the condition with alarming matter-of-factness. Barkley, who had been paid $118,000 by Lilly from 2009 to 2012 for consulting and speaking engagements, remarked in a subsequent article that the study produced "an exciting finding." Even more exciting for Lilly, no doubt. If SCT ever does become identified as a medical condition, and Strattera approved as treatment, Lilly's patent and profitability would get the customary extension.

Asked about these efforts, an Eli Lilly spokesperson stared straight ahead. "Sluggish cognitive tempo," she said, "is one of many conditions that Lilly scientists continue to study to help satisfy unmet medical needs around the world."

Ah, yes. The world.

*　　　*　　　*

MOST COUNTRIES HAVE cringed at America's approach to difficult children. To varying degrees they have viewed ADHD's explosion as an
American travesty borne of parental impatience and corporate greed.
Global doctors have been quite blunt in their criticism, as in a 1973
editorial in the globally influential journal *The Lancet*: "Are the Americans ahead of the British, or behind them, or do their children's brains
dysfunction in such an ostentatiously exotic transatlantic fashion that
they require drug therapy?" A British psychiatrist told the London
Times in 1981, soon before Ritalin use Stateside mushroomed: "I don't
practice chemical warfare against children."

This contempt did wane as more, often younger, international
experts concluded that diagnosing and medicating the most severely
hyperactive kids really could be justified. But criteria for pharmacological intervention were kept far more restrictive. The international community has rejected the American Psychiatric Association's expanding
ADHD definitions and instead relied upon what the World Health
Organization defines as hyperkinetic syndrome. That diagnosis requires
a child to have significant problems in all three of ADHD's symptom
groups—hyperactivity, impulsivity, and inattention—and includes
other barriers to haphazard diagnosis. When applied appropriately, this
definition results in 1 to 2 percent of children being told they have the
disorder; even by-the-book use of America's ADHD guidelines captures
four times that.

Not surprisingly, each country's value system affects its medicalization of children's behavioral issues. Most have gradually, if sometimes
grudgingly, recognized some form of ADHD and stimulant therapy
since the 1990s. Some nations, such as Brazil, France, Italy, and Sweden, remain very conservative toward the diagnosis, and especially the
medications in cases anything less than dire. (Canada, Italy, and Sweden have at one time or another banned stimulant medications outright.) The United Kingdom, the Netherlands, and Germany have
been more liberal in accepting the ADHD concept, to the point that
some estimates of diagnosis rates in those countries have reached about

5 percent. China has been more ambivalent, on one hand questioning American fashions but on the other seeing medication as helping some children conform to strict classrooms. As for ADHD drugs in and of themselves, no country has anywhere near the enthusiasm of the United States, which until recently had prescribed more than 90 percent of the world's amphetamine and methylphenidate. But the rest of the world is catching up. From 2000 through 2010, its consumption of ADHD drugs almost doubled. The current decade will see similar or stronger growth.

Pharmaceutical companies have stoked other markets' growing comfort with ADHD medications, sometimes using tactics at which even the United States would blanch. Concerta's advertisements in Europe—always to doctors, as direct-to-consumer advertising remains banned there—have been particularly grotesque. One that ran in Germany depicts a boy sitting atop a table while he enthusiastically cuts it with a saw, the blade's teeth inches away from his exposed little leg—implying that if you don't prescribe Concerta to your impish young patients, they will self-amputate their limbs. Another from Portugal merely presented a letter written by a little boy to his doctor:

> *Hi, I'm Manuel. I'm 7 and I am already in 3rd grade. I am a bit of a difficult child but not for much longer. Miss Palmira, my teacher, talked to my parents, and they took me to the doctor and he, with a serious look, said a bunch of difficult words: "We are going to fight hyperactivity with Concerta, thanks to its active principle, methylfloridate [sic]." I never paid much attention during the classes, but from now on I will be like my friends. The doctor told me that I will start taking Concerta at breakfast time and I will behave like a good boy during the whole day. My mother jumped for joy when the doctor told her that now there is a medicine for me in Portugal.*

Shire has taken a less direct route to growing its offshore market, educating doctors about ADHD itself so that prescriptions follow. In 2013, relying on what it called an expert panel from about ten European countries, the company commissioned and oversaw the publication of a paper entitled "ADHD: Making the Invisible Visible." While

predictably suggesting that all nations use America's widening definition of ADHD, it recommended that each country "initiate awareness
campaigns to inform and educate the wider public and policy makers
about the impact, long-term outcomes and cost of ADHD." (The group
also proposed that stakeholders "identify celebrities with ADHD to
provide testimonials on the successful management of their disorder.")
The paper's recommendations got even worse, up to and including suggesting that possibly ADHD children be held out of school until they
get examined. Shire CEO Flemming Ørnskov explained in a media
interview that measures like these were necessary for Shire to grow the
global market for Vyvanse, which in Europe is branded Elevanse: "The
next year to two years is going to be a significant educational effort on
our part. The climate in Europe is a bit more negative. It will take us
some time."

In 2015, a medical conference at the National Institutes of Health
in Bethesda, Maryland, staged a panel called "ADHD Around the
World." The audience had traveled from all over the globe, from Japan
to New Zealand to Spain, to discuss what some feared to be a tidal wave
of ADHD diagnoses approaching their own shores. A British doctor
called the growing number of parents expecting him to diagnose the
disorder in one short session "lunacy," while an Australian clinician
quite sweetly warned that however important it is to correctly diagnose
children with ADHD and help them, misdiagnoses can matter just as
much. "Our diagnostic decisions," she said, "affect the lives of children
whose own, and their family's, narrative changes irrevocably."

The third speaker, though, was the man most came to see. The host
playfully introduced him:

"And now, the creator of ADHD—Keith Conners!"

All but unfit to travel, Conners had hobbled his way onto a plane
at Raleigh-Durham airport and gotten to the conference, where he was
wheelchaired to the room in which he made what could become his last
public talk on ADHD. (When the PowerPoint screen flashed "low battery," he quipped, "How does it know my health?") Once again Conners
recounted his decades in the field, from his work with Leon Eisenberg to
minimal brain dysfunction to what he now declared were "outrageous
rates" of ADHD diagnoses. He warned against the imminent world-

wide influence of pharmaceutical companies, and all but apologized for his having worked on their behalf for decades. "When I was invited to a round table by Shire, all of my most respected colleagues were usually there," he said. "So it was fun to go to these drug-sponsored meetings just to meet my companions. But looked at a different way, you could say that me and my companions were just serving Big Pharma." He described the meeting with the obstinate school superintendent in North Carolina the year before who had brushed off how a quarter of the boys in her district were being diagnosed as disordered, and the challenge of handling adults asking for prescriptions.

"ADHD is a wonderful concept in the abstract, and it's very easy to accept it and all parts of it," Conners said. "When someone comes into your office with the book *Driven to Distraction* under his arm and says 'I have ADHD and here are all the symptoms and here are all the problems in my life, can I have some Adderall,' it's pretty hard to dissuade that person because they're seeking something. I think this idea has a powerful influence above any rational or empirical data. The data don't account for the hold that certain concepts have on us."

SIX HUNDRED MILES south, in Georgia, some health officials had been growing concerned about how many young children in the state were on ADHD medication. Georgia's rate, 6.1 percent, wasn't that out of whack with the rest of the United States—in fact, it was dead average. But the number was growing, and disturbing. They wanted to learn more, particularly in the youngest children. So they called the Centers for Disease Control and Prevention, just down the road in Atlanta, and its epidemiologist for ADHD, Dr. Susanna Visser. They asked her to run the numbers on four- and five-year-olds. They didn't think to ask about any kids younger than that, mere toddlers; none would be diagnosed with ADHD, they figured, let alone medicated for it. No drug has ever been tested in that age group, and the American Academy of Pediatrics guidelines do not even address three-year-olds as candidates for a diagnosis in the first place.

Dr. Visser ran the data on toddlers anyway. She checked them twice. Then she met with ten officials over dinner at a French restaurant near the CDC headquarters. When she mentioned the toddler number, a doctor, enjoying his trout almondine, literally dropped his fork.

"What?" he gasped.

Dr. Visser had discovered that more than ten thousand toddlers—kids ages two and three, still in diapers—across the United States had been diagnosed as ADHD and put on Adderall, Concerta, and the like.

These weren't just one or two tots diagnosed by renegades who lamentably, yet inevitably, exist in all fields. It was ten thousand crib-sleeping, all-but babies diagnosed with a behavior disorder impossible to pinpoint reliably in children that young. Hyperactivity and impulsivity are developmentally appropriate for toddlers, and while some might wind up warranting an ADHD diagnosis in coming years, deciding that early is simply reckless. No one knows what effects the drugs have on the Play-Doh brains of two-year-olds.

Dr. Visser wrote up a formal report and presented it at a conference on children's mental health at the Carter Center in Atlanta. Former first lady Rosalynn Carter herself made sure to be there. No one could believe the ten thousand number. Anita Zervigon-Hakes, the Carter Center's consultant on pediatric psychiatry issues, spoke for most of the dumbfounded audience when she said: "People are just feeling around in the dark. We obviously don't have our act together for little children."

Whether kids as young (or in this context old) as four and five can have ADHD has been debated for decades. Minimal brain dysfunction in the 1960s and 1970s was figured to manifest at age six, when a child's behavior issues could be confirmed in first grade's more organized classrooms. As more children entered nursery school in the 1980s and 1990s, the most hyperactive and impulsive began being diagnosed with ADHD and put on medication. Experts at the American Academy of Pediatrics ultimately convened to evaluate whether the trend was appropriate; in 2010, they issued guidelines authorizing the diagnosis. (Although it's hard not to wonder if they were merely green-lighting what was already happening and bound to increase anyway.)

As for the inevitable question of how to treat these children, the guidelines made it clear: Methylphenidate such as Ritalin and Concerta—not amphetamines like Adderall, for reasons unexplained—were to be considered a last resort, only after behavioral therapy for the child and parent and teacher training were tried and ineffective. This was a little puzzling given that Adderall, not methylphenidate, is the only ADHD drug approved by the FDA for children under six, by being quasi-grandfathered in from its old Dexedrine/Obetrol days.* The only "off-label" trial of stimulants in the youngest kids was the 2006 Preschool ADHD Treatment Study, which examined how children from age three to five reacted to methylphenidate only. The trial showed some encouraging short-term results among four- and five-year-olds, a reasonably predictable result given the drug's influence on slightly older humans. But only about a dozen three-year-olds were included in the study, so the medication's effectiveness and safety in those youngest children were simply not assessable.

Dr. Visser's data was shocking not just because ten thousand two- and three-year-olds nationally were nonetheless being fed ADHD drugs, but also the number was almost certainly conservative, and growing. The report begged a response from government health agencies to address just what in the world was going on here. A few days later, one arrived, quite appropriately, from Dr. Tom Insel, director of the National Institute of Mental Health. Certainly, the man most responsible for cultivating and protecting children's psychological well-being would have something to say about all this. He did.

In a blog post, Dr. Insel called the toddler numbers "notable." He then slipped into perhaps the most tone-deaf and ultimately dispiriting monologue in the history of ADHD. "While blaming psychiatrists, parents, schools, or drug companies might seem legitimate, some of the facts just don't fit," he wrote. He examined the overall ADHD explosion with logic as twisted as it was tired:

- Were medications being prescribed too often? No, he said, because, "Most of the prescriptions for stimulant drugs and antidepressants are not from psychiatrists." He left unaddressed just

---

*Just because a drug is approved by the FDA for one condition, or age group, does not make it illegal for a doctor to prescribe it for something else. Such "off-label" prescriptions, while often benefiting patients, can become try-this-and-see-if-it-helps medicine with little knowledge of efficacy or side effects.

who, then, were writing all those prescriptions, and why the distinction mattered.

• Regarding parents, he wrote that most "resist medication rather than request it"—another time-honored ADHD line that has never made any sense. First, quite clearly, the point is how such vast numbers of them get over their resistance and fill the prescription. Second, to the extent that Dr. Insel's image of parents can be true at times—some do delay putting their kids on medication, occasionally to the youngsters' detriment—if so many parents are in fact declining the prescriptions, then how many are being offered them?

• Insel correctly noted that elementary schools' cutting recess time has left the most bursting-at-the-seams kids with little outlet for their energy during the school day. "But," he countered with pretzeled logic, "the increase in medication is now seen in toddlers, years before children begin school." He offered no thoughts—there or elsewhere—on whether toddlers should be taking ADHD medications at all.

• As for the pharmaceutical industry, don't point fingers there: "Drug companies, while frequently maligned, have reduced, not increased, their marketing budgets in the US," Insel explained.

"The problem," Insel concluded, "may be both over-treatment and under-treatment."

That was the response from America's highest mental health official to the news that ten thousand toddlers were being prescribed ADHD drugs well outside medical guidelines.

IF IT SEEMS like many doctors don't know enough about what ADHD actually is and how its medications work, that's because they don't. The vast majority do care deeply about kids and most don't take a penny from Big Pharma. But painfully few physicians who diagnose and treat

ADHD received any training in the area during medical school, or from any reliable source since.

Dr. Insel did get one thing right: Most diagnoses in children are indeed made by pediatricians and family doctors, rather than better-trained and more experienced child psychiatrists, who must receive two extra years of schooling in order to practice; some discussion of ADHD and stimulants has long been included in this supplemental program and, although some graduates stray from those lessons, at least they received them. But the United States has only about eight thousand practicing child psychiatrists. Some rural families must drive a hundred miles to see one (if they can endure long waiting lists and higher fees). It's no wonder that parents prefer seeing someone closer, cheaper, and more familiar with their child to begin with: their pediatrician.

Unfortunately, through their seven years in medical school and residency, most pediatricians were taught about ADHD and stimulants for only a few hours. Psychiatry courses are often optional and tend to focus on more severe issues like adolescent schizophrenia and suicidality. Any pediatrician who graduated before ADHD began to explode in the mid-1990s, meaning those now in their fifties or older, might have gotten nothing. Most simply do their best, guided by their concern for children rather than any expertise. Like countless pediatricians across the United States, Dr. William Wittert, a pediatrician in Libertyville, Illinois, just went down the Conners Scale symptom list with the parent; he later said regretfully, "If you had enough yesses then you pretty much got the diagnosis of ADHD." A pediatric nurse practitioner on Long Island admitted that she had to rely merely on instinct, what she called a "hair-on-the-back-of-your-neck feeling."

Many clinicians, parents, and pundits believe that rising ADHD rates derive from children spending much of their waking hours pickled in synapse-stirring video screens. This explanation, actually proffered since the primordial days of Pong and Pac-Man, does hold some validity. Video games, interactive touchscreens, and social media immerse children in worlds that instantly respond to their every whim. Those activities are pleasurable in part because they release dopamine in the brain; too much of it and the brain can feel underserved during relatively dopamine-free pursuits, like math. But even though research has suggested that too much technology can impede young attention spans, the resulting deficiency should not be mistaken for true ADHD, which we've been told is a disorder with which one is born. (Not to mention that if a child is getting too much dopamine through gadgetry, the solution is not to even things out through stimulants.) Yet some ADHD folks insist on muddying this technology connection, making it hard for anyone to make sense of the issue. A *Time* magazine article claimed that ADHD children "are usually ridiculed and ostracized, and that isolation sends them back to those gadgets"—after which "electronics are likely their only consistent companion." Not to be outdone, one published study claimed that children with ADHD who took methylphenidate actually spent *less* time playing video games. So to get your kid to play less Minecraft, get him diagnosed with ADHD.

AS DISHEARTENING AS this messaging can be, some genuine hope does exist for doctors to receive better education about ADHD and its proper treatment. In perhaps the ultimate sign that the field needs reform, two longtime members of ADHD's horn section have joined Keith Conners and are changing their tune, at least somewhat. The doctors have taken it upon themselves to hold seminars across the nation to teach pediatricians how to diagnose ADHD—and, in a new twist, how *not* to diagnose it, too.

One of them, Peter Jensen, is the former NIMH official who oversaw the spurious MTA study back in the mid-1990s, and whose papers and interviews downplayed evidence of overdiagnosis. The other is the *Driven to Distraction* Ned Hallowell, who had repeatedly declared stimulants "safer than aspirin." But he decided to retire that catchphrase in 2013 after accepting an invitation to appear on *The Dr. Oz Show* to yet again discuss all things ADHD. His fellow guests that day were Rick and Kathy Fee, whose son, Richard, had recently killed himself after faking the disorder and getting addicted to Adderall. Hallowell talked with the Fees in the green room before taping and, visibly moved by how the ADHD machine had failed Richard, later looked into the cameras and told the audience that he would never use the aspirin line again.

Jensen and Hallowell haven't shed their skins by any means. Jensen remains fond of calling ADHD both overdiagnosed and underdiagnosed. Hallowell still describes a diagnosis as "good news" and, ever the marketer, has an iPhone app with the infamous six-question quiz to see if you should head to the doctor. But to their credit they are among the few prominent ADHD voices to adjust their message in light of the evidence before them. They recognize that even if medical schools were to adjust their curricula to improve coverage of ADHD—some are considering doing so—any real-life improvements won't be meaningfully felt for twenty years or more. Better education is needed right now, and not from traditional, pharma-controlled channels. So about ten times a year, for forty pediatricians at a time, Jensen and Hallowell step forward to help.

Rather than stand at a podium and lecture—their typical pose at industry conferences—they literally stage typical office scenarios in which they role-play actual children. The stocky and gray-haired Hallowell will pretend to be a hyperactive six-year-old boy, climbing under chairs and squiggling dreamily across the carpet during pretend evaluations. Actors portray other identifiable ADHD characters: the pushy father who wants a prescription for his Harvard-aspiring daughter; a girl who really does seem to have hallmark ADHD and legitimately needs treatment; and a boy whose distractibility quite possibly derives from bullying at school rather than any congenital brain disorder. A dozen of these scenes allow pediatricians in the audience to experience the challenge of giving a child a thoughtful and ultimately correct diagnosis. One clinician remarked during a class in New York: "I'd love a blood test where you draw the blood and there it is. But it doesn't exist." A graduate of the program said that he and other doctors back home had previously used the Conners Scale only, circling numbers and adding them up to see if a kid passed the magic ADHD threshold. He was almost embarrassed: "This isn't something you can diagnose in fifteen or twenty minutes. Now I spend the time to try and find out what's really going on with the kid."

The program helps clinicians serve both the "overdiagnosed" and "underdiagnosed" populations of children so seemingly irreconcilable. Doctors are not dissuaded from making a diagnosis when appropriate—

just to be more discerning during such an important juncture in a youngster's life. And, just as vitally to children, clinicians who had once felt uncomfortable handling ADHD leave feeling more qualified to do so, providing services to families and communities who otherwise couldn't get them.

This last benefit was perfectly illustrated by a pediatrician from a poor section of the Bronx, whose lack of training had left her unwilling to diagnose ADHD and prescribe medication for children who might need it. After taking the Jensen-Hallowell class, she had a different outlook. When a struggling third-grade girl on Medicaid came to her office, the doctor spent several weeks conducting a proper evaluation—using a Conners-like rating scale, yes, but also deeply investigating the girl's educational history and interviewing her parents and teachers. In the end the girl really did appear to have ADHD and was prescribed medication.

"She just had that textbook ADHD issue where she could not sit still or focus," the doctor said. "Now she's reaching her potential. Her whole way about her has changed."

Given the long history of ADHD, the decades of mounting forces and fallacies that led America to tell one in seven children nationwide that they have a brain disorder—and in some communities one in four—perhaps it's a bit odd to suggest that diagnosing yet another kid is a sign of progress.

But it actually is. It can continue being so, too, if enough of ADHD's major players realize how easy reform can be, one child at a time.

Chapter 18

PRESCRIPTION

All of us are unique combinations of hundreds of traits that lie on remarkably wide ranges, spectra that shift with context and culture. When you get down to it, we all are short and tall, rich and poor, perceptive and obtuse. Thankfully, we live in an era of empathy for people on the unenviable end of many scales, helping them climb the bell curve through means from wheelchairs to welfare. Only recently have those on man's emotional extremes—the despondent, the manic—been identified as worthy of similar services and support. That list includes people whose severe hyperactivity and inattention jeopardize their education or employment. Perhaps our terming that tail of the spectrum "attention deficit hyperactivity disorder" derives less from compassion than commerce, but the concept is not, at its core, unreasonable.

Whatever ADHD is, it has always had the right—the responsibility, even—to pursue medical and societal legitimacy. There should be studies of possible treatments, pharmacological or otherwise. Any drug with a reasonable balance of benefits and risks, communicated to the patient or parent, should be available for their consideration as with any other medical condition. Advocacy groups should educate families in crisis and even lobby legislatures to respect patients' rights, particularly those of children.

It's the grown-ups who have—one decade at a time—either bungled or exploited this mandate. Our culture's handling of the disorder could very well be diagnosed with ADHD itself. From parents to teachers to doctors, we have been too impulsive, jumping at easy labels and even easier medication. We have hyperactively bounced from one definition to the next, scrambling to rationalize the newest ADHD symptom roster that is then swiftly judged insufficient. And the zeal for diagnosing and medicating children, and now adults, has distracted us from the abundantly obvious evidence that ADHD long ago jumped its tracks.

Restoring order to the disorder will take years of both education and effort among many groups. Even incremental improvements, from enough angles, can finally balance ADHD between the real and realistic.

PARENTS

NO ONE UNDERSTANDS and loves any individual child more than mom and dad. Unfortunately, when discussion of ADHD begins, no one understands less about the process and its pitfalls. Parents should be neither scared nor discouraged—not even by this book—to consider whether their child truly has the disability and would benefit from carefully monitored medication. But they should also consider the forces and biases, including their own, that can act upon them as they do.

Simply asking a doctor about his or her approach to ADHD can be both unthreatening and illuminating. What goes into making a diagnosis? What are the benefits and risks of medication? And what about all this talk about children being overdiagnosed and underdiagnosed? Although most doctors' answers will be reasonable, some could demonstrate a harmful ignorance, or mere intolerance, of ADHD's complexities. Any doctor who says anything remotely approaching "Well, let's try Concerta and see if it helps" does not know what he is doing, period.

Most of all, no parent should accept any diagnosis made in fifteen or even forty-five minutes. A proper appraisal requires several appointments, long discussions with family members and teachers about the exact behaviors at issue, and the consideration of other causes like trauma or anxiety. Many doctors will discourage this, thinking it's a waste of your time or theirs, in part because most insurance companies will not pay them for anything more than a brief assessment. One of Richard Fee's doctors tried to rationalize his mishandling of the case by saying: "I hate to say this, but when you put in five hours and get paid for only one, it's hard to make a living." You wouldn't tolerate a mechanic telling you, "Well, I skipped some steps on your brakes because Ford doesn't reimburse me." If it's not good enough for your car, it's not good enough for your child.

Similarly, some teachers, under their own tremendous pressure to perform, will encourage diagnoses by asking parents veiled questions like "Have you talked with your pediatrician?" Many mean well and you might even agree with their suggestion. But if you feel bullied, say so.

Speaking of pressure, when a teenager claims to have trouble concentrating in school or on homework, parents must consider whether the child actually has other issues. As we've seen, even "good" kids who have avoided other drugs will be drawn to Adderall to maintain their academic pace.* Probe this possible rationale. Discuss their fears of failure and, when they acknowledge them, motivations for meds. Of course, some children have inherent, lifelong ADHD that just didn't become truly impairing until adolescence; that possibility should never be dismissed. But they also could be pulling strings, and heartstrings, to get what they think they need to compete.

Whenever an appropriate diagnosis is made, great care must be taken to explain to the child what ADHD is and is not, and what taking medication means. Children aren't stupid—by second grade they will have heard from a friend or five that they have this brain thing, and have to take pills to "behave better" or "pay attention." As they get older, ADHD children can search the Internet and read about how their disorder results from neurochemical issues and is linked to terrible lifelong problems. They worry. Kids have just as many feelings and fears about all this as parents do.

Navigating ADHD is hard, made only harder by a system left unchecked for so long. Kids who don't quite qualify for the diagnosis

---

*In 2013, while keynoting a round table discussion on drug abuse on college campuses—held at NYU during Kristin Parber's junior year—Bill Clinton admitted that he had no idea how many young people took Adderall to deal with academic pressure. He shook his head and said, "A lot of students have scheduling issues that would break Einstein's brain."

look awfully similar to those who have already received it, so parents are entitled to think, "My Ethan is much worse than Zack, and Zack takes Adderall. Ethan probably should, too." And so it goes. Telling a mother to turn down a chance to help her child academically just because other kids are misdiagnosed? That's a tough sell only getting tougher.

DOCTORS

DOCTORS WANT TO help people, especially kids. When a family is in distress, immediate and proven solutions are sought. Restless waiting rooms and insurance companies tighten the vise. And what if this kid becomes one of those friendless, drug-addled, drive-into-a-tree adolescents the studies (and advertisements) depict? Adderall has helped so many people that it understandably feels worth trying. Yet to diagnose ADHD without proper training and assessment is to wield a scalpel with one eye closed. Getting it right is noble. Getting it wrong is child abuse.

Required or not, pediatricians asked to evaluate ADHD should put it on themselves to learn more—and not from the Continuing Medical Education modules strewn with Big Pharma marketing. The Peter Jensen and Ned Hallowell course is a nice step. The next is for medical schools to add courses to teach upcoming physicians about the ADHD diagnoses and stimulant prescriptions patients will regularly ask them to consider. When a request becomes fishily vehement, doctors should remember what they themselves were told about drugs as kids: Just Say No.

As for medical organizations like the American Psychiatric Association and the American Academy of Child and Adolescent Psychiatry, they are absolutely correct about one thing: In general, a child whose real ADHD goes unhelped can be harmed more than a child mislabeled and even mismedicated. But the groups must understand that these are *both* mistakes, both costly, and demand that each be minimized. Preliminary work on the next version of the *DSM* will probably start soon. Negotiations should, at long last, center on tightening—or at least clarifying—criteria to set ADHD on a more healthy course.

NEWS MEDIA

MEDIA OUTLETS PAY little attention to illogic and agenda when relaying health news. Sometimes this is actually humorous. In 2015, just to illustrate the media's dopeyness in parroting scientific medical claims, one journalist fabricated a study that "proved" that eating chocolate can help you lose weight; the story of candy's newfound healthiness went viral and was picked up by media outlets worldwide, including the *Huffington Post*. ADHD and children's mental health are no joke, but remain just as vulnerable to downright false information. In 1990, a federally funded study claimed to have pinpointed the primary brain defects that caused kids to have ADHD. The *Washington Post* and *New York Times* ran large stories with doctors and parents alike relieved at the mystery finally being solved; *Time*'s headline declared, "Why Junior Won't Sit Still: Researchers Link Hyperactivity to an Abnormality in the Brain." The study was ultimately debunked. So many confident ADHD findings have been ultimately incorrect over the years that one researcher actually looked into it and found that six of ten ADHD studies most written about in nationwide newspapers were eventually disproven, or their results at least seriously clouded, by other research.

Perhaps that isn't the mass media's fault; it reported on what presumably credible journals had printed. But journalists must be more vigilant when discussing ADHD. Many continue to cite a 2012 study that reported the economic cost of the disorder to society to be about $200 billion; few, if any, mention that the study was run by Shire, with four of the authors owning stock or stock options in the company. (On the other side of the ledger, few discuss what diagnosing and medicating millions of children *erroneously* is costing us, too.)

The fervor to profile female ADHD has been sketchy, as well. A January 2016 article in *Quartz* said that the underdiagnosis of ADHD in girls has created "a lost generation of women," and quoted a doctor frantically warning that one study showed that girls with ADHD were "four to five times" more likely to attempt suicide or intentionally hurt themselves; the actual study, however, which no one apparently bothered to check, reported rates nowhere remotely that high. Lisa Ling, hosting a show on CNN, invited cameras to chronicle her getting her own diagnosis, when she casually told her doctor about pretty common behaviors: "I have always had a bit of a difficult time focusing on things that aren't interesting to me, and I get really, really anxious before taking any kind of test or having any kind of evaluation." Two minutes later, after a few tests, the doctor said Ling had ADHD and discussed medication. The gender competition reached new heights when an *NBC Nightly News* report decried underdiagnosis in girls mainly because their rates trailed boys'—without noticing that girls already are diagnosed far more often than the *DSM* suggests.

ADVOCATES

CHADD'S EFFORTS YEARS ago were vital in empowering parents and others touched by ADHD, both protecting their children's rights and reducing both medical and societal aversion to the disorder's significance. The group's strategy was to unveil and expand the ADHD population to prove to doubters just how many people needed help, and invite all comers under their umbrella to bolster their ranks. Yet CHADD did its job too well. The dynamics have essentially reversed. The news media no longer disrespects ADHD—it typically runs virtual ads for the disorder. Parents can't be scared by the so-called label that much if they're applying that label to 15 percent of their children. That war is over.

After three decades of inclusivity, CHADD must become more *exclusive*. It should discourage those with scant or nonexistent attention issues from continuing to dilute their ranks beyond recognition. People with the real, severe problem will be far better served, and respected, if they aren't outnumbered two to one—as they are now—by millions of people with specious diagnoses. The effort will require the organization to educate parents and the public as much about what ADHD is as what it simply is not. Its members deserve that.

CHADD states that its work is based on the best science, but its credibility is undermined by foolish and misleading messaging, often through its online and print magazine, *ADDitude*. The first sentence of a column to teach parents about nondrug treatments for ADHD said, "There is little evidence that cognitive behavior therapy (CBT) is helpful for young children with ADHD," a shockingly untrue and irresponsible statement. E-mails tell parents about "travel secrets" for ADHD children and explain to ADHD adults "why you hate cocktail parties." The website's "Do I Have ADD?" tests veer far from official *DSM* symptoms; in one whopper, answering yes to enough categories like "get bored easily," "procrastinate," or "can't seem to reach my goals" results in users being told "It is likely that you have attention deficit disorder." Having columnists and board members such as William Dodson and Larry Silver, doctors who over the years have written appalling materials on behalf of Big Pharma, only invites and justifies skepticism of its mission.

THE GOAL OF any worthwhile medical effort must be to serve legitimate needs. ADHD can be one of them: People who truly qualify for the diagnosis should get it, while those who don't qualify should not. (People with other difficulties absolutely deserve assistance, just not the ADHD label and medication.) Firebrands who deny that the disorder exists or decry all use of stimulant medications are not just unfair to the children and adults with severe problems—that strategy is simply doomed. ADHD is here to stay, a vehicle we now can either drive responsibly or continue swerving all over the road.

No one should expect the system to function perfectly. Until a blood test or brain scan can somehow confirm the presence of the disorder, humans as fallible as ever will make mistakes. Reform in the ADHD world will not be measured by the percentage of children diagnosed, although that number would have to drastically decrease. True success will derive from the percentage of children diagnosed *correctly*.

The *DSM* says that number should be about 5 percent. Many people could live with 7 or 8. But at 15 percent and rising, we have a long way to go. Any chance of getting there requires us all to reconsider what we expect not from children, but from ourselves.

EPILOGUE

In response to coverage of Kyle Craig's suicide, Vanderbilt University has updated its student handbook to feature a full message about the dangers of Adderall abuse, warning students about addiction, hallucinations, and "risk of self-harm." Student health departments at many other colleges are also reforming their approach toward diagnosing ADHD and prescribing stimulants; some universities require students to submit to drug testing, while others require doctors to consult a student's parents to make a more thorough and accurate evaluation.

SHIRE IS CURRENTLY conducting two formal trials on Vyvanse. One will assess whether the four hundred thousand annual prescriptions currently written to four- and five-year-olds per year are in fact safe. The other, in partnership with NYU's Len Adler, will explore how the drug can relieve adult symptoms of sluggish cognitive tempo.

HEALTH OFFICIALS IN Louisiana, stunned at how about one-third of the state's boys covered by Medicaid get put on ADHD drugs, have begun the slow process of improving how the disorder is handled there. Medicaid is streamlining families' access to trained behavioral health providers, who will be encouraged to make the ADHD diagnosis more judiciously and discuss with families options for therapy beyond medication.

ROGER GRIGGS, THE pharmaceutical executive who launched Adderall in 1994 and now laments its effect on American culture, has developed a natural vitamin supplement that he hopes can improve attention issues in some children before they get an ADHD diagnosis and put on stimulants. "It's like pain management," Griggs said. "If a person is in pain you don't go slamming them with morphine." Addivance is expected to go on sale in late 2016.

THE US CENTERS for Disease Control and Prevention has classified ADHD misdiagnosis as a "winnable battle," its official term for a national health problem for which reform is not only imperative but attainable. Dr. Susanna Visser's next report on national rates of ADHD diagnoses in children is expected to be published in 2017.

DR. JOSEPH BIEDERMAN remains director of the Pediatric Psychopharmacology Unit at Massachusetts General Hospital. Having gotten the 2013 *DSM* to raise the age by which ADHD symptoms must appear from seven to twelve, he has coauthored another paper that claims the age requirement should be thrown out altogether so that more adults can be diagnosed. An early version of the study, presented at an annual meeting of the American Professional Society of ADHD and Related Disorders, received a gold ribbon.

IN SEPTEMBER 2015, Jamison Monroe and Kristin Parber opened Newport Academy's third location, a private high school in New York City dedicated to helping teenagers recover from substance-use disorders and other psychiatric troubles. Recognizing academic pressure's role in many kids' problems, the school assigns no homework. Newport plans to open a high school in Philadelphia in late 2016, and then one more each year in different cities.

KEITH CONNERS LIVES on a beautiful, seven-acre estate in Durham with Carolyn and their two Labradoodles, Puppy and Rosie. He is working with Multi-Health Systems, the publisher of the still-thriving Conners Scale series, to adjust the forms' language and scoring methods to discourage misdiagnoses, particularly among adults. He plays with the dogs, catalogs his thousands of books, and listens to his favorite Russian tenors.

He taught himself to watercolor. His favorite painting hangs in his bedroom, a self-portrait. An old man on his cane, back to the world, walks plaintively down an open trail and into the woods.

ACKNOWLEDGMENTS

This book owes its existence to interviews with more than a thousand people, primarily doctors, parents, students, researchers, government officials, and other experts in ADHD. I thank each of them for taking so much time to share their experiences and perspectives, providing their little pixel to what came to form the larger picture.

I am most moved by and appreciative of the scores of kids, some no longer kids, who opened up to me about their ADHD diagnoses or experiences with medication. Their names are not used, usually to protect family relationships and occasionally for legal reasons. But I hope some of the most helpful will recognize their initials here: GD, CZ, KM, J at LM, SP, JS, and TH. The parents of kids who could not speak for themselves were staggeringly brave in telling their stories to benefit other families, in particular Rick and Kathy Fee, Chip and Andrea Craig, Kathy Cavucci, and Kathy Aplington.

Of the hundreds of doctors and other clinicians who provided insight as unique as their patients, none deserves more thanks than Liz Jorgensen, who introduced me to an amazing teenager without whose candor my initial investigation into high school Adderall abuse might very well have stalled. Nancy Rappaport, DeAnsin Parker, and Allan Lans gave early encouragement to trust my instincts. Larry Diller and Stephen Hinshaw showed the intellectual integrity to defend their profession and criticize it, each invaluable for me to understand both sides. I am under no delusion that Ned Hallowell will like some parts of the book, but I thank him specifically for giving me multiple interviews despite knowing full well that he would take some lumps.

Jamison Monroe candidly and patiently spent more than twenty hours of interviews recalling the system he had exploited and is now trying to help fix. I am humbled by the courage of Kristin Parber, who relived her struggles in excruciating detail for the sole purpose of helping others. She requested a pseudonym not out of embarrassment, but out of respect for her parents, who deserve no blame for her struggles; like so many families, the Parbers merely got swept up by the growing ADHD current in ways they could not have foreseen. And, of course, no one gave me more time and insight than Keith Conners. His willingness to share his lifetime of work, and current misgivings, will ultimately go down as downright heroic.

Special thanks go to the Centers for Disease Control and Prevention—especially their primary epidemiologist covering ADHD, Susanna Visser, to whom some important people are finally listening. The CDC director, Tom Frieden, took me seriously from the start, as did Nora Volkow and Wilson Compton of the National Institute on Drug Abuse. Michael Botticelli and Gil Kerlikowske of the White House Office of National Drug Control Policy carved out time for me whenever I needed it. Vital counsel before and during this project came from Elliot Kaye, chairman of the US Consumer Product Safety Commission.

As I trust these pages made clear, the growth of ADHD and stimulant medications had been discussed for decades before I ever took notice. I salute the brilliant historical work—and prescience—of Rick Mayes, Nick Rasmussen, Elaine Moore, and Ilina Singh in excellent books of their own.

My colleagues at the *New York Times*, under whose auspices much of my research was conducted, are by far the smartest, nicest, do-the-right-thingest people for whom one could ever work. Jill Abramson, Glenn Kramon, Sam Sifton, Alison Mitchell, Hilary Stout, and Jim Dao entrusted me to find good stories regarding children's mental health and tell them in ways deserving of our pages. Before that, Tom Jolly and Jason Stallman oversaw my investigation into concussions in sports, cultivating my appreciation for inexplicably veiled issues of public health. And thank you, Arthur Sulzberger Jr., for giving us all the philosophical and financial support to pursue such important stories.

Ryan Morrison, Dylan Blanke-White, and Alisha Fillip were fantastic research assistants, transcribing hundreds of hours of interviews and unearthing long-lost studies, articles, and advertisements. Michael Finkel, Randall Lane, and Adam Cohen are longtime writing advisors, while conversations with my pals Omar Minaya, Dan Okrent, Marv Goldklang, John Haldi, John Abbamondi, David Neft, Robert Easton, and David Weiss always make me think as much as smile. I thank the Starbucks at 92nd and Third for its hospitality, and Debbie Harry and Jane Wiedlin for the soundtrack.

My editor at Scribner, Colin Harrison, came exactly as Dan had advertised: as astute as he is kind. I am also indebted to his colleagues Susan Moldow, Nan Graham, Roz Lippel, Jaya Micelli, Sarah Goldberg, Lisa Rivlin, Laura Wise, and Jill Putorti. David Black provided unparalleled guidance and friendship, without either of which this book would not exist.

No wife should have to put up with the two years my wonderful Laura did. Even while building her own thriving business from scratch, she met every one of my exasperatingly frequent professional and emotional crises with "What can I do to help?," holding my head as much as my hand. And Teddy, we spent more vacations and weekends apart than father and son ever should, but I was buoyed by your love—and by watching you play sports, my purest joy. I did this for you, buddy.

Finally, I thank the late Sam Vaughan, a family friend and editing legend at Doubleday and Random House, who twenty winters ago gave me the best piece of life advice I have ever received. "The people who write books," he said, "are the people who write books."

APPENDIX

The American Psychiatric Association's most recent definition and diagnostic criteria for ADHD, as presented by the US Centers for Disease Control and Prevention:

People with ADHD show a persistent pattern of inattention and/or hyperactivity-impulsivity that interferes with functioning or development:

1. Inattention: Six or more symptoms of inattention for children up to age 16, or five or more for adolescents 17 and older and adults; symptoms of inattention have been present for at least 6 months, and they are inappropriate for developmental level:

   - Often fails to give close attention to details or makes careless mistakes in schoolwork, at work, or with other activities.
   - Often has trouble holding attention on tasks or play activities.
   - Often does not seem to listen when spoken to directly.
   - Often does not follow through on instructions and fails to finish schoolwork, chores, or duties in the workplace (e.g., loses focus, side-tracked).
   - Often has trouble organizing tasks and activities.
   - Often avoids, dislikes, or is reluctant to do tasks that require mental effort over a long period of time (such as schoolwork or homework).

- Often loses things necessary for tasks and activities (e.g., school materials, pencils, books, tools, wallets, keys, paperwork, eyeglasses, mobile telephones).
- Is often easily distracted.
- Is often forgetful in daily activities.

2. Hyperactivity and Impulsivity: Six or more symptoms of hyperactivity-impulsivity for children up to age 16, or five or more for adolescents 17 and older and adults; symptoms of hyperactivity-impulsivity have been present for at least 6 months to an extent that is disruptive and inappropriate for the person's developmental level:

- Often fidgets with or taps hands or feet, or squirms in seat.
- Often leaves seat in situations when remaining seated is expected.
- Often runs about or climbs in situations where it is not appropriate (adolescents or adults may be limited to feeling restless).
- Often unable to play or take part in leisure activities quietly.
- Is often "on the go" acting as if "driven by a motor."
- Often talks excessively.
- Often blurts out an answer before a question has been completed.
- Often has trouble waiting his/her turn.
- Often interrupts or intrudes on others (e.g., butts into conversations or games).

In addition, the following conditions must be met:

- Several inattentive or hyperactive-impulsive symptoms were present before age 12 years.
- Several symptoms are present in two or more settings (such as at home, school, or work; with friends or relatives; in other activities).

- There is clear evidence that the symptoms interfere with, or reduce the quality of, social, school, or work functioning.
- The symptoms are not better explained by another mental disorder (such as a mood disorder, anxiety disorder, dissociative disorder, or a personality disorder). The symptoms do not happen only during the course of schizophrenia or another psychotic disorder.

Population surveys suggest that ADHD occurs in most cultures in about 5 percent of children and about 2.5 percent of adults.

GLOSSARY

AACAP The American Academy of Child and Adolescent Psychiatry. Primary association of child mental health professionals.

ADD Attention deficit disorder. Added to *DSM* in 1980 to replace minimal brain dysfunction.

Adderall Amphetamine medication for ADHD, originally a diet pill named Obetrol, released by Richwood Pharmaceutical in 1994. Rights transferred to Shire in 1997.

Adderall XR Long-acting version of Adderall released by Shire in 2002.

ADHD Attention deficit hyperactivity disorder. Added to *DSM* in 1987 to replace attention deficit disorder.

ADHD (Combined Type) Form of ADHD in which someone has both hyperactivity/impulsivity and attention deficits. Added to *DSM* in 1994.

ADHD (Inattentive Type) Form of ADHD in which someone has few symptoms of hyperactivity. Added to *DSM* in 1994.

ALZA California-based pharmaceutical company that released Concerta in 2000. Later sold rights to Johnson & Johnson.

APSARD American Professional Society of ADHD and Related Disorders. Founded in 2009.

atomoxetine Generic name for Strattera, a nonstimulant medication manufactured by Eli Lilly.

attention deficit disorder See ADD.

attention deficit hyperactivity disorder See ADHD.

Barkley, Dr. Russell Longtime ADHD researcher, speaker, and author of more than ten books on the disorder.

Benzedrine Breakthrough amphetamine medication first marketed in the 1930s by Smith, Kline & French.

Biederman, Dr. Joseph Psychiatrist at Massachusetts General Hospital and Harvard University who has written hundreds of papers regarding ADHD and stimulant medications while being paid millions of dollars by pharmaceutical companies. Became the public face of such conflicts of interest during a 2008 congressional inquiry.

Bradley, Dr. Charles Rhode Island doctor who in the 1930s and 1940s discovered that amphetamine could calm hyperactive children and improve their focus.

Celltech Pharma Small drug company that released Metadate, a long-acting form of Ritalin, in 2001. Ad for Metadate in August edition of *Ladies' Home Journal* was first US direct-to-consumer marketing for a controlled substance.

CHADD The advocacy group Children and Adults with Attention Deficit Disorder, founded in 1987.

CIBA Swiss pharmaceutical company that launched Ritalin to the United States market in 1956. Acronym stood for "Chemical Industries of Basel," the city in which the company was based. Firm later merged with another to form Ciba-Geigy.

Concerta Extended-release methylphenidate for ADHD launched by ALZA in 2000. Currently marketed by Janssen Pharmaceuticals, a subsidiary of Johnson & Johnson.

Conners, Dr. C. Keith Psychologist who first investigated the effects of Ritalin (methylphenidate) on hyperactive children. Published what became the most widely used symptom checklist for diagnosing ADHD. (See Conners Scale.) Practiced and taught child psychiatry at Harvard University, the University of Pittsburgh, George Washington University, and Duke University.

Conners Scale Questionnaire first published in 1969 by Dr. Keith Conners to help clinicians assess a child's behaviors associated with ADHD (then called minimal brain dysfunction). Conners distributed the scales for free until he sold the rights in the 1980s to Multi-Health Systems, a Canadian publishing firm that has sold them ever since.

Cylert See pemoline.

Daytrana A medication launched by Shire in 2006 in which methylphenidate is delivered from a patch through the skin, similar to nicotine patches. Shire sold rights to the medication to Noven Pharmaceuticals in 2010.

Dexedrine Amphetamine product patented by Smith, Kline & French in 1939 and later released as the company's successor to Benzedrine. Even after going generic, remained the primary name by which prescription amphetamines were known until Adderall's emergence in the 1990s.

DSM *The Diagnostic and Statistical Manual of Mental Disorders.* Official publication of the American Psychiatric Association that lists what the organization considers all psychiatric conditions and their diagnostic criteria. Latest edition, called *DSM V*, was published in 2013. Other editions were: *DSM I* (1952), *DSM II* (1968), *DSM III* (1980), *DSM-III Revised* (1987), and *DSM IV* (1994).

Eisenberg, Dr. Leon Keith Conners's mentor at Johns Hopkins in the 1960s and a key pioneer in child psychiatry.

Focalin Methylphenidate ADHD medication launched by Novartis in 2002.

Griggs, Roger Founded Richwood Pharmaceutical and launched Adderall in 1994. Sold interest in company to Shire in 1997 for $186 million.

guanfacine. See Intuniv.

Hallowell, Dr. Edward Coauthor of *Driven to Distraction* (1994) and frequent ADHD media commentator.

hyperkinetic reaction of childhood Name for the disorder now known as ADHD listed in the *DSM* from 1968 through 1980.

Intuniv Nonstimulant medication for ADHD manufactured by Shire. Generic name: guanfacine.

Metadate Long-acting form of Ritalin released by Celltech Pharma in 2001.

methylphenidate Chemical with stimulant effects similar to amphetamine first synthesized by CIBA chemist Leandro Panizzon in mid-1940s. Released to US market by CIBA as Ritalin in 1956.

minimal brain damage Name in the 1950s and 1960s for what is now termed ADHD. Fell out of favor because many patients did not have any signs of physical brain damage. Became minimal brain dysfunction.

minimal brain dysfunction Name popular in 1960s and 1970s for what it is now termed ADHD. Never appeared in the *DSM*, which from 1968 to 1980 called the disorder "hyperkinetic reaction of childhood."

MTA Study The Multimodal Treatment of Children with ADHD study. Massive research effort in mid-1990s to investigate which treatments (stimulant medication and/or behavioral therapy) were most effective for children with ADHD. Even though using both treatments was shown to be most effective, results published in 1999 were communicated as supporting the use of medication alone.

NIH National Institutes of Health.

NIMH National Institute of Mental Health.

Novartis Manufacturer of Focalin.

Obetrol Amphetamine pill for weight loss so abused in 1960s that it helped spawn the Controlled Substances Act.

Panizzon, Leandro Chemist for CIBA who first synthesized methylphenidate in the mid-1940s. Named it Ritaline after his wife, Rita, whose energy was boosted by the drug.

pemoline Generic name for Cylert, a medication for minimal brain dysfunction introduced by Abbott Pharmaceuticals in early 1970s. Neither methylphenidate nor amphetamine, and less popular than Ritalin and Dexedrine, it was banned by the FDA in 2005 for links to liver damage.

psychiatrist Mental health professional who is an MD and therefore can prescribe medication.

psychologist Mental health professional who is not an MD and, in most states, therefore cannot prescribe medication.

Ritalin Brand name of methylphenidate first marketed in America by CIBA in 1956. Experiments by Keith Conners and Leon Eisenberg in the mid-1960s established how Ritalin could help calm hyperactive children.

Shire Irish pharmaceutical company which obtained Adderall's exclusive rights by purchasing Richwood Pharmaceutical in 1997 for $186 million. Later developed Adderall XR, Vyvanse, and Intuniv.

sluggish cognitive tempo Name some prominent ADHD researchers have proposed for what they assert is a newly discovered disorder marked by daydreaminess and lethargy. Although researched to varying extents since the 1980s, has never appeared in the *DSM*.

Strattera Nonstimulant medication for ADHD launched in 2006 by Eli Lilly. Generic name atomoxetine. Considered less addictive, but also less effective, than amphetamine or methylphenidate.

Vyvanse Amphetamine-based medication for ADHD launched by Shire in 2008. Approved by FDA for binge eating disorder in 2015.

NOTES

xi *"Argue with success":* Wender, *Minimal Brain Dysfunction in Children,* 10.

INTRODUCTION

1 *Synapses in the brain:* Castellanos et al., "Developmental trajectories of brain volume abnormalities in children and adolescents with attention-deficit/hyperactivity disorder," 1740.

2 *Almost one in three:* Author analysis of data from Visser, "Trends in the parent-report of health care provider–diagnosed and medicated attention-deficit/hyperactivity disorder."; Schwarz and Cohen, "A.D.H.D seen in 11% of U.S. Children as Diagnoses Rise," A1.

2 *Taking ADHD medications:* Bilbo et al., "Demographic & Geographic Patterns of ADHD Prescriptions among Louisiana's Medicaid Children."

3 *"Behavior drugs":* Maynard, "Omaha Pupils Given 'Behavior' Drugs," A1.

3 *"Diagnosed with ADHD": The Colbert Report.*

3 *"Youthful Tendency Disorder":* "More U.S. Children Being Diagnosed With Youthful Tendency Disorder, September 27, 2000."

3 *"Impair[s] life functioning":* ADDitude, Oct. 22, 2015. As archived at https://freshpickeddeals.com/additudemag.com/why-youre-always-tired-the-adhd-sleep-link-and-sound-solutions-559245.

3 *"Famous People with ADHD":* Grohol, "Famous People with A.D.H.D."

4 *"ADHD Superpowers":* Editors and Readers of *ADDitude,* "12 Amazing ADHD Superpowers."

4 *"All good news":* Walkup et al., "Beyond rising rates," 14.

CHAPTER 1: FIDGETY PHIL'S ARITHMETIC PILLS

13 *Nobody else wanted:* M. Johnston, *Out of Sorrow and into Hope,* 21.

14 *"Arithmetic pills":* Mayes et al., *Medicating Children,* 54.

14 *"Too active":* Weikard, as translated by Barkley and Peters in "The earliest reference to ADHD in the medical literature?," 627.

15 *"Affections of the human mind":* Tansey, "The life and works of Sir Alexander Crichton," 244.

15 *Knighted him:* Ibid., 251.

15 *"Nature of delirium":* Crichton, *An Inquiry into the Nature and Origin of Mental Derangement,* 272.

16 *"Of their lives":* Ibid., 277–78.

17 *"I am getting cross":* Hoffmann, *Struwwelpeter.*

17 *Official definition of ADHD:* American Psychiatric Association, *DSM 5,* 59–60.

17 *"Good of self":* Still, "Some abnormal psychical conditions in children," 1009.

18 *Primordial ADHD:* Conners, "Attention-deficit/hyperactivity disorder: historical development and overview," 176; Lange et al., "The history of attention deficit hyperactivity disorder," 3–4.

19 *Bell Telephone Company: Bell Telephone Quarterly,* 145; M. Johnston, *Out of Sorrow and into Hope,* 8–9.

19 *Mentally retarded:* Johnston, *Out of Sorrow and into Hope,* 11.

19 *"In like manner":* Bradley will, 18.

19 *Eskay's Neuro Phosphates:* Rasmussen, *On Speed,* Fig. 8.

20 *Postpartum depression:* Ibid., 27–31. Rasmussen's book is by far the most authoritative source on the history of amphetamine—a must-read for anyone wanting to learn more.

21 *"From a practical viewpoint":* Bradley, "The behavior of children receiving Benzedrine," 582.

21 *"More careful work":* Bradley and Bowen, "School performance of children receiving amphetamine (Benzedrine) sulfate," 785.

22 *Basic safety tests:* Rasmussen, *On Speed,* 47; Mogull, "Chronology of direct-to-consumer advertising regulation in the United States," 107–8.

22 *Demonstrated to be safe:* Rasmussen, *On Speed,* 47.

22 *For the high:* Moore, *Amphetamine Debate,* 35.

22 *Nights on end to study:* "Pep-Pill Poisoning."

23 *One of the first times the federal government:* Conners interview with author, 2016.

23 *Oil drum:* Conners interview with author, 2014.

CHAPTER 2: DR. CONNERS

24 *Old Mrs. Howarth:* Conners interview with author. Unless noted, all biographical information regarding Conners derives from author interviews, 2012–16.

24 *Temple of Israel:* 1 Kings 10:11.

25 *Killed Rudolph Valentino:* "Rudolph Valentino Biography," Biography.com, http://www.biography.com/people/rudolph-valentino-9514591#tragic -death.

27 *Gender identity:* Carey, "John William Money, 84, Sexual Identity Researcher, Dies."

27 *Gender-reassignment surgery:* "fe_sexchange_jf07."

28 *"Adjustment Reaction of Childhood":* DSM-I, 41–42.

28 *Described autism:* Harris, "Leon Eisenberg."

28 *Predict their autistic behaviors:* Safford, "Leon Eisenberg."

28 *"Psychiatrist who can count":* David Healy interview with Eisenberg (unpublished, provided by Healy).

28 *"Minimal brain damage":* Lange et al., "The history of attention deficit hyperactivity disorder," 250.

29 *"Under school conditions":* Denhoff et al., "Hyperkinetic impulse disorder in children's behavior problems," 38.

29 *"Responsibility for the problem":* Laufer and Denhoff, "Hyperkinetic behavior syndrome in children," 473.

29 *Tanks drive sideways:* Rasmussen, *On Speed*, 70–71.

29 *Giddily addicted housewife:* Schaar, "Witty Songs"; for audio of song see https://www.youtube.com/watch?v=l2WJqnK3gAY&app=desktop.

29 *"Little patients too":* Singh, "Not Just Naughty: 50 Years of Stimulant Drug Advertising," 136.

29 *"Lengthening the child's attention span":* Ibid., 137.

30 *Remained frowned upon:* Freed and Peifer, "Treatment of hyperkinetic emotionally disturbed children with prolonged administration of chlorpromazine," 24.

30 *"Pushing them in":* Mayes et al., *Medicating Children,* 60.

31 *Named it Ritaline:* Myers, *The 100 Most Important Chemical Compounds,* 178.

31 *Caused by senility:* Leonard et al., "Methylphenidate: a review of its neuropharmacological, neuropsychological and adverse clinical effects," 151.

31 *"Help psychiatric patients talk":* Singh, "Not Just Naughty: 50 Years of Stimulant Drug Advertising," 136.

32 *The paper Conners and Eisenberg wrote up:* Conners and Eisenberg, "The effects of methylphenidate on symptomatology and learning in disturbed children," 458–64.

32 *"Not understanding it":* Sinclair, *I, Candidate for Governor,* 107.

32 *Knocked on the open door:* Conners interview with author, 2014.

33 *More than thirty:* Clements, *Minimal Brain Dysfunction in Children: NINDB Monograph,* 9.

33   New England Journal of Medicine: Pincus and Glaser, "The syndrome of 'minimal brain damage' in childhood," 27.
33   *"Minimal brain damage":* Clements and Peters, "Minimal Brain Dysfunctions in the School-Age Child," 185.
33   *"Hyperkinetic reaction of childhood":* DSM II, 50.
33   *"Beyond doubt":* Editorial, *Public Health*, 59–61.
34   *In child psychiatry:* Safford, "Leon Eisenberg."
34   *Science is made:* Sutton-Smith and Rosenberg, "A scale to identify impulsive behavior in children," 211–16.
35   *"Available to them":* Conners et al., "Effect of dextroamphetamine on children," 478–85.
36   *"All three":* Mayes et al., *Medicating Children,* 60.

CHAPTER 3: FROM MBD TO ADD

37   *Inner-city riots:* Locke, "Robert Maynard, Publisher, Powerful Black Journalist."
37   *Page-one headline blared:* Maynard, "Omaha Pupils Given 'Behavior' Drugs," A1.
38   *Twenty apiece:* Rasmussen, *On Speed,* 178.
38   *Abusers and addicts:* Ibid., 191.
38   *Average housewives:* Ibid., 179.
39   *An astonishing 90 percent:* Ibid., 220.
39   Huntley-Brinkley Report: Murray, "Drugs to Control Classroom Behavior?," 21.
39   *Responded with an article:* Reinhold, "Rx for Child's Learning Malady," 27.
40   *Massachusetts General Hospital:* Carey, "Dr. Leon Eisenberg, Pioneer in Autism Studies, Dies at 87," A39.
40   *"Nothing new about it":* Maynard, "Can Drugs Help a 'Wild Child'?," B1.
40   *"Safer than penicillin":* Reinhold, "Rx for Child's Learning Malady," 27.
40   *Bundles from parents and doctors:* Von Hoffman, "Student Pep Talk: A Commentary," B1.
40   *Called the hearing to order: Federal Involvement in the Use of Behavior Modification Drugs,* 1.
43   *Ross Youngs is now:* Youngs interview with author, 2015.
44   *Lenny:* Conners interview with author, 2014.
45   *"Virtually constitutes malpractice":* Wender, *Minimal Brain Dysfunction in Children,* 130.
46   *Cylert was later linked:* Conners et al., "Magnesium Pemoline and Dextroamphetamine," 335; Moon, "The Amphetamine Years," 207.

46 *In a journal essay:* Schmitt, "The Minimal Brain Dysfunction Myth," 1313.

47 *It was insufficient* attention: Douglas, "Stop, Look and Listen," 259.

47 *Two thousand studies:* Carter, "Paying Attention."

48 *"Krankheit's syndrome":* Wender, "Minimal Brain Dysfunction: An Overview," 1429.

49 *"I urge restraint":* Decker, *The Making of DSM-III,* 273. Decker's book provides the best history of the negotiations behind the development of *DSM-III,* which in many ways changed the course of psychiatry.

CHAPTER 4: COLLISION COURSE

53 *"Behavioral or learning problem":* Shaywitz and Shaywitz, "Increased medication use in attention-deficit hyperactivity disorder," 2271.

53 *Bumped diagnosis rates:* Lahey et al., "Comparison of DSM-III and DSM-III-R diagnoses for prepubertal children," 620.

53 *"Less than ten seconds": Dennis the Menace,* cartoon, *The Indianapolis Star,* Sept. 11, 1990, 27.

54 *"Thinking pill":* Sperling, "Families Struggle with Kids' Hyperactive Behavior."

54 *"Now he's on the student council":* Associated Press, Apr. 5, 1988.

54 *"Sweet little boy":* "Attention Deficit Disorder Stirs Debate Among Parents," 3.

54 *"Before we help them":* Brecher, "Why Johnny Can't Behave," E1.

54 *"Kiss you on both cheeks":* Haney, "Drug Helps Hyperactive Kids; No One Knows Why," G-3.

54 *Going on medication:* Associated Press, Apr. 5, 1988.

54 *Children were given posters:* Sappell and Welkos, "Suits, Protests Fuel a Campaign Against Psychiatry," A1.

55 *Some kids hallucinated:* Mosholder, *Psychiatric Adverse Events in Attention Deficit Hyperactivity Disorder (ADHD) Clinical Trials;* Mosholder et al., "Hallucinations and other psychotic symptoms associated with the use of attention-deficit/hyperactivity disorder drugs in children," 611.

55 *Growth being suppressed:* Swanson et al., "Effects of stimulant medication on growth rates across 3 years in the MTA follow-up," 1015; DeNoon, "ADHD Drug Does Stunt Growth."

56 *"They would do so":* Sappell and Welkos, "Suits, Protests Fuel a Campaign Against Psychiatry," A1.

56 *At least 20 percent:* Safer and Krager, "Effect of a media blitz and a threatened lawsuit on stimulant treatment," 1004.

57 *"Guilt off them"*: Borzi, "Group Comforts Parents of Hyperactive Children," D1.

57 *"You're not alone"*: Ibid.

58 *About two million:* Borzi, "Group Aids Parents of Special Kids," BR-3.

58 *640 chapters nationwide:* CHADD 1995 Annual Report.

59 *The film was so controversial:* Merrow interview with author, 2013.

59 *400 percent:* National Public Radio, Nov. 18, 1998.

60 *Edward was born:* Hallowell interview with author, 2014.

60 *He is self-diagnosed:* Ibid.

60 *"Powerfully positive"*: Hallowell and Ratey, *Driven to Distraction*, 43.

62 *"Filling my waiting room"*: Hallowell interview with author, 2015.

62 *"Good-news diagnosis"*: Hales and Hales, "Finally, I Know What's Wrong," 8.

62 *"A nation full of ADHD"*: *CNN Newsroom*, Nov. 13, 2010.

62 *"I want to"*: *Talkback Live*, CNN, May 26, 1999, 3 p.m.

63 *Forty thousand copies:* Diller interview with author, 2014.

64 *"I had a child back"*: *CBS Evening News*, Apr. 21, 1998.

64 *"One of the leading developments"*: *CBS Evening News*, Nov. 15, 1998.

65 *Conners's opening:* Author transcription of event video that has since been removed from https://www.youtube.com/watch?v=SvdxW_T01lk.

68 *"The diagnosis is a mess"*: Ibid.

68 *"The rest of their lives"*: Vedantam, "Industry Role in Medical Meeting Decried," A01.

69 *"Quite safe and effective"*: *Good Morning America*, ABC News, Nov. 19, 1998.

69 *Devote its cover: Time*, Nov. 30, 1998.

CHAPTER 5: KRISTIN

74 Newsweek's *cover story:* Hancock, "Mother's Little Helper," 52.

75 *"Happens in some schools"*: Cohen, "Letter to Fox Broadcasting about Simpson's [*sic*] Episode."

76 *Congress clarified its regulations:* Individuals with Disabilities Education Act (IDEA), https://www.gpo.gov/fdsys/pkg/PLAW-108publ446/html/PLAW-108publ446.htm.

76 *Some argued that the fuzziness:* Mayes, *Medicating Children,* 109.

76 *More than doubled:* Swanson et al., "More frequent diagnosis of attention deficit–hyperactivity disorder," 944.

81 *Dopamine moved across:* Hinshaw and Scheffler, *The A.D.H.D. Explosion,* 54–55; Volkow et al., "Evaluating dopamine reward pathway in ADHD: clinical implications," 1084–91.

CHAPTER 6: JAMISON

85 *How's it work for you?:* This and all other such conversations recalled in detail by Jamison Monroe in author interviews, 2013–16.

87 *Hall of Fame:* "TCU Lettermen's Association Hall Of Fame Members," Texas Christian University website, http://www.gofrogs.com /genrel/032102aaa.html.

87 *Hated his father:* Jim Monroe interview with author, 2014.

93 *"See if it helps":* Kay Monroe interview with author, 2014.

CHAPTER 7: ADD FOR ALL

95 *Chose his words carefully:* All Griggs recollections and dealings with Adderall from interviews with author, 2013–16.

102 *There was no Nolan:* E-mail from Swanson to author, Dec. 14, 2015.

103 *"Medicine Over Therapy":* Thomas, "Study of Attention Deficit Disorder Supports Medicine Over Therapy," 14D.

103 *"Help for Attention Deficit":* World News Tonight, ABC News, Dec. 14, 1999.

103 *Of No Benefit:* Schwarz, "The Selling of Attention Deficit Disorder," A1.

104 *"For Attention-Disorder Kids":* Kotulak, "Major Study Rebuts Critics of Drugs for Attention-Disorder Kids," 5.

104 *"Hands-down winner":* Kotulak, Ibid.

104 *"It is still surprising":* Noble, "Study Backs a Drug for Hyperactive Children," A18.

CHAPTER 8: THE HIJACKING

109 *"If you say this":* Wilson, "Side Effects May Include Lawsuits," B1.

109 *But it did:* Wazana, "Physicians and the pharmaceutical industry," 373–80.

110 *"We are extremely encouraged":* ALZA press release, Oct. 25, 1999.

110 *$250 million:* Zernike and Petersen, "Schools' Backing of Behavior Drugs Comes Under Fire."

111 *"Often in error":* Conners's notes from the presentation.

111 *In the early 1980s:* Biederman, Testimony, Vol. 1, 36–39.

112 *He responded flatly: "God":* Ibid., 48.

112 *Almost three hundred papers:* "An Interview with Dr. Joseph Biederman."

112 *"These data provide support":* Mccracken et al., "Analog classroom assessment of a once-daily mixed amphetamine formulation, SLI381 (Adderall XR), in children with ADHD," 673.

112 *"Family studies":* Biederman, "Attention-Deficit/Hyperactivity Disorder: A Life-Span Perspective," 4–16.

112 *"Well tolerated and effective":* Bostic et al., "Pemoline treatment of adolescents with attention deficit hyperactivity disorder," 205.

112 *Cautioned against:* Wilens et al., "Controlled trial of high doses of pemoline for adults with attention-deficit/hyperactivity disorder," 257.

113 *"Brilliantly at school":* Gale, "Ritalin requests often deemed inappropriate," Sept. 14, 2006.

113 *Best interests at heart:* Joel Adamson interview with author, 2013.

113 *Increased by forty times:* Harris and Carey, "Researchers Fail to Reveal Full Drug Pay," A1.

113 *"Funding from conventional sources":* Allen, "Backlash on bipolar diagnoses in children MGH psychiatrist's work stirs debate," A1.

113 *While speaking at one conference:* Conners recollection of Biederman lecture at Yokohama, 2002.

114 *Grassley's team unearthed:* Harris and Carey. "Researchers Fail to Reveal Full Drug Pay, A1.

114 *According to internal documents:* Harris, "Drug Maker Told Studies Would Aid It, Papers Say."

116 *People with ADHD:* Barkley et al., "International consensus statement on ADHD," 90.

116 *One-third of his income:* Barkley website page on Internet Archive Wayback Machine: https://web.archive.org/web/20081211060716/http://www.russellbarkley.org/about-dr-barkley.htm.

116 *Barkley had a twin brother:* Barkley, "I Lost My Brother to ADHD."

117 *Even some drug companies:* Celltech, *Metadate CD Visiting Faculty Program*, 3.

117 *"Getting away with it":* Tennant, "Combating A.D.D.," E1.

117 *"Fringe doctors":* Barkley et al., "International consensus statement on ADHD," 90.

117 *Local newspaper told-you-sos:* Sizemore, "Did Study Miss the Mark?," A14.

118 *Going down a hill:* Traffic Collision Report, Berkeley Police Department, Report Number 06-20357, Apr. 26, 2006.

119 *Just like MBD kids:* Rapoport et al., "Dextroamphetamine: cognitive and behavioral effects in normal prepubertal boys," 560.

119 *"Concerta helped improve interactions":* Concerta ad, 2006.

119 *"ADDERALL XR enhances Social Functioning":* Adderall XR ad, 2003.

119 *"Control and Confidence":* Strattera ad, 2005.

119 *When could ADHD symptoms:* Strattera ad, 2007.

120 *"The Comfort of UNDENIABLE SAFETY":* Concerta ad, 2003.

120 *"Experience life's successes":* Concerta ad, year unknown.

121 *10 percent of kids:* CDC data.

CHAPTER 9: THERE'S SOMETHING THEY KNOW ABOUT US

123 *Four million readers:* "Reaching More Subscribers More Efficiently," *Better Homes & Gardens,* http://www.meredith.com/mediakit/print/print_circ _demo.html.

123 *Imperiled public safety:* United Nations, Single Convention on Narcotic Drugs, 1961.

124 *Their third-grade son:* All information regarding the Parry family from interviews with author, 2013–14.

126 *More than one per issue:* Author examination of *Family Circle, Good House-keeping, Ladies' Home Journal, Redbook,* and *Parenting* from 1998 through 2010.

127 *Acquired ALZA:* Johnson & Johnson press release, *Johnson & Johnson to Merge With ALZA Corporation In $10.5 Billion Stock-for-Stock Transaction,* http://www.investor.jnj.com/releasedetail.cfm?releaseid=63833.

128 *"Ice cream party with team":* Concerta ad, 2009.

130 *"Data on file":* Concerta ad, 2008.

130 *Approached two million:* Derived from CDC data.

130 *$3 billion:* Armstrong, "Will Success Rock Shire Pharma?," 6.

131 *Counted as if they did:* FDA warning letter to Alliant, Sept. 25, 2008.

132 *"Inquiries from the government":* Ibid.

132 *It came from doctors:* Kaufman, "Ransom-Note Ads About Children's Health Are Canceled."

CHAPTER 10: HIGHER AND HIGHER

138 *In a 1983 episode:* "Speed Trap."

138 *"Feeling of omnipotence":* Michael Weithorn interview with author, 2015.

141 *10-milligram blue pills:* Pill color from personal correspondence with Roger Griggs, 2015.

142 *"I felt like going to class":* Stepp, "A Wonder Drug's Worst Side Effect," A1.

142 *Snorted it en masse:* Mitchell, "DA Charges 2 More in Ritalin Case," B5.

142 *Injected it:* DeGrandpre, *Ritalin Nation,* 184.

143 *"Very widespread application":* Klein and Wender, "The role of methylphenidate in psychiatry," 431.

143 *"Is not happening":* Attention Deficit/Hyperactivity Disorder—Are We Overmedicating Our Children?, 79.

CHAPTER 11: LESS THAN

149 *Antics of George and Harold:* Pilkey, *Captain Underpants and the Perilous Plot of Professor Poopypants,* 14–15.

150 *"Swinging from a tree":* Pilkey interview with author, 2015.

154 *Little effect at all:* Molina et al., "Adolescent substance use in the multimodal treatment study of attention-deficit/hyperactivity disorder,"
250; Lee et al., "Prospective association of childhood attention-deficit/
hyperactivity disorder (ADHD) and substance use and abuse/dependence,"
328; Schwarz, "No Link Seen Between Child Stimulant Use and Later
Drug Abuse."

157 *Without a doctor's prescription:* Johnston et al., "Monitoring the Future
National Survey Results on Drug Use"; McCabe and West, "Medical and
nonmedical use of prescription stimulants," 1272.

157 *"They're always looking for it":* Interview with author, 2012.

158 *A little over nine hours:* National Sleep Foundation, "Teens and Sleep,"
https://sleepfoundation.org/sleep-topics/teens-and-sleep.

158 *Only seven hours:* Nationwide Children's Hospital, "Sleep in Adolescents
(13–18 Years)," http://www.nationwidechildrens.org/sleep-in-adolescents.

158 *"Make my parents happy?":* Interview with author, 2012.

158 *Confidential survey of students:* Author interview with member of board of
education, 2012.

159 *Self-medicating their undiagnosed ADHD:* McCabe and West, "Medical
and nonmedical use of prescription stimulants," 1278.

CHAPTER 12: BRIGHT COLLEGE DAYS

161 *What "trying" means to them:* Author interviews with students at Vanderbilt University, Mar. 19–21, 2013.

162 *A sophomore named Kyle Craig:* Author interviews with Chip and Andrea
Craig, 2013.

163 *"What we have learned":* E-mail from Chip Craig to Vanderbilt University,
June 28, 2010.

163 *"Campuses across the country":* Bishop, "Adderall at Vanderbilt: Causes,
Integrity and Safety."

163 *Studies generally do not find:* Lakhan and Kirchgessner, "Prescription stimulants in individuals with and without attention deficit hyperactivity disorder," 661.

164 *Cranking out papers overnight:* Volkow and Swanson, "The action of
enhancers can lead to addiction."

164 *Vanderbilt, for example:* Vanderbilt University, *2012/2013 Student Handbook Policies & Regulations in Co-Curricular Matters*, updated Dec. 13,
2012.

164 *A reasonable estimate:* Smith and Farah, "Are prescription stimulants
'smart pills'?," 717–41; DeSantis et al., "Illicit use of prescription ADHD
medications on a college campus," 315; National Survey on Drug Use

and Health, "Nonmedical Use of Adderall among Full-Time College Students," Apr. 7, 2009.

164 *One 2006 study:* Kroutil et al., "Nonmedical use of prescription stimulants in the United States," 135.

164 *Even Supreme Court justices:* Sherman, "Justices Sympathetic to Man Deported for Carrying Adderall in Sock."

165 *Couldn't tell the groups apart:* Sollman et al., "Detection of feigned ADHD in college students," 325.

165 *Depose the clinician involved:* Testimony of Marianne Cannon, *Edwards v. Harvard College.*

165 *Her absurd 80 percent claim:* Faraone et al., "Molecular genetics of attention deficit/hyperactivity disorder," 1313.

166 *"Thorough and appropriate":* Schwarz, "Harvard Student's Suicide as a Case Study," A12.

166 *Wrote a column:* Servantes, "If I Did It: Academics and Adderall."

166 *"Magic pill":* "Magic Pill Can Enhance Focus, Drive."

166 *"Take advantage of pills":* Pursell, "Stressed-Out Students Should Take Advantage of Pills."

167 *A short press release:* University of Miami press release, Nov. 16, 2012.

167 *"Are not addictive":* "ADD—A Dubious Diagnosis."

167 *People with heart disease:* Huang et al., "Long-term use of aspirin and the risk of gastrointestinal bleeding," 426.

167 *"If each injury is managed properly":* National Football League, "What is a Concussion?," 2007.

168 *"A user can become dependent":* United States Patent No. 7,662,788.

169 *Stimulant-related suicides:* Similar suicides have included Marcus Cavucci (Youngstown State) and Will Cuva (University of Missouri). Circumstances of deaths were confirmed through author interviews with both families.

169 *"Attention to detail":* Richard Fee medical records courtesy of the Fee family.

171 *This is the same city:* Gretchen LeFever interviews with author, 2012.

171 *"Anyone in the state":* As recalled by Rick Fee in multiple interviews as well as in his court testimony.

171 *He made a proposal:* Philip Morris Companies Inter-Office Correspondence, Dec. 8, 1994.

173 *They decided to go:* Author present with Fee family at CHADD event.

173 *"Unlikely to lead to addiction":* Hughes, "Substance Abuse, ADHD, and Medications: The Real Issues."

174 *"Care to struggling children":* Miller, "Stimulants and Suicide."

174 *"Effective treatment is available":* Drell, Letter to the Editor.

CHAPTER 13: AND NOW, A WORD FROM OUR SPONSORS

175 *Out ran Ty Pennington: The Revolution.*

179 *More than a million viewers:* Block, "ABC Renews 'General Hospital' and 'The Chew,' Cancels 'The Revolution.'"

180 *"That was better":* Author interview with Shire sales representative who spoke on condition of anonymity, 2013.

180 *Constituted malpractice:* Wender, *Minimal Brain Dysfunction in Children,* 130.

180 *Like a child's problem:* Decker, *The Making of DSM-III,* 274.

182 *"Gave me my life back":* Morrow, "Attention Disorder Is Found in Growing Number of Adults."

183 *"Like erectile dysfunction was":* Tortora, "It's Not Just Kids: ADHD Affects Adults, Too."

183 *"You shouldn't have said that":* Conversation recalled by Conners, Jan. 2015.

186 *He had computed:* Shire press release, 2005.

186 *Reproduced on medical websites:* "Behavioral Briefs: ADHD Has Repercussions Throughout Adulthood."

186 *Checklist of only six questions:* Kessler et al., "The World Health Organization Adult ADHD Self-Report Scale (ASRS)," 245.

187 *"Highly consistent with ADHD":* Surman, "Clinical Assessment of ADHD in Adults," 23.

187 *Researchers determined:* Kessler et al., "The prevalence and correlates of adult ADHD in the United States," 716.

188 *"Screen for ADHD":* Shire ads, various years.

189 *Goofed by putting it online:* George, "Promotional ADHD Drug Video Draws FDA's Rebuke."

190 *Concerta campaign "Genius":* L2 Digital IQ Index: Pharma & Healthcare Providers, Apr. 18, 2011, 27.

190 *Almost 100,000 people:* E-mail from Shire representative to author, July 16, 2013.

190 *Forty-nine percent:* Schwarz, "The Selling of Attention Deficit Disorder," A1.

190 *To 16 million:* Data from IMS Health in Schwarz, "The Selling of Attention Deficit Disorder," A1.

191 *"Adults who were never diagnosed":* Russell interview on Bloomberg TV, May 11, 2011, 3:31 p.m.

191 *40 million times:* "Best TV Advertising Campaign."

CHAPTER 14: AWAKENING

195 *Letter to the Editor:* Kollins, *The Raleigh News & Observer.*

195 *Eisenberg wrote an essay:* Eisenberg and Guttmacher, "Were we all asleep at the switch?," 89–102.

195 *"I think it's dreadful":* Eisenberg interview with Healy.

196 *In a Florida newspaper:* Loftus, "Ritalin Use Poses Questions; What Do You Think?," A1.

196 *Used it among themselves:* Fink, "The Challenge of Treating ADHD," 15.

196 *Unremarkable fact:* Kagan, *CNN Morning News*; Lodge, "Kids' Health Hazards," 5C.

197 *3 percent had the disorder:* American Psychiatric Association *DSM-III*, 42.

197 *Inched its estimate upward:* American Psychiatric Association *DSM-IV*, 82.

197 *5 percent:* American Psychiatric Association *DSM 5*, 61.

198 *"To get more funding":* Interview with author at REACH training session, Jan. 2014.

198 *Interviewed a representative group:* The standard survey used by CDC researchers is called the Diagnostic Interview Schedule for Children, which assesses many more psychiatric conditions beyond ADHD.

198 *Cincinnati Children's Hospital:* Froehlich et al., "Prevalence, recognition, and treatment of attention-deficit/hyperactivity disorder in a national sample of US children," 857.

198 *Drug makers rejoiced:* Shire promotional booklet, "You Have Our Full Attention," 3.

199 *ADHD* they did not have: Data from Froehlich et al. study provided to author.

200 *The paper's front page:* Schwarz and Cohen, "A.D.H.D. Seen in 11% of U.S. Children as Diagnoses Rise," A1.

200 *"Overestimate true prevalence":* Getahun et al., "Recent trends in childhood attention-deficit/hyperactivity disorder," 286.

200 *"Not a lot of value":* Gupta on *Anderson Cooper 360°*.

200 *"Not of overtreatment":* Walkup et al., "Beyond Rising Rates," 14.

201 *Shire had paid for the study:* Lowry, "Drug Therapy for Parents' ADHD Improves Kids' Behavior."

201 *About one in three:* CDC, "Key Findings of the Prevalence of Attention-Deficit/Hyperactivity Disorder."

202 *"It's Everywhere YOU Want to Be":* APSARD 2013 Meeting Program.

204 *It did not go well:* Author present at meeting with Alamance County officials, May 9, 2014.

206 *Some remarkable scenes:* Author present during seminars.

207 *Especially valuable for pediatricians:* Notes taken by meeting attendee, Oct. 23, 2013.

CHAPTER 15: CONNECTION

212 *Led him into their meeting room:* Meeting among Keith Conners, Jamison Monroe, and Kristin Parber took place on June 8, 2015.

214 *One in five boys:* Nolan et al., "Teacher reports of DSM-IV ADHD, ODD, and CD symptoms in schoolchildren," 241.

214 *One of the youngest in their grade:* Elder, "The importance of relative standards in ADHD diagnoses," 641.

214 *"Prescribed to treat ADHD":* Ibid.

CHAPTER 16: THIS IS YOUR BRAIN ON CAPITALISM

222 *"Basement of the YMCA":* Vedantam, "Industry Role in Medical Meeting Decried," A10.

222 *Didn't mince words:* Goodman, "Unmasking ADHD in Adults."

223 *One middle-aged woman:* Schwarz, "Report Says Medication Use Is Rising for Adults With Attention Disorder," A16.

223 *"Hit on all cylinders":* "Efficiency of Brain Held Due to Its 'Fuel'; Cells Found Speeded Up by Synthetic Drug," 6.

223 *Initiative and efficiency:* Reifenstein and Davidoff, "The Psychological Effects of Benzedrine Sulfate," 56–64.

223 *"Nothing seemed impossible":* Nathanson, "The central action of beta-aminopropylbenzene (Benzedrine)," 528.

223 *"With a wood racquet":* Schwarz, "Abuse of Attention Deficit Pills Graduates into the Workplace," A1.

223 *Jump on the competition:* Lane, *The Zeroes*, 236.

224 *All of them adding:* Author interviews, 2012 through 2015.

224 *Even video gamers:* Wingfield and Dougherty, "Drug Testing Is Coming to E-Sports," B1.

224 *An article on academic misuse:* Sahakian and Morein-Zamir, "Professor's Little Helper," 1157.

224 *"Doctor Robert":* Turner, *A Hard Day's Write*, 166.

225 *No signs of slowing down:* Express Scripts, "Turning Attention to ADHD."

225 *"Plenty of supply":* Harris, "F.D.A. Finds Short Supply of Attention Deficit Drugs," A1.

225 *Risen substantially:* U.S. Substance Abuse and Mental Health Services Administration, "Treatment Episode Data Set (TEDS)," 43.

226 *"It becomes a crutch immediately":* Kroutil et al., "Nonmedical use of prescription stimulants in the United States," 135.

226 *Rammed through a locked gate:* Mazik interviews with author, 2013 through 2015.

227 *"Spend time with my husband":* Vyvanse ad, 2010.

227 *More quickly among women than men:* Schwarz, "Report Says Medication Use Is Rising for Adults with Attention Disorder," A16.

227 *"How positive these findings were":* Brauser, "ADHD Med May Offer Drug Option for Binge Eating Disorder."

227 *Monica Seles:* Thomas, "Shire, Maker of Binge-Eating Drug Vyvanse, First Marketed the Disease," B1.

227 *"Talking about it":* Calderone, "Monica Seles Opens Up About Binge Eating Disorder."

228 *Cleaning dishes:* Author interview with Dr. Nathan Herrmann, 2014.

228 *The most prolific mathematician:* Huffman, "The Man Who Loves Only Numbers," 64.

229 *Dr. Goodman described:* Berck, "Is It Old Age, or A.D.H.D.?"

230 *Subsequently banned by the FDA:* Moore, *Amphetamine Debate*, 13.

230 *Improper advertising:* U.S. Food and Drug Administration press release, *Pharmaceutical Company Cephalon to Pay $425 Million for Off-label Drug Marketing*, Sept. 28, 2008.

231 The Wizard of Oz: "Provigil: The Secret Success Drug?"

231 *Shooting schedules:* "Judy Garland."

CHAPTER 17: COMING SOON TO A DOCTOR NEAR YOU

232 *Primer on the subject:* Becker et al., "Sluggish cognitive tempo in abnormal child psychology," 1.

233 *"They know what you're talking about":* Schwarz, "Idea of a New Attention Disorder Spurs Research, and Debate," A12.

233 *"April Fool's issue":* Author interview with US government official speaking on condition of anonymity, Feb. 14, 2014.

234 *"Has become the second attention disorder":* Barkley, "ADHD Cutting Edge Understanding & Management."

234 *For doctors to diagnose adults:* Attention Deficit Disorder Association, "A Q&A with Psychologist and ADHD Expert, Russell Barkley."

234 *SCT's name to be changed:* Barkley, *Attention Deficit Hyperactivity Disorder: A Handbook for Diagnosis and Treatment*, 435.

234 *"Effects of any medication on SCT":* Wietecha et al., "Atomoxetine improved attention in children and adolescents with attention-deficit/hyperactivity disorder and dyslexia in a 16 week, acute, randomized, double-blind trial," 605.

234 *Consulting and speaking engagements:* ProPublica, *Dollars for Docs*.

234 *"Medical needs around the world":* Eli Lilly spokesperson e-mail to author, Feb. 27, 2014.

235 *"They require drug therapy?":* Editorial, *Lancet*, 488.

235 *"Chemical warfare:"* As quoted in Smith, *Hyperactive*, 165.

235 *Hyperkinetic syndrome: International Statistical Classification of Diseases, 1992 edition.*

235 *Captures four times that:* National Institute for Clinical Excellence, "Attention Deficit Hyperactivity Disorder," 6.

235 *Canada, Italy, and Sweden:* Conrad and Bergey, "The Impending Globalization of ADHD," 35.

236 *China:* Hinshaw and Scheffler, *A.D.H.D. Explosion*, 125.

236 *Almost doubled:* Ibid., 126.

236 *Another from Portugal:* Concerta ad, 2003.

236 *Publication of a paper:* Young et al., "ADHD: Making the Invisible Visible."

237 *"It will take us some time":* Kelley, "The Big Bucks in Keeping Kids Focused."

238 *It was dead average:* CDC, "State Profile: Georgia," http://www.cdc.gov /ncbddd/adhd/stateprofiles/stateprofile_georgia.pdf.

238 *Pediatrics guidelines:* "Wolraich et al., "ADHD: clinical practice guideline for the diagnosis, evaluation, and treatment of attention-deficit/ hyperactivity disorder in children and adolescents," 1015.

239 *"Act together for little children":* Schwarz, "Thousands of Toddlers Are Medicated for A.D.H.D., Report Finds, Raising Worries," A11.

239 *Authorizing the diagnosis:* Ibid.

239 *Considered a last resort:* Wolraich et al., "ADHD: clinical practice guideline for the diagnosis, evaluation, and treatment of attention-deficit/ hyperactivity disorder in children and adolescents."

240 *The only "off-label" trial:* Greenhill et al., "Efficacy and safety of immediate-release methylphenidate treatment for preschoolers with ADHD," 1284.

240 *Dispiriting monologue:* Insel, "Director's Blog: Are Children Overmedicated?"

242 *Made by pediatricians:* Garfield, "Trends in attention deficit hyperactivity disorder ambulatory diagnosis and medical treatment in the United States, 2000–2010," 110; Visser et al., "Diagnostic Experiences of Children with Attention-Deficit/Hyperactivity Disorder."

242 *Only about eight thousand:* 2014 AACAP Annual Report, 9, http://www .aacap.org/App_Themes/AACAP/docs/about_us/annual_report/2014 _Annual_Report_Updated.pdf.

242 *"Got the diagnosis of ADHD":* Schwarz, "Doctors Train to Spot Signs of A.D.H.D. in Children," A10.

242 *Dopamine in the brain:* Friedman, "A Natural Fix for A.D.H.D."

243 *Research has suggested:* Klass, "Fixated by Screens, but Seemingly Nothing Else," D5.

243 *"Only consistent companion":* Rock, "A Nation of Kids with Gadgets and ADHD."

243 *Spent less time:* Klass, "Fixated by Screens, but Seemingly Nothing Else."

243 *Downplayed evidence of overdiagnosis:* Jensen et al., "Are Stimulants Over-prescribed?," 797.

243 *His fellow guests: Dr. Oz Show.*

243 *Visibly moved:* Author present in green room with Hallowell and Fee family before and after show was taped.

244 *"What's really going on with the kid":* Schwarz, "Doctors Train to Spot Signs of A.D.H.D. in Children," A10.

CHAPTER 18: PRESCRIPTION

248 *"Hard to make a living":* Schwarz, "Drowned in a Stream of Prescriptions," A1.

248 *Bill Clinton admitted:* Author present at event held by Clinton Foundation and NYU Law School, May 6, 2013.

250 *Eating chocolate:* Bohannon, "I Fooled Millions into Thinking Chocolate Helps Weight Loss. Here's How."

250 *Primary brain defects:* Elmer-Dewitt, "Behavior: Why Junior Won't Sit Still," 59.

250 *Were eventually disproven:* Gonon et al., "Why most biomedical findings echoed by newspapers turn out to be false."

250 *The study was run by Shire:* Doshi et al., "Economic impact of childhood and adult attention-deficit/hyperactivity disorder in the United States," 990.

250 *"Lost generation of women":* Anderson, "Decades of Failing to Recognize ADHD in Girls Has Created a 'Lost Generation' of Women."

250 *The actual study:* Hinshaw et al., "Prospective follow-up of girls with attention-deficit/hyperactivity disorder into early adulthood," 1041.

250 *Invited cameras to chronicle:* "Our America with Lisa Ling."

251 *Decried underdiagnosis in girls: NBC Nightly News,* Dec. 12, 2014.

251 *Based on the best science:* Author interviews and correspondence with Ruth Hughes, 2013 and 2014.

251 *"For young children with ADHD":* Newmark, "Does CBT Help Kids?"

252 *"You have attention deficit disorder":* "Do I Have ADD? An ADHD Test for Adults."

EPILOGUE

253 *Updated its student handbook:* Vanderbilt University, "The Vanderbilt Community Creed."

253 *Some universities require students:* Schwarz, "Attention-Deficit Drugs Face New Campus Rules," A10.

253 *Are in fact safe:* Shire press release, *Shire Agrees to FDA Request to Conduct Clinical Trials Investigating the Potential Use of Vyvanse (lisdexamfetamine dimesylate) in Preschool-Age Children with ADHD,* June 2014, http://www .shire.com/~/media/shire/shireglobal/shirecom/pdffiles/newsroom/2014 /june/20140612-shire-vyvanseannouncement.pdf?la=en.

253 *Explore how the drug:* Clinicaltrials.gov, "Shire SCT: Lisdexamfetamine Treatment for ADHD and SCT," https://clinicaltrials.gov/ct2/show /NCT02635035.

254 *A natural vitamin supplement:* Author interviews with Griggs, 2015 and 2016.

254 *An early version of the study:* Chandra et al., "Assessing Validity of 'age of onset' Criteria for Diagnosis of ADHD in DSM-5," Poster presentation at meeting of the American Professional Society of ADHD and Related Disorders, January 2015.

BIBLIOGRAPHY

BOOKS

Abramson, John. *Overdo$ed America: The Broken Promise of American Medicine.* New York: HarperCollins, 2004.

American Psychiatric Association. *Diagnostic and Statistical Manual of Mental Disorders (DSM-I, 1952).*

———. *Diagnostic and Statistical Manual of Mental Disorders (DSM-II, 1968).*

———. *Diagnostic and Statistical Manual of Mental Disorders (DSM-III, 1980).*

———. *Diagnostic and Statistical Manual of Mental Disorders (DSM-III-R, 1987).*

———. *Diagnostic and Statistical Manual of Mental Disorders (DSM-IV, 1994).*

———. *Diagnostic and Statistical Manual of Mental Disorders (DSM-IV, 2000).*

———. *Diagnostic and Statistical Manual of Mental Disorders (DSM 5, 2013).*

Angell, Marcia. *The Truth About Drug Companies: How They Deceive Us and What to Do About It.* New York: Random House, 2005.

Archer, Dale. *The ADHD Advantage.* New York: Hudson Street Press, 2015.

———. *Attention Deficit Hyperactivity Disorder: A Handbook for Diagnosis and Treatment.* New York: Guilford Press, 1990.

———. *Attention Deficit Hyperactivity Disorder: A Clinical Workbook.* New York: Guilford Press, 1991.

Barkley, Russell. *ADHD and the Nature of Self-control.* London: Guilford Press, 1997.

Barkley, Russell, et al. *ADHD in Adults: What the Science Says.* New York: Guilford Press, 2008.

Bible: First Book of Kings, 10:11.

Bosco, James J. and Stanley S. Robin, eds. *The Hyperactive Child and Stimulant Drugs.* Chicago: University of Chicago Press, 1976.

Bouton, Jim. *Ball Four.* New York: Macmillan, 1990.

Brawley, Otis Webb with Paul Goldberg. *How We Do Harm.* New York: St. Martin's Press, 2011.

Chilman-Blair, Kim, and Shawn deLoache. *What's Up with Josh? Medikidz Explain ADHD*. London: Medikidz Limited, 2012.

Clements, Sam D. *Minimal Brain Dysfunction in Children: NINDB Monograph*. U.S. Public Health Service, 1966.

———. *Minimal Brain Dysfunction in Children: Terminology and Identification: Phase One of a Three-Phase Project*. Washington, DC: U.S. Department of Health, Education and Welfare, 1966.

Conners, C. Keith, ed. *Clinical Use of Stimulant Drugs in Children: Proceedings of a Symposium Held at Key Biscayne, Florida, 5–8 March, 1972*. Princeton, N.J.: Excerpta Medica, 1974.

Conners, C. Keith, and Juliet L. Jett. *Attention Deficit Hyperactivity Disorder (in Adults and Children): The Latest Assessment and Treatment Strategies*. Kansas City, Mo.: Compact Clinicals, 1999.

Conners, C. Keith, and Karen C. Wells. *Hyperkinetic Children: A Neuropsychosocial Approach*. Beverly Hills, Calif.: Sage Publications, 1986.

Corman, Clifford L., and Esther Trevino. *Eukee the Jumpy Jumpy Elephant*. Plantation, Fla.: Specialty Press, 1995.

Crichton, Alexander. *An Inquiry into the Nature and Origin of Mental Derangement: Comprehending a Concise System of the Physiology and Pathology of the Human Mind and a History of the Passions and their Effects*. London: T. Cassell Jr. & W. Davies; 1798. http://books.google.com/books?id=Tq xaAAAAcAAJ&printsec=frontcover&dq=%22inquiry+into+the+nature +and+origin+of+mental+derangement%22&hl=en&sa=X&ei=ysy2U7X RJMGSyAS78IGgBA&ved=0CB4Q6AEwAA#v=onepage&q=%22inqu iry%20into%20the%20nature%20and%20origin%20of%20mental%20 derangement%22&f=false.

Decker, Hannah S. *The Making of DSM-III: A Diagnostic Manual's Conquest of American Psychiatry*. New York: Oxford University Press, 2013.

DeGrandpre, Richard. *Ritalin Nation: Rapid-Fire Culture and the Transformation of Human Consciousness*. New York: W.W. Norton, 1999.

Diller, Lawrence H. *Running on Ritalin: A Physician Reflects on Children, Society and Performance in a Pill*. New York: Bantam, 1998.

Dykman, R. A. "Specific Learning Disabilities: An Attentional Deficit Syndrome." In *Progress in Learning Disabilities*, Vol. 2, edited by H. Myklebust, 56–93. New York: Grune and Stratton, 1971.

Frances, Allen. *Saving Normal: An Insider's Revolt Against Out-of-Control Psychiatric Diagnosis, DSM-5, Big Pharma, and the Medicalization of Ordinary Life*. New York: HarperCollins, 2013.

Galvin, Matthew. *Otto Learns about His Medicine: A Story about Medication for Children with ADHD* Washington, DC: Magination Press, 1995.

Gazzinga, Michael S. *Tales from Both Sides of the Brain*. New York: HarperCollins, 2015.

Grinspoon, Lester, and Peter Hedblom. *The Speed Culture: Amphetamine Use and Abuse in America*. Cambridge, Mass.: Harvard University Press, 1975.

Gross, Mortimer D., and William C. Wilson. *Minimal Brain Dysfunction*. New York: Brunner/Mazel, 1974.

Hallowell, Edward M. *Driven to Distraction at Work*. Boston: Harvard Business Review Press, 2015.

Hallowell, Edward M., and John J. Ratey. *Driven from Distraction: Getting the Most out of Life with Attention Deficit Disorder*. New York: Ballantine Books, 2006.

————. *Driven to Distraction: Recognizing and Coping with Attention Deficit Disorder from Childhood through Adulthood*. New York: Pantheon Books, 1994.

Healy, David. *The Psychopharmacologists: Interviews by Dr. David Healy*. New York: Chapman and Hall, 1997.

Hinshaw, S. P. "Is ADHD an impairing condition in childhood and adolescence?" In *Attention-Deficit Hyperactivity Disorder: State of the Science, Best Practices*, edited by P. S. Jensen & J. R. Cooper. Kingston, N.J.: Civic Research Institute, 2002.

Hinshaw, Stephen P., and Richard M. Scheffler. *The ADHD Explosion: Myths, Medication, Money and Today's Push for Performance*. New York: Oxford University Press, 2014.

Hoffmann, Heinrich. *Struwwelpeter: Merry Stories and Funny Pictures*. http://www.gutenberg.org/files/12116/12116-h/12116-h.htm#The_Story_of_Fidgety_Philip.

Kraus, Jeanne. *Cory Stories: A Kid's Book about Living with ADHD* Washington, DC: Magination Press, 2005.

Lambert, Nadine M. "Stimulant treatment as a risk factor for nicotine use and substance abuse." In *Attention-Deficit Hyperactivity Disorder: State of the Science, Best Practices*, edited by P. S. Jensen & J. R. Cooper. Kingston, N.J.: Civic Research Institute, 2002.

Lane, Randall. *The Zeroes: My Misadventures in the Decade Wall Street Went Insane*. New York: Portfolio, 2010.

Mayes, Rick, Catherine Bagwell, and Jennifer Erkulwater. *Medicating Children: ADHD and Pediatric Mental Health*. Cambridge, Mass.: Harvard University Press, 2009.

Moon, Nathan William. "The Amphetamine Years: A Study of the Medical Applications and Extramedical Consumption of Psychostimulant Drugs in the Postwar United States, 1945–1980." Thesis, Georgia Institute of Technology, 2009.

Moore, Elaine A. *The Amphetamine Debate: The Use of Adderall, Ritalin and Related Drugs for Behavior Modification, Neuroenhancement and Anti-Aging Properties*. Jefferson, N.C.: McFarland & Company, 2011.

Moss, Deborah M. *Shelley the Hyperactive Turtle*. Rockville, Md.: Woodbine House, 1989.

Moynihan, Ray, and Alan Cassels. *Selling Sickness: How the World's Biggest Pharmaceutical Companies Are Turning Us All into Patients*. New York: Perseus Books Group, 2005.

Myers, Richard L. *The 100 Most Important Chemical Compounds*. Westport, Conn.: Greenwood Press, 2007.

Peters, John, et al. *Screening for MBD: Physician's Handbook*. Summit, N.J.: CIBA Medical Horizons, 1973.

Pilkey, Dav. *Captain Underpants and the Perilous Plot of Professor Poopypants*. New York: Scholastic, 2000.

———. *Captain Underpants and the Sensational Saga of Sir Stinks-A-Lot*. New York: Scholastic, 2015.

Rasmussen, Nicolas. *On Speed: The Many Lives of Amphetamine*. New York: New York University Press, 2008.

Ross, Dorothea M., and Sheila A. Ross. *Hyperactivity: Research, Theory and Action*. New York: John Wiley & Sons, 1976.

Safer, Daniel J., and Richard P. Allen. *Hyperactive Children: Diagnosis and Management*. Baltimore: University Park Press, 1976.

Schrag, Peter, and Diane Divoky. *The Myth of the Hyperactive Child*. New York: Pantheon Books, 1975.

Sinclair, Upton. *I, Candidate for Governor: and How I Got Licked*. Oakland: University of California Press, 1994.

Singh, Ilina. "Not Just Naughty: 50 Years of Stimulant Drug Advertising." In *Medicating Modern America: Prescription Drugs in History*, edited by Andrea Tone and Elizabeth Siegel Watkins. New York: New York University Press, 2007.

Smith, Matthew. *Hyperactive: The Controversial History of ADHD* London: Reaktion Books, 2012.

Surman, Craig B. H., ed. *ADHD in Adults: A Practical Guide to Evaluation and Management*. New York: Current Clinical Psychiatry, 2013.

Timimi, Sami, and Jonathan Leo, eds. *Rethinking ADHD: From Brain to Culture*. New York: Palgrave Macmillan, 2009.

Turner, Steve. *A Hard Day's Write: The Stories Behind Every Beatles Song*. New York: HarperCollins, 2005.

Wedge, Marilyn. *A Disease Called Childhood: Why ADHD Became an American Epidemic*. New York: Penguin, 2015.

Wegmann, Joseph. *Psychopharmacology: Straight Talk on Mental Health Medications*. Eau Claire, Wis.: Premier Publishing & Media, 2012.

Weikard, Melchior Adam. *Der Philosophische Arzt: Philosophische Arzeneykunst oder von Gebrechen der Sensationen, des Verstandes, und des Willens*. Frankfurt am Main, Andreäische Buchhandlung, 1799. books.google.com /books?id=gYUjAAAAcAAJ&hl=en.

Weiss, Gabrielle, and Lily Hechtman. *Hyperactive Children Grown Up*. New York: Guilford Press, 1993.

Wender, Paul. "Hypothesis for a Possible Biochemical Basis of Minimal Brain Dysfunction." In *Neuropsychology of Learning Disorders: Theoretical Approaches*, edited by Robert M. Knights and Dirk J. Bakker. Baltimore: University Park Press, 1976.

———. *Minimal Brain Dysfunction in Children*. New York: John Wiley, 1971.

Wender, Paul H. "Minimal Brain Dysfunction: An Overview." In *Psychopharmacology: A Generation of Progress*, edited by M. A. Lipton et al. New York: Ravel Press, 1978, 1429–35.

Whitaker, Robert. *Anatomy of an Epidemic*. New York: Broadway Paperbacks, 2010.

Whitaker, Robert, and Lisa Cosgrove. *Psychiatry Under the Influence: Institutional Corruption, Social Injury, and Prescriptions for Reform*. New York: Palgrave Macmillan, 2015.

PERIODICAL AND WEB ARTICLES

"ADHD Has Repercussions Throughout Adulthood." *Medscape*, undated. http://www.medscape.com/viewarticle/488329.

Allen, Scott. "Backlash on bipolar diagnoses in children: MGH psychiatrist's work stirs debate." *Boston Globe*, June 17, 2007, A1.

Anderson, Jenny. "Decades of Failing to Recognize ADHD in Girls Has Created a 'Lost Generation' of Women." *Quartz*, Jan. 19, 2016. http:// qz.com/592364/decades-of-failing-to-recognize-adhd-in-girls-has-created -a-lost-generation-of-women/.

Armstrong, Walter. "Will Success Rock Shire Pharma?" *Pharmaceutical Executive*, Mar. 10, 2010, 6–10. digital.findpharma.com/nxtbooks/advanstaruk /pee_digest_20100310/index.php?startid=8#/7.

"Attention Deficit Disorder Stirs Debate Among Parents" (photo caption) in *Chicago Tribune*, Dec. 9, 1990, 3.

Barkley, Russell. "I Lost My Brother to ADHD." *ADDitude*, undated. http:// www.additudemag.com/adhd/article/9673.html.

BIBLIOGRAPHY

Battista, Judy. "Drug of Focus Is at Center of Suspensions." *NYT*, Dec. 1, 2012. http://www.nytimes.com/2012/12/02/sports/football/adderall-a-drug-of-increased-focus-for-nfl-players.html.

Beck, Melinda. "Mind Games." *Wall Street Journal*, Apr. 6, 2010. http://www.wsj.com/articles/SB10001424052702304620304575165902933059076.

"Behavioral Briefs: ADHD Has Repercussions Throughout Adulthood." Medscape, undated. http://www.medscape.com/viewarticle/488329.

Berck, Judith. "Is It Old Age, or A.D.H.D.?" *NYT*, Sept. 28, 2015. http://well.blogs.nytimes.com/2015/09/28/is-it-alzheimers-or-a-d-h-d/.

"Best TV Advertising Campaign." Medical Marketing & Media, Oct. 9, 2012. http://www.mmm-online.com/best-tv-advertising-campaign/article/262846/.

Bishop, Tyler. "Adderall at Vanderbilt: Causes, Integrity and Safety." *Vanderbilt Hustler*, Dec. 5, 2012. http://www.vanderbilthustler.com/news/safety/article_dd8e73a8-3f31-11e2-845e-001a4bcf6878.html.

Block, Alex Ben. "ABC Renews 'General Hospital' and 'The Chew,' Cancels 'The Revolution.'" *Hollywood Reporter*, Apr. 11, 2012. http://www.hollywoodreporter.com/news/abc-general-hospital-revolution-chew-cancellation-renewal-311092.

Boeck, Scott. "MLB Drug Report: Nearly 1 in 10 Get ADD Exemption." *USA Today*, Nov. 30, 2012. http://www.usatoday.com/story/sports/mlb/2012/11/30/mlbs-annual-drug-report-adderall/1738371/.

Bohannon, John, "I Fooled Millions into Thinking Chocolate Helps Weight Loss. Here's How." *io9*. http://io9.gizmodo.com/i-fooled-millions-into-thinking-chocolate-helps-weight-1707251800.

Borzi, Patrick. "Group Comforts Parents of Hyperactive Children." *Miami Herald*, Apr. 28, 1988, BR-3.

Brauser, Deborah. "ADHD Med May Offer Drug Option for Binge Eating Disorder." *Medscape Medical News*, Jan. 20, 2015. http://www.medscape.com/viewarticle/838410.

Brecher, Elinor J. "Why Johnny Can't Behave." *Miami Herald*, Aug. 3, 1990, E1.

Caher, J. "Ritalin Case Puts Parents, Courts on a Collision Course." *New York Law Journal*, Aug. 17, 2000, 1.

Calderone, Ana. "Monica Seles Opens Up About Binge Eating Disorder." *People*, Feb. 3, 2015. http://www.people.com/article/monica-seles-opens-up-about-eating-disorder.

Carey, Benedict. "Dr. Leon Eisenberg, Pioneer in Autism Studies, Dies at 87." *NYT*, Sep. 24, 2009, A39.

———. "John William Money, 84, Sexual Identity Researcher, Dies." *NYT*, July 11, 2006. http://www.nytimes.com/2006/07/11/us/11money.html.

Carter, Matthew. "Paying Attention: ADHD, and Our Children, Inside and Out." GoodTherapy.org, Nov. 10, 2009. http://www.goodtherapy.org/blog/paying-attention-to-adhd/.

Cassels, Caroline. "FDA Okays First Orally Disintegrating Tablet for ADHD in Kids." Medscape, Jan. 28, 2016. http://www.medscape.com/viewarticle/857892?nlid=98264_3901&src=wnl_newsalrt_160128_MSCPEDIT&uac=190940BY&impID=972066&faf=1.

CDC. "Key Findings of the Prevalence of Attention-Deficit/Hyperactivity Disorder: Its Diagnosis and Treatment in a Community Based Epidemologic Study."2014.http://www.cdc.gov/ncbddd/adhd/features/adhd-key-findings-play.html.

Connor, Daniel F. "Problems of overdiagnosis and overprescribing in ADHD." *Psychiatric Times*, Aug. 11, 2012. http://www.psychiatrictimes.com/display/article/10168/1926348.

Dell'Antonia, K. J. "How Many People Believe A.D.H.D. Is Caused by Poor Parenting?" *NYT* (*Motherlode* blog), May 4, 2012. parenting.blogs.nytimes.com/2012/05/04/how-many-people-believe-a-d-h-d-is-caused-by-poor-parenting/.

DeNoon, Daniel. J. "ADHD Drug Does Stunt Growth." WebMD Health News, July 20, 2007. http://www.webmd.com/add-adhd/childhood-adhd/news/20070720/adhd-drug-does-stunt-growth.

"Do I Have ADD? An ADHD Test for Adults." *ADDitude*, http://www.additudemag.com/adhd/article/1041.htm.

Drell, Martin J. Letter to the Editor. *NYT*, Feb. 6, 2013. http://www.nytimes.com/2013/02/07/opinion/treatment-of-adhd.html.

Editorial. *Lancet* 301 (1973): 488.

Editors and Readers of *ADDitude*. "12 Amazing ADHD Superpowers." http://www.additudemag.com/slideshow/135/slide-1.html?utm_source=eletter&utm_medium=email&utm_campaign=October.

"Efficiency of Brain Held Due to Its 'Fuel'; Cells Found Speeded Up by Synthetic Drug." *NYT*, Apr. 10, 1937, 6.

Elliott, Carl. "The Secret Lives of Big Pharma's 'Thought Leaders.'" *Chronicle of Higher Education*, Sept. 12, 2010. http://chronicle.com/article/The-Secret-Lives-of-Big/124335/.

Elmer-Dewitt, Philip. "Behavior: Why Junior Won't Sit Still." *Time*, Nov. 26, 1990, 59.

Express Scripts. "Turning Attention to ADHD." Express Scripts, Mar. 12, 2014. http://lab.express-scripts.com/lab/insights/industry-updates/report-turning-attention-to-adhd.

"fe_sexchange_jf07." http://baltimorestyle.com/3347/fe_sexchange_jf07/.

BIBLIOGRAPHY

Fields, Lisa. "FDA Says ADHD Drug Shortage to End in April." *Consumer Reports*, Apr. 5, 2012. news.consumerreports.org/health/2012/04/fda -says-adhd-drug-shortage-to-end-in-april.html.

Fink, Paul J. "The Challenge of Treating ADHD." *News*, Apr. 1, 2004, 15.

Friedman, Richard. "A Natural Fix for A.D.H.D.," *New York Times*, Nov. 2, SR-1. http://www.nytimes.com/2014/11/02/opinion/sunday/e-natural-fix-for -adhad.html.

Gale, Karla. "Ritalin requests often deemed inappropriate." Reuters Health, Sept. 14, 2006.

George, John. "Promotional ADHD Drug Video Draws FDA's Rebuke." *Philadelphia Business Journal*, Oct. 13, 2008. Accessed Nov. 29, 2015. http://www.bizjournals.com/philadelphia/stories/2008/10/13/story3 .html?b=1223870400%255E1713865.

Goode, Erica. "Arnold Hutschnecker, 102, Therapist to Nixon." *NYT*, Jan. 3, 2001.http://www.nytimes.com/2001/01/03/us/arnold-hutschnecker-102 -therapist-to-nixon.html.

Goodman, David W. "Unmasking ADHD in Adults." *Medscape Education Psychiatry & Mental Health*, released Aug. 10, 2012. http://www.medscape .org/viewarticle/768677.

Grohol, John M. "Famous People with A.D.H.D." PsychCentral. psychcentral .com/lib/famous-people-with-adhd/.

Hales, Dianne, and Robert E. Hales. "Finally, I Know What's Wrong." *Parade*, Jan. 7, 1996, 8. Retrieved from the Reading Eagle through Google: https:// news.google.com/newspapers?nid=1955&dat=19960107&id=yIsxAAAAI BAJ&sjid=jaYFAAAAIBAJ&pg=5126,2283738&hl=en.

Hamblin, James. "ER Visits Related to Brain Stimulants Have Quadrupled." *Atlantic*, Aug. 12, 2013. http://www.theatlantic.com/health/archive/2013 /08/er-visits-related-to-brain-stimulants-have-quadrupled/278568/.

Hancock, LynNell. "Mother's Little Helper." *Newsweek*, Mar. 18, 1996, 51–56.

Haney, Daniel Q. "Drug Helps Hyperactive Kids; No One Knows Why." *The Nashua Telegraph*, Apr. 10, 1988, G-3.

Harris, Gardiner. "Drug Maker Told Studies Would Aid It, Papers Say." *NYT*, Mar. 19, 2009. http://www.nytimes.com/2009/03/20/us/20psych. html?ref=topics&_r=0.

———. "F.D.A. Finds Short Supply of Attention Deficit Drugs." *NYT*, Dec. 31, 2011, A1. http://www.nytimes.com/2012/01/01/health/policy /fda-is-finding-attention-drugs-in-short-supply.html.

Harris, Gardiner, and Benedict Carey. "Researchers Fail to Reveal Full Drug Pay." *NYT*, June 8, 2008, A1.

Healy, Michelle. "Childhood ADHD Often Can Linger into Adulthood."

USA Today, Mar. 4, 2013. http://www.usatoday.com/story/news/nation /2013/03/04/adhd-adults-childhood/1953789/.

Hochman, Stan. "Victorino's Positive Spirit Has Helped Him Deal with ADD." Philly.com, May 5, 2011. articles.philly.com/2011-05-05/sports /29513110_1_attention-deficit-disorder-parents-kid/.

Huffman, Paul. "The Man Who Loves Only Numbers." *Vanity Fair*, Nov. 1987, 64.

Hughes, Ruth. "Substance Abuse, ADHD, and Medications: The Real Issues." *CHADD Leadership Blog*, Feb. 4, 2013. chaddleadershipblog.blogspot .com/2013/02/substance-abuse-adhd-and-medications.html.

Insel, Thomas. "Director's Blog: Are Children Overmedicated?" National Institute of Mental Health, June 6, 2014. http://www.nimh.nih.gov/about /director/2014/are-children-overmedicated.shtml.

"An Interview with Dr. Joseph Biederman." *Essential Science Indicators Special Topics*, July 2005. Accessed Nov. 27, 2015. http://www.esi-topics.com/add /interviews/JosephBiederman.html.

Kaufman, Joanne. "Ransom-Note Ads About Children's Health Are Canceled." *NYT*, Dec. 20, 2007. http://www.nytimes.com/2007/12/20/business /media/20child.html.

Kelley, Trista. "The Big Bucks in Keeping Kids Focused." *Bloomberg Business-week*, Oct. 10, 2013. http://www.bloomberg.com/news/articles/2013-10-10 /shires-adhd-drugs-face-resistance-in-a-skeptical-europe.

Ketchum, Hank. *Dennis the Menace*. Cartoon. *The Indianapolis Star*, Sept. 11, 1990, 27.

Kitamura, Makiko. "Preschoolers to Get ADHD Drug Vyvanse in Shire Study." *BloombergBusinessweek*, June 12, 2014. http://www.bloomberg.com/news /articles/2014-06-12/preschoolers-to-get-adhd-drug-vyvanse-in-shire-study.

Klass, Perri. "Fixated by Screens, but Seemingly Nothing Else." *NYT*, May 10, 2011, D5. http://www.nytimes.com/2011/05/10/health/views/10 klass.html.

Kotulak, Ronald. "Major Study Rebuts Critics of Drugs for Attention-Disorder Kids." *Chicago Tribune*, Dec. 15, 1999, 5.

Locke, Michelle. "Robert Maynard, Publisher, Powerful Black Journalist." *Seattle Times*, Aug. 18, 1993. http://community.seattletimes.nwsource.com /archive/?date=19930819&slug=1716618.

Lodge, Michelle. "Kids' Health Hazards; Childhood Illnesses Are Increasing and Getting Harder to Treat." *Dallas Morning News*, Jan. 20, 1998, 5C.

Loftus, Mary J. "Ritalin Use Poses Questions; What Do You Think?" *Ledger* (Lakeland, Florida), Aug. 22, 1996, A1.

Lowry, Fran. "Drug Therapy for Parents' ADHD Improves Kids' Behavior." *Medscape Family News*, May 31, 2013. http://www.medscape.com/view article/805071.

"Magic Pill Can Enhance Focus, Drive." Editorial. *Miami Hurricane*, Nov. 11, 2012. http://www.themiamihurricane.com/2012/11/11/magic-pill-can -enhance-focus-drive/.

Maynard, Robert. "Can Drugs Help a 'Wild Child'?" *Washington Post*, Aug. 23, 1970, B1.

———. "Nixon Asks about Criminal Testing of 6 Year Olds." *Milwaukee Journal*, Apr. 5, 1970, 14.

———. "Omaha Pupils Given 'Behavior' Drugs." *Washington Post*, June 29, 1970, A1.

Miller, Caroline. "Stimulants and Suicide: A Tragic Story with Misleading Implications." Childmind.org, Feb. 4, 2013. http://childmind.org/blog /stimulants-and-suicide-a-tragic-story-with-misleading-implications/.

Mitchell, Lynette. "DA Charges 2 More in Ritalin Case." *Raleigh News & Observer*, Mar. 14, 1996, B5.

"More U.S. Children Being Diagnosed with Youthful Tendency Disorder." *The Onion*, Sept. 27, 2000. Accessed Nov. 29, 2015. http://www.theonion .com/article/more-us-children-being-diagnosed-with-youthful-ten-248.

Morrow, David J. "Attention Disorder Is Found in Growing Number of Adults." *NYT*, Sept. 2, 1997.

Murray, Joseph N. "Drugs to Control Classroom Behavior?" *Educational Leadership*, Oct. 1973, 21.

Newmark, Sandy. "Does CBT Help Kids?" *ADDitude*, http://www.additude mag.com/adhdblogs/11/10525.html.

Noble, Holcomb B. "Study Backs a Drug for Hyperactive Children." *NYT*, Dec. 15, 1999, A18.

National Sleep Foundation. "Teens and Sleep." https://sleepfoundation.org /sleep-topics/teens-and-sleep.

Park, Alice. "ADHD: Why the Youngest Kids in a Class Are Most Likely to Be Diagnosed." *Time*, Mar. 6, 2012. healthland.time.com/2012/03/06 /adhd-why-the-youngest-students-in-a-class-are-most-likely-to-be-diag nosed/.

"Pemoline Removed from U.S. Market." *Modern Medicine Network*, Nov. 1, 2005. formularyjournal.modernmedicine.com/formulary-journal/news/clinical /pediatrics/pemoline-removed-us-market.

"Pep-Pill Poisoning." *Time*, May 10, 1937. content.time.com/time/magazine /article/0,9171,757775,00.html.

Pursell, Robert. "Stressed-Out Students Should Take Advantage of Pills."

Miami Hurricane, Nov. 11, 2012. http://www.themiamihurricane.com /2012/11/11/stressed-out-students-should-take-advantage-of-pills/.

Reinhold, Robert. "Rx for Child's Learning Malady." *NYT*, July 3, 1970, 27.

Reuters staff. "Alcobra ADHD Drug Meets Goals, after Excluding Some Data." *Medscape*, Oct 7, 2014. http://www.psychcongress.com/article/alcobras -adhd-drug-meets-goals-after-excluding-some-data-19233.

Rock, Margaret. "A Nation of Kids with Gadgets and ADHD." *Time*, July 8, 2013. techland.time.com/2013/07/08/a-nation-of-kids-with-gadgets-and -adhd/.

Sahakian, Barbara, and Sharon Morein-Zamir. "Professor's Little Helper." *Nature*, Dec. 20, 2007, 1157–59. http://www.nature.com/nature/journal /v450/n7173/full/4501157a.html.

Sappell, Joel, and Robert W. Welkos. "Suits, Protests Fuel a Campaign Against Psychiatry." *Los Angeles Times*, June 29, 1990, A1. http://www.latimes.com /news/local/la-scientology062990a,1,6085874,full.story?coll=la-news -comment.

Schaar, Ted. "Witty Songs." http://www.wittysongs.com/3whoputthebenzedrine .html.

Schwarz, Alan. "Abuse of Attention Deficit Pills Graduates into the Workplace." *NYT*, April 19, 2015, A1.

———. "Attention-Deficit Drugs Face New Campus Rules." *NYT*, May 1, 2013, A10.

———. "Attention Disorder or Not, Pills to Help in School." *NYT*, Oct. 9, 2012. http://www.nytimes.com/2012/10/09/health/attention-disorder-or -not-children-prescribed-pills-to-help-in-school.html.

———. "Doctors Train to Spot Signs of A.D.H.D. in Children." *NYT*, Feb. 19, 2014, A10.

———. "Drowned in a Stream of Prescriptions." *NYT*, Feb. 3, 2013, A1. http://www.nytimes.com/2013/02/03/us/concerns-about-adhd-practices -and-amphetamine-addiction.html.

———. "Harvard Student's Suicide as a Case Study." *NYT*, May 1, 2013, A12.

———. "Idea of a New Attention Disorder Spurs Research, and Debate." *NYT*, April 12, 2014, A12.

———. "No Link Seen Between Child Stimulant Use and Later Drug Abuse." *NYT*, May 30, 2013. http://www.nytimes.com/2013/05/30/health/no -impact-found-for-stimulants-on-later-drug-abuse.html.

———. "Report Says Medication Use Is Rising for Adults With Attention Disorder." *NYT*, Mar. 12, 2014, A16. http://www.nytimes.com/2014/03/12 /us/report-says-medication-use-is-rising-for-adults-with-attention-disorder .html.

————. "Risky Rise of the Good-Grade Pill." *NYT*, June 9, 2012. http://www
.nytimes.com/2012/06/10/education/seeking-academic-edge-teenagers
-abuse-stimulants.html.

————. "The Selling of Attention Deficit Disorder." *NYT*, Dec. 15, 2013, A1.
http://www.nytimes.com/2013/12/15/health/the-selling-of-attention
-deficit-disorder.html.

————. "Thousands of Toddlers Are Medicated for A.D.H.D., Report Finds,
Raising Worries." *NYT*, May 17, 2014, A11.

Schwarz, Alan, and Sarah Cohen. "A.D.H.D. Seen in 11% of U.S. Children as
Diagnoses Rise." *NYT*, Apr. 1, 2013. http://www.nytimes.com/2013/04/01
/health/more-diagnoses-of-hyperactivity-causing-concern.html.

Servantes, Ian. "If I Did It: Academics and Adderall." *Maneater*, Apr. 17, 2012.
http://www.themaneater.com/stories/2012/4/17/if-i-did-it-academics-and
-adderall/.

Sherman, Mark. "Justices Sympathetic to Man Deported for Carrying Adderall in Sock." *PBS Newshour*, Jan. 14, 2015. http://www.pbs.org/newshour
/rundown/justices-sympathetic-man-deported-carrying-adderall-sock/.

Sizemore, Bill. "Did Study Miss the Mark?" *Virginian-Pilot*, Jan. 23, 2005, A14.

Sperling, Dan. "Families Struggle with Kids' Hyperactive Behavior." *USA
Today*, Feb. 6, 1990, 4D.

Stepp, Laura Sessions. "A Wonder Drug's Worst Side Effect." *Washington Post*,
Feb. 5, 1996, A1.

Stix, Gary. "Should Ritalin Be Distributed to Everyone Taking the SATs?" *Scientific American* (*Observations* blog), June 13, 2012. blogs.scientificamerican
.com/observations/2012/06/13/should-ritalin-be-distributed-to-everyone
-taking-the-sats.

————. "Turbocharging the Brain—Pills to Make You Smarter?" *Scientific American*, Oct. 1, 2009. http://www.scientificamerican.com/article
/turbocharging-the-brain/.

Talbot, Margaret. "Brain Gain: The Underground World of 'Neuroenhanc-
ing' Drugs." *New Yorker*, Apr. 27, 2009. http://www.newyorker.com
/reporting/2009/04/27/090427fa_fact_talbot.

Tennant, Diane. "Combating A.D.D.: Expert Says Children Are Not Being
Overdiagnosed or Overtreated for Disorder, Which Is Genetic." *Virginian-
Pilot*, Apr. 9, 1996, E1.

Thakkar, Vatsal G. "Diagnosing the Wrong Deficit." *NYT*, Apr. 27, 2013.
http://www.nytimes.com/2013/04/28/opinion/sunday/diagnosing-the
-wrong-deficit.html.

Thomas, Karen. "Study of Attention Deficit Disorder Supports Medicine Over
Therapy." *USA Today*, Dec. 15, 1999, 14D.

Thomas, Katie. "Shire, Maker of Binge-Eating Drug Vyvanse, First Marketed the Disease." *NYT*, Feb. 25, 2015, B1.

Tortora, Andrea. "It's Not Just Kids: ADHD Affects Adults, Too." *Cincinnati Business Courier*, June 30, 2003. http://www.bizjournals.com/cincinnati /stories/2003/06/30/story6.html.

Vedantam, Shankar. "Federal Conferees Clash on Attention Deficit Disorder." *Philadelphia Inquirer*, Nov. 19, 1998, A01.

———. "Industry Role in Medical Meeting Decried." *Washington Post*, May 26, 2002. http://www.washingtonpost.com/archive/politics/2002/05/26 /industry-role-in-medical-meeting-decried/fabdd7dd-ee9d-4056-8b3a -093a97ef4ffd/.

Visser, Susanna, et al. "Diagnostic Experiences of Children with Attention-Deficit/Hyperactivity Disorder." *National Health Statistics Reports*, Sept. 3, 2015. http://www.cdc.gov/nchs/data/nhsr/nhsr081.pdf.

Von Hoffman, Nicholas. "Student Pep Talk: A Commentary." *Washington Post*, July 22, 1970, B1.

Wilson, Duff. "Side Effects May Include Lawsuits." *NYT*, Oct. 2, 2010, BU1.

Wingfield, Nick, and Conor Dougherty. "Drug Testing Is Coming to E-Sports." *NYT*, July 23, 2015, B1. http://www.nytimes.com/2015/07/24/technology /drug-testing-is-coming-to-e-gaming.html.

———. "Drug Testing Is Coming to E-Sports." *NYT*, July 24, 2015, B1.

Zernike, Kate, and Melody Petersen. "Schools' Backing of Behavior Drugs Comes Under Fire." NYT, Aug. 19, 2001. http://www.nytimes.com/2001 /08/19/us/schools-backing-of-behavior-drugs-comes-under-fire.html.

JOURNAL ARTICLES

Adams, SK, and TS Kisler. "Sleep quality as a mediator between technology-related sleep quality, depression, and anxiety." *Cyberpsychol Behav Soc Netw.* 2013; 16(1): 25–30.

Adler, LA, DW Goodman, SH Kollins et al. "Double-blind, placebo -controlled study of the efficacy and safety of lisdexamfetamine dimesylate in adults with attention-deficit/hyperactivity disorder." *J Clin Psychiatry.* 2008; 69(9): 1364–73.

Barbaresi, WJ, SK Katusic, RC Colligan, AL Weaver, and SJ Jacobsen. "Long-term school outcomes for children with attention-deficit/hyperactivity disorder: a population-based perspective." *J Dev Behav Pediatr.* 2007; 28(4): 265–73.

Barkley, RA. "The effects of methylphenidate on the interactions of preschool ADHD children with their mothers." *J Am Acad Child Adolesc Psychiatry.* 1988; 27(3): 336–41.

BIBLIOGRAPHY

————. "The relevance of the still lectures to attention-deficit/hyperactivity disorder: a commentary." *J Atten Disord.* 2006; 10(2): 137–40.

Barkley, RA., and eighty-four other behavioral scientists. "International consensus statement on ADHD." *Clinical Child and Family Psychology Review.* 2002; 5(2): 89–111.

Barkley, RA., and 20 co-endorsers. "Critique or misrepresentation? A reply to Timimi et al." *Clinical Child and Family Psychology Review.* 2004; 7(1): 65–69.

Barkley, RA, M Fischer, L Smallish, and K Fletcher. "Does the treatment of attention-deficit/hyperactivity disorder with stimulants contribute to drug use/abuse? A 13-year prospective study." *Pediatrics.* 2003; 111(1): 97–109.

————. "The persistence of attention-deficit/hyperactivity disorder into young adulthood as a function of reporting source and definition of disorder." *J Abnorm Psychol.* 2002; 111(2): 279–89.

Barkley, RA, DC Guevremont, AD Anastopoulos, GJ Dupaul, and TL Shelton. "Driving-related risks and outcomes of attention deficit hyperactivity disorder in adolescents and young adults: a 3- to 5-year follow-up survey." *Pediatrics.* 1993; 92(2): 212–18.

Barkley, RA, KR Murphy, GI Dupaul, and T Bush. "Driving in young adults with attention deficit hyperactivity disorder: knowledge, performance, adverse outcomes, and the role of executive functioning." *J Int Neuropsychol Soc.* 2002; 8(5): 655–72.

Barkley, RA, and H Peters. "The earliest reference to ADHD in the medical literature? Melchior Adam Weikard's description in 1775 of 'attention deficit' (Mangel der Aufmerksamkeit, Attentio Volubilis)." *J Atten Disord.* 2012; 16(8): 623–30.

Barry, CL, A Martin, and SH Busch. "ADHD medication use following FDA risk warnings." *J Ment Health Policy Econ.* 2012; 15(3): 119–25.

Becker, SP, SA Marshall, and K McBurnett. "Sluggish cognitive tempo in abnormal child psychology: an historical overview and introduction to the special section." *J Abnorm Child Psychol.* 2014; 42(1): 1–6.

Biederman, J. "Attention-Deficit/Hyperactivity Disorder: A Life-Span Perspective," *J Clin Psychiatry.* 1998; 59 (suppl 7): 4–16.

Biederman, J, SW Boellner, A Childress, et al. "Lisdexamfetamine dimesylate and mixed amphetamine salts extended-release in children with ADHD: a double-blind, placebo-controlled, crossover analog classroom study." *Biol Psychiatry.* 2007; 62(9): 970–76.

————. "Attention-deficit hyperactivity disorder." *Lancet.* 2005; 366(9481): 237–48.

Biederman, J, and SV Faraone. "The effects of attention-deficit/hyperactivity disorder on employment and household income." *MedGenMed.* 2006; 8(3): 12.

Biederman, J, SV Faraone, K Keenan et al. "Further evidence for family-genetic risk factors in attention deficit hyperactivity disorder. Patterns of comorbidity in probands and relatives psychiatrically and pediatrically referred samples." *Arch Gen Psychiatry.* 1992; 49(9): 728–38.

Biederman, J, SV Faraone, K Keenan, D Knee, and MT Tsuang. "Family-genetic and psychosocial risk factors in DSM-III attention deficit disorder." *J Am Acad Child Adolesc Psychiatry.* 1990; 29(4): 526–33.

Biederman, J, SV Faraone, MC Monuteaux, and JR Grossbard. "How informative are parent reports of attention-deficit/hyperactivity disorder symptoms for assessing outcome in clinical trials of long-acting treatments? A pooled analysis of parents' and teachers' reports." *Pediatrics.* 2004; 113(6): 1667–71.

Biederman, J, SV Faraone, TJ Spencer, et al. "Functional impairments in adults with self-reports of diagnosed ADHD: a controlled study of 1001 adults in the community." *J Clin Psychiatry.* 2006; 67(4): 524–40.

Biederman, J, S Krishnan, Y Zhang, JJ McGough, and RL Findling. "Efficacy and tolerability of lisdexamfetamine dimesylate (NRP-104) in children with attention-deficit/hyperactivity disorder: a phase III, multicenter, randomized, double-blind, forced-dose, parallel-group study." *Clin Ther.* 2007; 29(3): 450–63.

Biederman, J, E Mick, C Surman et al. "A randomized, placebo-controlled trial of OROS methylphenidate in adults with attention-deficit/hyperactivity disorder." *Biol Psychiatry.* 2006; 59(9): 829–35.

Biederman, J, MC Monuteaux, E Mick et al. "Young adult outcome of attention deficit hyperactivity disorder: a controlled 10-year follow-up study." *Psychol Med.* 2006; 36(2): 167–79.

Biederman, J, CR Petty, M Evans, J Small, and SV Faraone. "How persistent is ADHD? A controlled 10-year follow-up study of boys with ADHD." *Psychiatry Res.* 2010; 177(3): 299–304.

Biederman, J, T Wilens, E Mick et al. "Is ADHD a risk factor for psychoactive substance use disorders? Findings from a four-year prospective follow-up study." *J Am Acad Child Adolesc Psychiatry.* 1997; 36(1): 21–29.

Biederman, J, T Wilens, E Mick, T Spencer, and S Faraone. "Pharmacotherapy of attention-deficit/hyperactivity disorders reduces risk for substance abuse disorder." *Pediatrics.* Aug. 1999; 104(2): e20. pediatrics.aappublications. org/content/pediatrics/104/2/e20.full.pdf.

Bokhari, F, R Mayes, and RM Scheffler. "An analysis of the significant variation in psychostimulant use across the U.S." *Pharmacoepidemiol Drug Saf.* 2005; 14(4): 267–75.

BIBLIOGRAPHY

Bostic, JQ, J Biederman, TJ Spencer et al. "Pemoline treatment of adolescents with attention deficit hyperactivity disorder: a short-term controlled trial." *J Child Adolesc Psychopharmacol.* 2000; 10(3): 205–16.

Bradley, C. "The behavior of children receiving Benzedrine." *Am J of Psychiatry.* 1937; 94(3): 577–85.

———. "Benzedrine and dexedrine in the treatment of children's behavior disorders." *Pediatrics.* 1950; 5(1): 24–37.

Bradley, C, and M Bowen. "School performance of children receiving amphetamine (Benzedrine) sulfate." *Am J of Orthopsychiatry.* 1940; 10(4): 782–88.

Carroll, BC, TJ McLaughlin, and DR Blake. "Patterns and knowledge of nonmedical use of stimulants among college students." *Arch Pediatr Adolesc Med.* 2006; 160(5): 481–85.

Castellanos, FX, PP Lee, W Sharp et al. "Developmental trajectories of brain volume abnormalities in children and adolescents with attention-deficit /hyperactivity disorder." *JAMA.* 2002; 288(14): 1740–48.

Centers for Disease Control and Prevention. "Increasing prevalence of parent-reported attention-deficit/hyperactivity disorder among children—United States, 2003 and 2007." *Morbidity and Mortality Weekly Report.* 2010; 59(44): 1439–43.

———. "Prevalence of diagnosis and medication treatment for ADHD—United States, 2003. *Morbidity and Mortality Weekly Report.* 2005; 54(34): 842–47.

Chandra S, S Faraone, and J Biederman. "Assessing Validity of 'age of onset' Criteria for Diagnosis of ADHD in DSM-5." Poster presented at 2015 APSARD annual meeting.

Christakis, DA, FJ Zimmerman, DL DiGiuseppe, and CA McCarty. "Early television exposure and subsequent attentional problems in children." *Pediatrics.* 2004; 113(4): 708–13.

Clements, SD, and JE Peters. "Minimal brain dysfunctions in the school-age child. Diagnosis and treatment." *Arch Gen Psychiatry.* 1962; 6(3): 185–97.

Conners, CK. "Attention-deficit/hyperactivity disorder: historical development and overview." *J Atten Disord.* 2000; 1: 173–91.

———. "Forty years of methylphenidate treatment in Attention-Deficit/Hyperactivity Disorder." *J Atten Disord.* 2002; 6(Suppl 1): S17–30.

Conners, CK, et al. "Psychological assessment of children with minimal brain dysfunction." *Annals of the New York Academy of Sciences.* 1973; 205(2): 283–302.

Conners, CK, and L Eisenberg. "The effects of methylphenidate on symptomatology and learning in disturbed children." *Am J Psychiatry.* 1963; 120(5): 458–64.

Conners, CK, L Eisenberg, and A Barcai. "Effect of dextroamphetamine on children. Studies on subjects with learning disabilities and school behavior problems." *Arch Gen Psychiatry.* 1967; 17(4): 478–85.

Conners, CK, JN Epstein, JS March et al. "Multimodal treatment of ADHD in the MTA: an alternative outcome analysis." *J Am Acad Child Adolesc Psychiatry.* 2001; 40(2): 159–67.

Conrad, Peter, and MR Bergey. "The impending globalization of ADHD: notes on the expansion and growth of a medicalized disorder." *Soc Sci Med.* 2014; 122: 31–43.

Cooper, WO, LA Habel, CM Sox et al. "ADHD drugs and serious cardiovascular events in children and young adults." *N Engl J Med.* 2011; 365(20): 1896–904.

Cosgrove, L, S Krimsky, M Vijayaraghavan, and L Schneider. "Financial ties between DSM-IV panel members and the pharmaceutical industry." *Psychother Psychosom.* 2006; 75(3): 154–60.

DeGrandpre R, and SP Hinshaw. "Attention-deficit hyperactivity disorder: psychiatric problem or American cop-out?" *Cerebrum: The Dana Foundation Journal on Brain Sciences.* 2000; 2: 12–38.

Denhoff, E, MW Laufer, and G Solomons. "Hyperkinetic impulse disorder in children's behavior problems." *Psychosom Med.* 1957; 19(1): 38–49.

DeSantis, AD, and AC Hane. "'Adderall is definitely not a drug': justifications for the illegal use of ADHD stimulants." *Subst Use Misuse.* 2010; 45(1-2): 31–46.

DeSantis, AD, EM Webb, and SM Noar. "Illicit use of prescription ADHD medications on a college campus: a multimethodological approach." *J Am Coll Health.* 2008; 57(3): 315–24.

Donohue, JM, M Cevasco, and MB Rosenthal. "A decade of direct-to-consumer advertising of prescription drugs." *N Engl J Med.* 2007; 357(7): 673–81.

Doshi, JA, P Hodgkins, J Kahle et al. "Economic impact of childhood and adult attention-deficit/hyperactivity disorder in the United States." *J Am Acad Child Adolesc Psychiatry.* 2012; 51(10): 990–1002.e2.

Douglas, VI. "Stop, Look and Listen: The Problem of Sustained Attention and Impulse Control in Hyperactive and Normal Children." *Can J Behav Sci.* 1972; 10: 259–82.

Editorial. *Public Health.* 1964; 78(2): 59–61.

Eisenberg, L, and LB Guttmacher. "Were we all asleep at the switch? A personal reminiscence of psychiatry from 1940 to 2010." *Acta Psychiatr Scand.* 2010; 122(2): 89–102.

Elder, TE. "The importance of relative standards in ADHD diagnoses: evidence based on exact birth dates." *J Health Econ.* 2010; 29(5): 641–56.

Faraone, SV. "The scientific foundation for understanding attention-deficit/ hyperactivity disorder as a valid psychiatric disorder." *Eur Child Adolesc Psychiatry*. 2005; 14(1): 1–10.

Faraone SV, and J Biederman. "Genetics of attention-deficit hyperactivity disorder." *Child and Adolescent Psychiatric Clinics of North America*. 1994; 3(2): 285–302.

Faraone, SV, J Biederman, BK Lehman et al. "Evidence for the independent familial transmission of attention deficit hyperactivity disorder and learning disabilities: results from a family genetic study." *Am J Psychiatry*. 1993; 150(6): 891–95.

Faraone, SV, J Biederman, and E Mick. "The age-dependent decline of attention deficit hyperactivity disorder: a meta-analysis of follow-up studies." *Psychol Med*. 2006; 36(2): 159–65.

Faraone, SV, and J Buitelaar. "Comparing the efficacy of stimulants for ADHD in children and adolescents using meta-analysis." *Eur Child Adolesc Psychiatry*. 2010; 19(4): 353–64.

Faraone, SV, RH Perlis, AE Doyle et al. "Molecular genetics of attention -deficit/hyperactivity disorder." *Biol Psychiatry*. 2005; 57(11): 1313–23.

Faraone, SV, J Sergeant, C Gillberg, and J Biederman. "The worldwide prevalence of ADHD: is it an American condition?" *World Psychiatry*. 2003; 2(2): 104–13.

Faraone, SV, T Spencer, M Aleardi, C Pagano, and J Biederman. "Meta-analysis of the efficacy of methylphenidate for treating adult attention -deficit/hyperactivity disorder." *J Clin Psychopharmacol*. 2004; 24(1): 24–29.

Freed, H, and CA Peifer. "Treatment of hyperkinetic emotionally disturbed children with prolonged administration of chlorpromazine." *Am J Psychiatry*. 1956; 113(1): 22–26.

Froehlich, TE, BP Lanphear, JN Epstein, et al. "Prevalence, recognition, and treatment of attention-deficit/hyperactivity disorder in a national sample of US children." *Arch Pediatr Adolesc Med*. 2007; 161(9): 857–64.

Fulton, BD, RM Scheffler, SP Hinshaw et al. "National variation of ADHD diagnostic prevalence and medication use: health care providers and education policies." *Psychiatr Serv*. 2009; 60(8): 1075–83.

Garfield, CF, ER Dorsey, S Zhu et al. "Trends in attention deficit hyperactivity disorder ambulatory diagnosis and medical treatment in the United States, 2000–2010." *Acad Pediatr*. 2012; 12(2): 110–16.

Getahun, D, SJ Jacobsen, MJ Fassett, et al. "Recent trends in childhood attention-deficit/hyperactivity disorder." *JAMA Pediatr*. 2013; 167(3): 282–88.

Gilbody, S, P Wilson, and I Watt. "Benefits and harms of direct to consumer advertising: a systematic review." *Qual Saf Health Care*. 2005; 14(4): 246–50.

Gonon, F, JP Konsman, D Cohen, and T Boraud. "Why most biomedical findings echoed by newspapers turn out to be false: the case of attention deficit hyperactivity disorder." *PLoS ONE*. 2012; 7(9): e44275.

Graf, WD, SK Nagel, LG Epstein, et al. "Pediatric neuroenhancement: ethical, legal, social, and neurodevelopmental implications." *Neurology*. 2013; 80(13): 1251–60.

Greely, H, B Sahakian, J Harris et al. "Towards responsible use of cognitive-enhancing drugs by the healthy." *Nature*. 2008; 456(7223): 702–5.

Greenhill, L, S Kollins, H Abikoff et al. "Efficacy and safety of immediate-release methylphenidate treatment for preschoolers with ADHD." *J Am Acad Child Adolesc Psychiatry*. 2006; 45(11): 1284–93.

Greenhill, LL, S Pliszka, MK Dulcan et al. "Practice parameter for the use of stimulant medications in the treatment of children, adolescents, and adults." *J Am Acad Child Adolesc Psychiatry*. 2002; 41(2 Suppl): 26S–49S.

Hale, L, and S Guan. "Screen time and sleep among school-aged children and adolescents: a systematic literature review." *Sleep Med Rev*. 2015; 21: 50–58.

Harris, J. "Leon Eisenberg, M.D. (1922–2009)." *J Am Acad Child Adolesc Psychiatry*. 2010; 49(2): 199–201.

Hinshaw, SP, EB Owens, C Zalecki et al. "Prospective follow-up of girls with attention-deficit/hyperactivity disorder into early adulthood: continuing impairment includes elevated risk for suicide attempts and self-injury." *J Consult Clin Psychol*. 2012; 80(6): 1041–51.

Hinshaw, SP, and A Stier. "Stigma as related to mental disorders." *Annu Rev Clin Psychol*. 2008; 4: 367–93.

Huang, ES, LL Strate, WW Ho, SS Lee, and AT Chan. "Long-term use of aspirin and the risk of gastrointestinal bleeding." *Am J Med*. 2011; 124(5): 426–33.

Huh, J, DE Delorme, LN Reid, and S An. "Direct-to-consumer prescription drug advertising: history, regulation, and issues." *Minn Med*. 2010; 93(3): 50–52.

Humphreys, KL, T Eng, and SS Lee. "Stimulant medication and substance use outcomes: a meta-analysis." *JAMA Psychiatry*. 2013; 70(7): 740–49.

Jasinski, LJ, JP Harp, DT Berry, et al. "Using symptom validity tests to detect malingered ADHD in college students." *Clin Neuropsychol*. 2011; 25(8): 1415–28.

Jensen, PS, SP Hinshaw, JM Swanson et al. "Findings from the NIMH Multimodal Treatment Study of ADHD (MTA): implications and applications for primary care providers." *J Dev Behav Pediatr*. 2001; 22(1): 60–73.

Jensen, PS, L Kettle, MT Roper et al. "Are stimulants overprescribed? Treatment of ADHD in four U.S. communities." *J Am Acad Child Adolesc Psychiatry*. 1999; 38(7): 797–804.

Kessler, RC, L Adler, M Ames et al. "The World Health Organization Adult ADHD Self-Report Scale (ASRS): a short screening scale for use in the general population." *Psychol Med*. 2005; 35(2): 245–56.

Kessler, RC, L Adler, R Barkley et al. "The prevalence and correlates of adult ADHD in the United States: results from the National Comorbidity Survey Replication." *Am J Psychiatry*. 2006; 163(4): 716–23.

Kessler, RC, P Berglund, O Demler, et al. "Lifetime prevalence and age-of-onset distributions of DSM-IV disorders in the National Comorbidity Survey Replication." *Arch Gen Psychiatry*. 2005; 62(6): 593–602.

Kessler, RC, JG Green, LA Adler et al. "Structure and diagnosis of adult attention-deficit/hyperactivity disorder: analysis of expanded symptom criteria from the Adult ADHD Clinical Diagnostic Scale." *Arch Gen Psychiatry*. 2010; 67(11): 1168–78.

Klein, RG, S Mannuzza, MA Olazagasti et al. "Clinical and functional outcome of childhood attention-deficit/hyperactivity disorder 33 years later." *Arch Gen Psychiatry*. 2012; 69(12): 1295–303.

Klein, RG, and Wender. "The role of methylphenidate in psychiatry." *Arch Gen Psychiatry*. 1995; 52(6): 429–33.

Kollins, S, L Greenhill, J Swanson et al. "Rationale, design, and methods of the Preschool ADHD Treatment Study (PATS)." *J Am Acad Child Adolesc Psychiatry*. 2006; 45(11): 1275–83.

Kroutil, LA, DL Van Brunt, MA Herman-Stahl, et al. "Nonmedical use of prescription stimulants in the United States." *Drug Alcohol Depend*. 2006; 84(2): 135–43.

Lacasse, J, and J Leo. "Consumer advertisements for psychostimulants in the United States: a long record of misleading promotion." *Psychiatric Times*. 2009; 26(2): 12.

Lahey, BB, B Applegate, K McBurnett et al. "DSM-IV field trials for attention deficit hyperactivity disorder in children and adolescents." *Am J Psychiatry*. 1994; 151(11): 1673–85.

Lahey, BB, R Loeber, M Stouthamer-Loeber et al. "Comparison of DSM-III and DSM-III-R diagnoses for prepubertal children: changes in prevalence and validity." *J Am Acad Child Adolesc Psychiatry*. 1990; 29(4): 620–26.

Lakhan, SE, and A Kirchgessner. "Prescription stimulants in individuals with and without attention deficit hyperactivity disorder: misuse, cognitive impact, and adverse effects." *Brain Behav*. 2012; 2(5): 661–77.

Lambert, NM, and CS Hartsough. "Prospective study of tobacco smoking and substance dependencies among samples of ADHD and non-ADHD participants." *J Learn Disabil.* 1998; 31(6): 533–44.

Lang, HC, RM Scheffler, and TW Hu. "The discrepancy in attention deficit hyperactivity disorder (ADHD) medications diffusion: 1994–2003—a global pharmaceutical data analysis." *Health Policy.* 2010; 97(1): 71–78.

Lange, KW, S Reichl, KM Lange, L Tucha, and O Tucha. "The history of attention deficit hyperactivity disorder." *Atten Defic Hyperact Disord.* 2010; 2(4): 241–55.

Larriviere, D, MA Williams, M Rizzo, and RJ Bonnie. "Responding to requests from adult patients for neuroenhancements: guidance of the Ethics, Law and Humanities Committee." *Neurology.* 2009; 73(17): 1406–12.

Laufer, MW, and E Denhoff. "Hyperkinetic behavior syndrome in children." *J Pediatr.* 1957; 50(4): 463–74.

Lebowitz, MS. "Stigmatization of ADHD: A Developmental Review." *J Atten Disord.* 2016; 20(3): 199–205.

Lee, SS, KL Humphreys, K Flory, R Liu, and K Glass. "Prospective association of childhood attention-deficit/hyperactivity disorder (ADHD) and substance use and abuse/dependence: a meta-analytic review." *Clin Psychol Rev.* 2011; 31(3): 328–41.

LeFever, G, A Arcona, and D Antonuccio. "ADHD among American schoolchildren: evidence of overdiagnosis and overuse of medication." *Scientific Review of Mental Health Practice.* 2003; 2(1): 49–60.

LeFever, GB, KV Dawson, and AL Morrow. "The extent of drug therapy for attention deficit–hyperactivity disorder among children in public schools." *Am J Public Health.* 1999; 89(9): 1359–64.

Lemola, S, N Perkinson-Gloor, S Brand, JF Dewald-Kaufmann, and A Grob. "Adolescents' electronic media use at night, sleep disturbance, and depressive symptoms in the smartphone age." *J Youth Adolesc.* 2015; 44(2): 405–18.

Leonard, BE, D McCartan, J White, and DJ King. "Methylphenidate: a review of its neuropharmacological, neuropsychological and adverse clinical effects." *Hum Psychopharmacol.* 2004; 19(3): 151–80.

Lichtenstein, P, L Halldner, J Zetterqvist et al. "Medication for attention deficit–hyperactivity disorder and criminality." *N Engl J Med.* 2012; 367(21): 2006–14.

Mannuzza, S, RG Klein, A Bessler, P Malloy, and M Lapadula. "Adult psychiatric status of hyperactive boys grown up." *Am J Psychiatry.* 1998; 155(4): 493–98.

Mayes, R, C Bagwell, J Erkulwater. "ADHD and the rise in stimulant use among children." *Harv Rev Psychiatry.* 2008; 16(3): 151–66.

Mayes, R, and AV Horwitz. "DSM-III and the revolution in the classification of mental illness." *J Hist Behav Sci*. 2005; 41(3): 249–67.

McCabe, SE, C Teter, and C Boyd. "The use, misuse, and diversion of prescription stimulants among middle and high school students." *Substance Use and Misuse*. 2004; 39(7): 1095–111.

McCabe, SE, and BT West. "Medical and nonmedical use of prescription stimulants: results from a national multicohort study." *J Am Acad Child Adolesc Psychiatry*. 2013; 52(12): 1272–80.

McCabe, SE, BT West, P Veliz, KA Frank, and CJ Boyd. "Social contexts of substance use among U.S. high school seniors: a multicohort national study." *J Adolesc Health*. 2014; 55(6): 842–44.

McCracken, JT, J Biederman, LL Greenhill et al. "Analog classroom assessment of a once-daily mixed amphetamine formulation, SLI381 (Adderall XR), in children with ADHD." *J Am Acad Child Adolesc Psychiatry*. 2003; 42(6): 673–83.

McGough, JJ, and RA Barkley. "Diagnostic controversies in adult attention deficit hyperactivity disorder." *Am J Psychiatry*. 2004; 161(11): 1948–56.

Mogull, S. "Chronology of direct-to-consumer advertising regulation in the United States." *Am Med Writers J*. 2008; 23(3): 106.

Molina, BS, SP Hinshaw, L Eugene Arnold et al. "Adolescent substance use in the multimodal treatment study of attention-deficit/hyperactivity disorder (ADHD) (MTA) as a function of childhood ADHD, random assignment to childhood treatments, and subsequent medication." *J Am Acad Child Adolesc Psychiatry*. 2013; 52(3): 250–63.

Molina, BS, SP Hinshaw, JM Swanson et al. "The MTA at 8 years: prospective follow-up of children treated for combined-type ADHD in a multisite study." *J Am Acad Child Adolesc Psychiatry*. 2009; 48(5): 484–500.

Molina, BS, and WE Pelham. "Childhood predictors of adolescent substance use in a longitudinal study of children with ADHD." *J Abnorm Psychol*. 2003; 112(3): 497–507.

Moreno C, G Laje, C Blanco, et al. "National trends in the outpatient diagnosis and treatment of bipolar disorder in youth." *Arch Gen Psychiatry*. 2007; 64(9): 1032–39.

Morrow, RL, EJ Garland, JM Wright, et al. "Influence of relative age on diagnosis and treatment of attention-deficit/hyperactivity disorder in children." *CMAJ*. 2012; 184(7): 755–62.

Mosholder, AD, K Gelperin, TA Hammad, K Phelan, and R Johann-Liang. "Hallucinations and other psychotic symptoms associated with the use of attention-deficit/hyperactivity disorder drugs in children." *Pediatrics*. 2009; 123(2): 611–16.

MTA Cooperative Group. "A 14-month randomized clinical trial of treatment strategies for attention-deficit/hyperactivity disorder." *Arch Gen Psychiatry.* 1999; 56(12): 1073–86.

Nathanson, MH. "The central action of beta-aminopropylbenzene (Benzedrine): clinical observations." *JAMA.* 1937; 108(7): 528–31.

National Institute for Clinical Excellence. "Attention Deficit Hyperactivity Disorder: Diagnosis and Management of ADHD in Children, Young People and Adults." NICE Clinical Guidelines. 2008; 72:6.

Nikolas, MA, and SA Burt. "Genetic and environmental influences on ADHD symptom dimensions of inattention and hyperactivity: a meta-analysis." *J Abnorm Psychol.* 2010; 119(1): 1–17.

Nolan, EE, KD Gadow, and J Sprafkin. "Teacher reports of DSM-IV ADHD, ODD, and CD symptoms in schoolchildren." *J Am Acad Child Adolesc Psychiatry.* 2001; 40(2): 241–49.

Okie, S. "ADHD in adults." *N Engl J Med.* 2006; 354(25): 2637–41.

Palmer, ED, and S Finger. "An early description of ADHD (Inattention Subtype): Dr. Alexander Crichton and the 'Mental Restlessness' (1798)." *Child Psychol Psychiatry Rev.* 2001; 6: 66–73.

Pelham, W. "The NIMH multimodal treatment study for attention-deficit/hyperactivity disorder: just say yes to drugs alone?" *Can J Psychiatry.* 1999; 44(10): 765–75.

Pelham, W, and GA Fabiano. "Evidence-based psychosocial treatments for attention-deficit/hyperactivity disorder." *J Clin Child Adolesc Psychol.* 2008; 37(1): 184–214.

Pelham, WE, EM Foster, and JA Robb. "The economic impact of attention-deficit/hyperactivity disorder in children and adolescents." *Ambul Pediatr.* 2007; 7(1 Suppl): 121–31.

Pincus, JH, and GH Glaser. "The syndrome of 'minimal brain damage' in childhood." *N Engl J Med.* 1966; 275(1): 27–35.

Polanczyk, G, A Caspi, R Houts, et al. "Implications of extending the ADHD age-of-onset criterion to age 12: results from a prospectively studied birth cohort." *J Am Acad Child Adolesc Psychiatry.* 2010; 49(3): 210–16.

Polanczyk, G, MS de Lima, BL Horta, J Biederman, and LA Rohde. "The worldwide prevalence of ADHD: a systematic review and metaregression analysis." *Am J Psychiatry.* 2007; 164(6): 942–48.

Polanczyk, G, LA Rohde, C Szobot, et al. "ADHD treatment in Latin America and the Caribbean." *J Am Acad Child Adolesc Psychiatry.* 2008; 47(6): 721–22.

Proal, E, PT Reiss, RG Klein et al. "Brain gray matter deficits at 33-year follow-up in adults with attention-deficit/hyperactivity disorder established in childhood." *Arch Gen Psychiatry.* 2011; 68(11): 1122–34.

BIBLIOGRAPHY

Quinn, P, and S Wigal. "Perceptions of girls and ADHD: results from a national survey." *MedGenMed.* 2004; 6(2): 2.

Rapoport, JL, MS Buchsbaum, H Weingartner, et al. "Dextroamphetamine. Its cognitive and behavioral effects in normal and hyperactive boys and normal men." *Arch Gen Psychiatry.* 1980; 37(8): 933–43.

Rapoport, JL, MS Buchsbaum, TP Zahn, H Weingartner, C Ludlow, and EJ Mikkelsen. "Dextroamphetamine: cognitive and behavioral effects in normal prepubertal boys." *Science.* 1978; 199(4328): 560–63.

Ray, L, and A Hinnant. "Media Representation of Mental Disorders: A Study of ADD and ADHD Coverage in Magazines from 1985–2008." *J of Magazine and New Media Research.* 2009; 11(1).

Reifenstein, EC, and E Davidoff. "The Psychological Effects of Benzedrine Sulfate." *Am J Psychol.* 1939; 52(1): 56–64.

Richters, JE, LE Arnold, PS Jensen et al. "NIMH collaborative multisite multimodal treatment study of children with ADHD: I. Background and rationale." *J Am Acad Child Adolesc Psychiatry.* 1995; 34(8): 987–1000.

Riddle, MA, K Yershova, D Lazzaretto et al. "The Preschool Attention-Deficit/ Hyperactivity Disorder Treatment Study (PATS) 6-year follow-up." *J Am Acad Child Adolesc Psychiatry.* 2013; 52(3): 264–78.e2.

Rowland, AS, BJ Skipper, DM Umbach et al. "The Prevalence of ADHD in a Population-Based Sample." *J Atten Disord.* 2015; 19(9): 741–54.

Safer, DJ, and JM Krager. "Effect of a media blitz and a threatened lawsuit on stimulant treatment." *JAMA.* 1992; 268(8): 1004–07.

Safer, DJ, JM Zito, and EM Fine. "Increased methylphenidate usage for attention deficit disorder in the 1990s." *Pediatrics.* 1996; 98(6 Pt 1): 1084–88.

Safford, N. "Leon Eisenberg." *Br Med J.* 2009; 339: b4615.

Scheffler, RM, TT Brown, BD Fulton, et al. "Positive association between attention-deficit/ hyperactivity disorder medication use and academic achievement during elementary school." *Pediatrics.* 2009; 123(5): 1273–79.

Scheffler, RM, SP Hinshaw, S Modrek, and P Levine. "The global market for ADHD medications." *Health Aff (Millwood).* 2007; 26(2): 450–57.

Schmitt, BD. "The Minimal Brain Dysfunction Myth." *Am J Dis Child.* 1975; 129(11): 1313–18.

Setlik, J, GR Bond, and M Ho. "Adolescent prescription ADHD medication abuse is rising along with prescriptions for these medications." *Pediatrics.* 2009; 124(3): 875–80.

Shaw, P, K Eckstrand, W Sharp et al. "Attention-deficit/hyperactivity disorder is characterized by a delay in cortical maturation." *Proc Natl Acad Sci USA.* 2007; 104(49): 19649–54.

Shaywitz, SE, and BA Shaywitz. "Increased medication use in attention-deficit hyperactivity disorder: regressive or appropriate?" *JAMA*. 1988; 260(15): 2270–72.

Singh, I, AM Filipe, I Bard, M Bergey, and L Baker. "Globalization and cognitive enhancement: emerging social and ethical challenges for ADHD clinicians." *Curr Psychiatry Rep*. 2013; 15(9): 385.

Sleator, EK, and RK Ullmann. "Can the physician diagnose hyperactivity in the office?" *Pediatrics*. 1981; 67(1): 13–17.

Smith, ME, and MJ Farah. "Are prescription stimulants 'smart pills'? The epidemiology and cognitive neuroscience of prescription stimulant use by normal healthy individuals." *Psychol Bull*. 2011; 137(5): 717–41.

Sollman, MJ, JD Ranseen, and DT Berry. "Detection of feigned ADHD in college students." *Psychol Assess*. 2010; 22(2): 325–35.

Spencer, T, J Biederman, and T Wilens. "Stimulant treatment of adult attention-deficit/hyperactivity disorder." *Psychiatr Clin North Am*. 2004; 27(2): 361–72.

Spencer, T, J Biederman, T Wilens et al. "Efficacy of a mixed amphetamine salts compound in adults with attention-deficit/hyperactivity disorder." *Arch Gen Psychiatry*. 2001; 58(8): 775–82.

———. "A large, double-blind, randomized clinical trial of methylphenidate in the treatment of adults with attention-deficit/hyperactivity disorder." *Biol Psychiatry*. 2005; 57(5): 456–63.

Spencer, T, J Biederman, TE Wilens, and SV Faraone. "Adults with attention-deficit/hyperactivity disorder: a controversial diagnosis." *J Clin Psychiatry*. 1998; 59(Suppl 7): 59–68.

Spencer, T, T Wilens, J Biederman, et al. "A double-blind, crossover comparison of methylphenidate and placebo in adults with childhood-onset attention-deficit hyperactivity disorder." *Arch Gen Psychiatry*. 1995; 52(6): 434–43.

Spencer, TJ, J Biederman, PE Ciccone et al. "PET study examining pharmacokinetics, detection and likeability, and dopamine transporter receptor occupancy of short- and long-acting oral methylphenidate." *Am J Psychiatry*. 2006; 163(3): 387–95.

Still, GF. "Some abnormal psychical conditions in children: excerpts from three lectures." *J Atten Disord*. 2006; 10(2): 126–36.

———. "Some abnormal psychical conditions in children: the Goulstonian lectures." *Lancet*. 1902; 1: 1008–12.

Strohl, MP. "Bradley's Benzedrine studies on children with behavioral disorders." *Yale J Biol Med*. 2011; 84(1): 27–33.

Sutton-Smith, B, and BG Rosenberg. "A scale to identify impulsive behavior in children." *J Genetic Psychol*. 1959; 95(2): 211–16.

Swanson, JM, GR Elliott, LL Greenhill et al. "Effects of stimulant medication on growth rates across 3 years in the MTA follow-up." *J Am Acad Child Adolesc Psychiatry*. 2007; 46(8): 1015–27.

Swanson, JM, M Lerner, and L Williams. "More frequent diagnosis of attention deficit–hyperactivity disorder." *N Engl J Med*. 1995; 333(14): 944.

Swanson, JM, K McBurnett, T Wigal, and LJ Pfiffner. "Effect of stimulant medication on children with attention deficit disorder: a 'review of reviews.'" *Exceptional Children*. 1993; 60(2): 154–61.

Swanson, JM, and ND Volkow. "Psychopharmacology: concepts and opinions about the use of stimulant medications." *J Child Psychol Psychiatry*. 2009; 50(1-2): 180–93.

Swanson, JM, TL Wigal, and ND Volkow. "Contrast of medical and non-medical use of stimulant drugs, basis for the distinction, and risk of addiction: comment on Smith and Farah (2011)." *Psychol Bull*. 2011; 137(5): 742–48.

Swensen, A, HG Birnbaum, R Ben Bamadi, et al. "Incidence and costs of accidents among attention-deficit/hyperactivity disorder patients." *J Adolesc Health*. 2004; 35(4): 346.e1–9.

Tansey, EM. "The life and works of Sir Alexander Crichton, F.R.S. (1763–1856): a Scottish physician to the Imperial Russian Court." *Notes Rec R Soc Lond*. 1984; 38(2): 241–59.

Timimi, S, and E Taylor. "ADHD is best understood as a cultural construct." *Brit J Psychiatry*. 2003; 184(1): 8–9.

Vande Voort, JL, JP He, ND Jameson, and KR Merikangas. "Impact of the DSM-5 Attention-Deficit/Hyperactivity Disorder Age-of-Onset Criterion in the US Adolescent Population." *J Am Acad Child Adolesc Psychiatry*. 2014; 53(7): 736–44.

Visser, SN, RH Bitsko, ML Danielson et al. "Treatment of Attention Deficit/Hyperactivity Disorder among Children with Special Health Care Needs." *J Pediatr*. 2015; 166(6): 1423–30.e1–2.

Visser, SN, ML Danielson, RH Bitsko et al. "Trends in the parent-report of health care provider–diagnosed and medicated attention-deficit/hyperactivity disorder: United States, 2003–2011." *J Am Acad Child Adolesc Psychiatry*. 2014; 53(1): 34–46.e2.

Volkow, ND, and JM Swanson. "The action of enhancers can lead to addiction." *Nature*. 2008; 451(7178): 520.

Volkow, ND, GJ Wang, SH Kollins et al. "Evaluating dopamine reward pathway in ADHD: clinical implications." *JAMA*. 2009; 302(10): 1084–91.

Volkow, ND, GJ Wang, D Tomasi et al. "Methylphenidate-elicited dopamine increases in ventral striatum are associated with long-term symptom improvement in adults with attention deficit hyperactivity disorder." *J Neurosci*. 2012; 32(3): 841–49.

Walkup, JT, L Stossel, and R Rendleman. "Beyond rising rates: personalized medicine and public health approaches to the diagnosis and treatment of attention-deficit/hyperactivity disorder." *J Am Acad Child Adolesc Psychiatry*. 2014; 53(1): 14–16.

Watson, GL, AP Arcona, DO Antonuccio, and D Healy. "Shooting the messenger: the case of ADHD." *J Contemp Psychother*. 2014; 44: 43–52.

Wazana, A. "Physicians and the pharmaceutical industry: is a gift ever just a gift?." *JAMA*. 2000; 283(3): 373–80.

Weiss, GG. "Interview with Dr. Gabrielle 'Gaby' Weiss. A personal history of the choice of child psychiatry as a career. Interview by Normand Carrey." *J Can Acad Child Adolesc Psychiatry*. 2009; 18(4): 340–43.

Whalen, CK, B Henker, D Buhrmester, et al. "Does stimulant medication improve the peer status of hyperactive children?" *J Consult Clin Psychol*. 1989; 57(4): 545–49.

White, BP, KA Becker-Blease, and K Grace-Bishop. "Stimulant medication use, misuse, and abuse in an undergraduate and graduate student sample." *J Am Coll Health*. 2006; 54(5): 261–68.

Wietecha, L, D Williams, S Shaywitz et al. "Atomoxetine improved attention in children and adolescents with attention-deficit/hyperactivity disorder and dyslexia in a 16 week, acute, randomized, double-blind trial." *J Child Adolesc Psychopharmacol*. 2013; 23(9): 605–13.

Wilens, TE, LA Adler, J Adams et al. "Misuse and diversion of stimulants prescribed for ADHD: a systematic review of the literature." *J Am Acad Child Adolesc Psychiatry*. 2008; 47(1): 21–31.

Wilens, TE, J Biederman, TJ Spencer et al. "Controlled trial of high doses of pemoline for adults with attention-deficit/hyperactivity disorder." *J Clin Psychopharmacol*. 1999; 19(3): 257–64.

Wilens, TE, TJ Spencer, and J Biederman. "A review of the pharmacotherapy of adults with attention-deficit/hyperactivity disorder." *J Atten Disord*. 2002; 5(4): 189–202.

Wolraich, M, L Brown, RT Brown et al. "ADHD: clinical practice guideline for the diagnosis, evaluation, and treatment of attention-deficit/hyperactivity disorder in children and adolescents." *Pediatrics*. 2011; 128(5): 1007–22.

Wood, DR, FW Reimherr, PH Wender, and GE Johnson. "Diagnosis and treatment of minimal brain dysfunction in adults: a preliminary report." *Arch Gen Psychiatry*. 1976; 33(12): 1453–60.

BIBLIOGRAPHY

OTHER SOURCES

AACAP 2014 Meeting Program.

"ADD—A dubious diagnosis." *The Merrow Report*. Public Broadcasting Service, Arlington, Va., 1995.

APSARD 2013 Meeting Program, Sept. 2013.

Attention Deficit Disorder Association. "A Q&A with Psychologist and ADHD Expert, Russell Barkley," 2010.

Attention Deficit/Hyperactivity Disorder—Are We Overmedicating Our Children? Hearing Before the Committee on Government Reform, U.S. House of Representatives, 107th Congress (Sept. 26, 2002). http://www.gpo.gov/fdsys/pkg/CHRG-107hhrg83516/pdf/CHRG-107hhrg83516.pdf.

Barkley, Russell. "ADHD Cutting Edge Understanding & Management." J&K Seminars video, 1:25. http://jkseminars.com/product_info.php?products_id=627; https://www.youtube.com/watch?v=1t7X6uhgB4E#action=share.

Bell Telephone Quarterly. New York: American Telephone and Telegraph Company, 1922, 145.

Biederman, Joseph. Testimony. Superior Court of New Jersey Law Division—Middlesex County, Feb. 26, 2009, Vol. 1.

Bilbo, Ryan et al. "Demographic & Geographic Patterns of ADHD Prescriptions among Louisiana's Medicaid Children." Presentation to Louisiana Department of Health and Hospitals A.D.H.D. Symposium, Dec. 9, 2014.

"Brother's Little Helper." *The Simpsons*. Fox. Originally aired on Oct. 3, 1999.

Cannon, Marianne. Testimony in *Edwards vs. President and Fellows of Harvard College et al.*, Superior Court of Massachusetts, No. 09-04695, 2012.

CBS Sunday Morning. "Rethinking Ritalin: Parents, Educators, and Researchers Debate the Use of Ritalin on Children with Behavioral Problems as Colleges Discover It's Used as a Study Aid by Students." CBS News transcripts, November 15, 1998.

CBS This Morning. "Many Say Ritalin Is Being Overpriced and ADHD is Overdiagnosed." CBS News transcripts. November 19, 1998.

CNN Newsroom, November 13, 2010.

Cohen, Matthew D. "Letter to Fox Broadcasting about Simpson's [*sic*] Episode." Dec. 3, 1999. https://web.archive.org/web/20000302155337/http://www.chadd.org/news/simpsons.htm.

The Colbert Report, Oct. 10, 2012. http://www.cc.com/video-clips/jur0u9/the-colbert-report-the-word-meducation.

The Dr. Oz Show, Feb. 13, 2013.

Federal Involvement in the Use of Behavior Modification Drugs on Grammar

School Children of the Right to Privacy Inquiry. Hearing before a Subcommittee of the Committee on Government Operations, U.S. House of Representatives, 91st Congress (Sept. 29, 1970).

Frank, R., E. R. Berndt, J. Donohue, A. Epstein, and M. Rosenthal. (2002, February 14). *Trends in direct-to-consumer advertising of prescription drugs* (Publication No. 3162). Retrieved from Kaiser Family Foundation website: http://www.researchgate.net/publication/24927320_Direct-to-consumer _advertising_of_ prescription_drugs/file/79e415134d69703553.pdf.

Gupta, Sanjay, on *Anderson Cooper 360°,* Apr. 1, 2013. http://ac360.blogs.cnn .com/2013/04/01/cdc-data-shows-increase-in-kids-with-adhd.

Johnston, Lloyd D., et al. "Monitoring the Future: National Survey Results on Drug Use." Ann Arbor: Institute for Social Research, University of Michigan, Feb. 2015. Accessed Nov. 29, 2015. http://www.monitoringthefuture .org/pubs/monographs/mtf-overview2014.pdf.

Johnston, Michelle Dally. *Out of Sorrow and into Hope: The History of the Emma Pendleton Bradley Hospital.*

"Judy Garland." YouTube video. https://www.youtube.com/watch?v=V0 -1r4nfSoI.

Kagan, Daryn. CNN Morning News, May 2, 2000.

Last Will and Testament with Codicils of George L. Bradley of Pomfret, Connecticut, 1906.

Mason, Oren. Professional website. http://www.attentionmd.com/Our _Practice.html.

Moones Mellouli v. Eric H. Holder, Jr., Attorney General. (Oral Arguments for Supreme Court case.) No. 13-1034 at 49. http://www.supremecourt.gov /oral_arguments/argument_transcripts/13-1034_i3dj.pdf.

Mosholder, A. D. *Psychiatric Adverse Events in Attention Deficit Hyperactivity Disorder (ADHD) Clinical Trials.* Slideshow Presentation to FDA Pediatric Advisory Committee, Mar. 22, 2006.

"Our America with Lisa Ling." *Huffington Post* OWN Video. June 12, 2014. http://www.huffingtonpost.com/2014/06/12/lisa-ling-add-adhd_n_ 5489924.html.

Philip Morris Companies, Inter-Office Correspondence, Dec. 8, 1994. https:// www.industrydocumentslibrary.ucsf.edu/tobacco/docs/#id-hmxw0019.

ProPublica. *Dollars for Docs.* https://projects.propublica.org/d4d-archive/.

ProPublica. *Dollars for Docs.* https://projects.propublica.org/docdollars/.

"Provigil: The Secret Success Drug?." YouTube video. https://www.youtube .com/watch?v=PAKS0aVhGto&feature=player_embedded.

The Revolution. ABC. Episode originally aired Mar. 22, 2012.

Shire. *$77 Billion in Lost Income Is Attributed to Attention-Deficit/Hyperactiv-*

ity Disorder (ADHD) Annually in the U.S. (Press release May 23, 2005). Retrieved from http://www.prnewswire.com/news-releases/77-billion-in-lost-income-is-attributed-to-attention-deficithyperactivity-disorder-adhd-annually-in-the-us-54493867.html.

"Speed Trap." *Family Ties*. NBC. Originally aired on Nov. 9, 1983.

Substance Abuse and Mental Health Services Administration (SAMHSA). "The DAWN Report: Emergency Department Visits Involving Attention Deficit/Hyperactivity Disorder Stimulant Medications." Jan. 24, 2013. http://www.samhsa.gov/data/sites/default/files/DAWN073/DAWN073/sr073-ADD-ADHD-medications.pdf.

Substance Abuse and Mental Health Services Administration (SAMHSA), Center for Behavioral Health Statistics. *Treatment Episode Data Set (TEDS) 2002–2012: National Admissions to Substance Abuse Treatment Services*. July 2014. Retrieved from http://archive.samhsa.gov/data/2k14/TEDS2012NA/TEDS2012N_Web.pdf.

This Week's Citation Classic. *Current Contents*, Feb. 23, 1987, 18.

United Nations. *Single Convention on Narcotic Drugs, 1961 (As amended by the 1972 Protocol amending the Single Convention on Narcotic Drugs, 1961)*. Retrieved from http://www.unodc.org/pdf/convention_1961_en.pdf.

United States ex rel. Torres et al. v. Shire Specialty Pharmaceuticals et al., No. 08-4795, 2008.

United States Patent No. 7,662,788. "Abuse-Resistant Amphetamine Prodrugs."

U.S. Food and Drug Administration. *Pharmaceutical Company Cephalon to Pay $425 Million for Off-label Drug Marketing* (Press release September 29, 2008). Retrieved from http://www.fda.gov/ICECI/CriminalInvestigations/ucm260715.htm.

Vanderbilt University. *2012/2013 Student Handbook Policies and Regulations in Cocurricular Matters*, updated Dec. 13, 2012.

———. "The Vanderbilt Community Creed," from "Student Handbook 2015/2016, Second Edition." http://www.vanderbilt.edu/student_handbook/print-handbook.

World News Tonight. ABC. Originally aired Dec. 14, 1999.

Young, Susan, Michael Fitzgerald, and Maarten J. Postma. "ADHD: Making the Invisible Visible." April 2013.

INDEX

ABOUT THE AUTHOR

Alan Schwarz is a Pulitzer Prize–nominated investigative reporter for *The New York Times* whose acclaimed series of more than one hundred articles exposed the seriousness of concussions in the NFL and led to safety reforms for young athletes nationwide. His work was profiled in *The New Yorker* and honored with a George Polk Award, the Associated Press award for project reporting (three times), and the 2013 Excellence in Statistical Reporting Award from the American Statistical Association. He and his family live in New York City.